P9-AGA-286

Susanne Vees-Gulani

Trauma and Guilt

Susanne Vees-Gulani

Trauma and Guilt

Literature of Wartime Bombing
in Germany

Walter de Gruyter · Berlin · New York

2003

∞ Printed on acid-free paper which falls within the guidelines
of the ANSI to ensure permanence and durability.

ISBN 3-11-017808-7

Bibliographic information published by Die Deutsche Bibliothek

Die Deutsche Bibliothek lists this publication in the Deutsche
Nationalbibliografie; detailed bibliographic data is available in the
Internet at <http://dnb.ddb.de>.

To Vikas and Maya

Acknowledgments

I owe thanks to many people whose assistance helped me complete this book. I would like to express my gratitude to Sari Aronson, Nancy Blake, Michael Palencia-Roth, Helmut Puff, and Mara Wade for their interest, support, and comments. Andrew Webb has been a great friend throughout the process and has also been a tremendous help with editing.

Thanks are also due to my parents who have shown deep interest in my research, and were always on the lookout for pertinent new material. I would like to express my heartfelt gratitude to my husband Vikas Gulani for showing such enthusiasm and interest in the project, which led to many fruitful discussions and ideas. In addition, he gave much of his time reading through various drafts, and provided valuable comments and editing.

Portions of this book have been previously presented and published. Parts of Chapter 4 were presented at the MLA conference in 2000 and at the Sebald Symposium at Davidson College in 2003. Parts of Chapter 6 were published in "Diagnosing Billy Pilgrim: A Psychiatric Approach to Kurt Vonnegut's *Slaughterhouse-Five*," *Critique* 44 (2003): 175-184. German quotations have been kept in the original with translation in footnotes. English translations are mine, unless otherwise noted.

Contents

Chapter 1
Introduction

Karl Kunz, *Im Keller*, 1945. Reproduced in black and white with permission from Bayerische Staatsgemäldesammlungen München.

Augsburg artist Karl Kunz' *Im Keller* from April 1945 offers graphic insight into the force of the World War II air raids. The painting gives a powerful and disturbing impression of the situation in the cellars where people are huddled together during a bombing attack.[1] Between two listless, faceless men who sit quietly on their benches awaiting their destiny, the inner turmoil of the experience unfolds. People of all ages are crouching together like animals, their faces marked by absolute terror and the fear of death. Some scream in panic, others raise their hands to the sky beseechingly, or try to protect themselves and their family against the destructive forces from above which they cannot see, but only hear and feel. The sole light source, the dim beam of the small flashlight in the front of the painting, illuminates only individual body parts, creating an image of fragmentation and destruction, and at the same time blending everything together into a collective experience of panic and chaos.

In the last years of the war, these scenes were played out in cities all over Germany. Night after night large bomber formations flew over the country leaving behind fire and destruction. There is no certainty about the number of people killed by the air raids. Some speak of 323,000 (Beseler and Gutschow IX), other estimates vary between 420,000 and 570,000 (Friedrich 63). People died suffocated in the cellars, burned beyond recognition by the firestorms, or buried under the debris. In the end, German cities were scenes of devastation, with their rubble measuring several hundred million cubic meters.

Going through a bombing attack was a never-forgotten experience. The roaring and rumbling of the planes, the loud bursts of the hits, and the noise of the anti-aircraft fire resonated in the ears while walls and floors were swinging and shaking as if the cellar were a ship on rough sea. There was no power, and the air was filled with dust and smoke. Those who made it out alive not only faced the destruction of their cities, but also had ample opportunity to observe those who had not been so lucky as to survive. Witness reports are full of descriptions of dead body parts littering the streets, or adult corpses burned to the size of children's bodies.

This devastating new form of warfare, which attacked the enemy not at the front line, but at home, and which played such an important role in World War II, was first outlined by the Italian general Giulio Douhet in a work on air war strategies, *Il Dominio dell'Aria*. Writing in 1921, he predicted how important the role of the air force would be for future warfare, since it was capable of quickly and effectively destroying both the enemy's war material and the population's will to fight, while at the same time minimizing losses to the attacker (Kurowski 10).

A demonstration of the power of this strategy of large area bombings was first shown in April of 1937 when the small, but historically significant, town of

---

[1] Karl Kunz (1905-1971) was not allowed to work or exhibit under National Socialism, but continued to paint secretly at night, while working during the day in his father's business in Augsburg. Kunz was a rescue worker during the air raids, and this gave him firsthand experience of the effects of the bombings. Augsburg was the site of much war-related industry and was heavily attacked. Much of the city was destroyed, and Kunz lost most of his paintings and sculptures.

Guernica became the site of a massive attack during the Spanish Civil War. This air raid was organized by the German Luftwaffe in support of the Fascist leader General Franco and flown by German and Italian pilots. Under the command of Lieutenant Colonel Wolfram von Richthofen, the unsuspecting Basque city was almost completely leveled to the ground in three phases. First, bombs destroyed the core of the city, then machine-gun fire mowed down people fleeing from the destruction and, in the third phase, planes set fire to the rubble with incendiary bombs (Martin 42). As *The Times* correspondent George Steer reported:

> "In the form of its execution and the scale of the destruction it wrought, no less than in the selection of its objective, [...] the raid on Gernika is unparalleled in military history. Gernika was not a military objective. [...] The object of the bombardment was seemingly the demoralization of the civil population and the destruction of the cradle of the Basque race." (quoted in Martin 50-51)

Guernica was, in some sense, the first 'morale bombing,' as the attacks aimed at breaking the civilian spirit were later called during World War II. It was also seen as an opportunity for the German military to try out its new air powers. Even though other cities were also bombed during the Spanish civil war, it is the destruction of Guernica that stands out today. Being reported widely by journalists who arrived in the city shortly after the attack took place, and also immortalized in Picasso's famous painting *Guernica*, the town came to symbolize the beginning of a new and cruel phase of warfare.[2]

Delighted by the success, bombing became an important tactic for Germany in World War II, predominantly against England, but also against such cities as Rotterdam and Warsaw. In response, starting in 1942 under the leadership of Sir Arthur Harris, also known as 'Bomber' Harris, the British Royal Air Force (with help from the U.S. Airforce) used target-area bombings against Germany on a large scale (Connelly 71-73). By having many planes attack one target together, instead of separating into small units, they hoped to cause the maximum amount of concentrated damage, and at the same time decrease support for the war within the German population. Consequently, air war was now not so much a way of supporting ground troops, as an independent and integral part of war strategy.

While some historians doubt whether the bombings truly succeeded in lowering morale, there is no question that the overall experience of the air war had an extremely strong impact on the population, and has become a lasting and haunting memory for many who went through it and survived its force. Yet, when early in 1998 feature writers in the culture sections of several German newspapers engaged in a debate about air raids in World War II, their effects on the population, and their depictions in literature, it was the first time since 1945 that

---

[2] For more information on the Guernica bombing and a history of Picasso's painting see Russell Martin's detailed account in *Picasso's War*.

there had been a wide and public deliberation on this subject in Germany. The discussion was sparked by a series of lectures on poetics entitled "Luftkrieg und Literatur" ("Air War and Literature") presented by W. G. Sebald (1944-2001) in Zurich in December of 1997. The German author and literary scholar explored why the bombings of German cities in World War II are so rarely talked about in Germany. He asserted that there are few literary accounts dealing with them, even though the events affected such a large number of people, both physically and psychologically. Sebald concludes that the establishment of a taboo about the events immediately after the war, an unspoken agreement by the German population, is responsible for what he perceives is silence of German authors with regards to the bombings:

> Der wahre Zustand der materiellen und moralischen Vernichtung, in welchem das ganze Land sich befand, durfte aufgrund einer stillschweigend eingegangenen und für alle gleichermaßen gültigen Vereinbarung nicht beschrieben werden. Die finstersten Aspekte des von der weitaus überwiegenden Mehrheit der deutschen Bevölkerung miterlebten Schlußakts der Zerstörung blieben so ein schandbares, mit einer Art Tabu behaftetes Familiengeheimnis, das man vielleicht nicht einmal sich selber eingestehen konnte. (Sebald 18)[3]

The debate after Sebald's lectures mostly followed one of two tracks. While all agreed, including Sebald (though he does not explore the question in detail), that the topic is necessarily difficult to discuss among those responsible for the murder of millions of people in concentration camps, the critics were split in their assessment of what kind of reactions were appropriate. One group applauded Sebald's move to speak out against the silence surrounding the events, since the topic deserves more attention from writers and readers because of its large impact on the population. In one of the first articles on the subject, for example, Volker Hage in *Der Spiegel* emphasizes that one obviously cannot write responsibly about the bombings without also writing about the Holocaust, but he does not see this fact as a valid reason not to talk about either one (Hage "Feuer vom Himmel" 141). In addition, he notes that the silence about the events has left German writing and writers with a sense of emptiness – a state he sees manifested both by Sebald's move to bring up the topic in his lectures on poetics and by the fact that German contemporary literature has been described by some as pale and unexciting because it does not explore the German past as much as it could (Hage "Feuer vom Himmel" 140-141).[4] Frank Schirrmacher in the *Frankfurter Allgemeine* confirms this assessment of the missing historical element in

---

[3] "There was a tacit agreement, equally binding on everyone, that the true state of material and moral ruin in which the country found itself was not to be described. The darkest aspects of the final act of destruction, as experienced by the great majority of the German population, remained under a kind of taboo like a shameful family secret, a secret that perhaps could not even be privately acknowledged" (trans. 10).

[4] Since the publication of his article, Hage himself has done much to keep the topic in public discussion, for example by making a TV documentary about it and by instigating the reissuing of the forgotten bombing novel *Vergeltung* by Gert Ledig.

German literature. He views the lack of descriptions of the bombings as part of a larger trend of avoiding important but painful and difficult historical events of the recent past. While Schirrmacher does not expect German postwar literature to find words to describe the Holocaust adequately, he sees the overall treatment of World War II by German authors as disappointing:

> Auch die Darstellung der langsamen Genese des Verbrechens inmitten der Städte, Familien und Schulen scheint den Schriftstellern immer wieder zu entraten. [...] [D]ie Verlustliste ist groß. Es gibt bis heute keine literarische Verarbeitung der Vertreibung; die Literatur weiß nichts von den Okkupationsjahren des Ostens durch die Rote Armee. [...] All das ist unerzählt, also: unerlöst. Es arbeitet weiter in den Tiefenstrukturen auch der vergeßlichsten Gesellschaft. (265)[5]

In contrast to these positive evaluations of Sebald's endeavor, a second group of critics questioned the legitimacy of writing literature about the air raids, since talking about the topic could send the general message that German crimes were atoned for by the suffering endured during and after the bombings or, even more dangerously, could be used by authors to try to divert attention away from their own involvement in the Nazi era by describing the suffering they had lived through during and immediately after the war. As Maxim Biller puts it: "Mit dem Krieg kam [...] die Lüge in unsere Literatur" (279).[6] According to these critics, the absence of literature about the bombings, and not discussing German suffering during the war is thus neither as surprising, nor as big a loss, as Sebald suggests: "Das Schweigen verbarg vielleicht eine Scham, die kostbarer ist als alle Literatur" (Harpprecht 269).[7] The objections raised against the exploration of a topic such as the bombing of German cities by writers, readers, and critics are understandable and not completely unfounded. They correctly point out that talking about German suffering is necessarily always under suspicion of trying to revise history in a way that could show Germans in a more favorable light or even as victims themselves, suppressing the idea that "So böse es war, das unsereiner überstanden haben mag: es gab immer das Bösere - es gab das Böse schlechthin" (Harpprecht 268).[8] The centrality that the air war occupied in Sebald's lectures, which went hand in hand with an almost complete neglect of crimes committed by Germans, was thus also of some concern. That this criticism was not completely without foundation showed itself in some audience

---

[5] "Writers repeatedly seem to fail to capture the slow emergence and acceptance of crime in cities, families, and schools. [...] The list of omissions is long. Up to this date there is no literary representation of the expulsion from the East; literature describes nothing about the years of occupation by the Red Army in the East. [...] All of this has not been told which means not resolved. It is still working itself out within the deep structures of even the most forgetful society."

[6] "With war, the lie entered [...] our literature."

[7] "The silence might have hidden a state of shame which is more precious than literature itself."

[8] "As bad as it was what we went through, there was always worse - there was true evil."

reactions who misunderstood Sebald as lending support to their ideas of German victimhood or Jewish conspiracy theories (Sebald 116-119).

A number of critics actually challenge the very notion of the supposed silence in German postwar society about the bombings and their effects. Early on, Joachim Güntner in the *Neue Zuercher Zeitung* insisted that there was never a literary taboo surrounding the bombings, even though he contends that there was no vast readership for the works concerned (275). Volker Ullrich in *Die Zeit* goes further and claims that the Allied bombings as well as the expulsion from the East were never a taboo in society: "Die Erinnerung an Bombenkrieg und Vertreibung blieb, mit unterschiedlicher Intensität, immer präsent" (45).[9] Studies of the Holocaust also frequently refer to the air raid experiences as Germany's way to suppress the suffering of the true victims of Nazi Germany.[10]

As the debate shows, there is not much agreement about the role of the bombings after 1945. While some consider the bombings to be overrepresented in the German psyche, others lament their complete neglect. It cannot be denied that there has always been some degree of local and private interest in the subject. There are publications dealing with the destructions of individual cities, and in family circles experiences of bombardments have been talked about and shared. There has not been, however, significant public discussion of the air war and its consequences until today. The bombings and their effects have not been studied systematically. If they are mentioned in scholarship, then they are usually only alluded to, or grouped together with other complex war experiences such as the expulsion from the East or the German soldiers' lot in Russian prison camps. Precise analysis of the events has indeed been rare.

So although Sebald's approach might contain some shortcomings, he was correct to call attention to the bombings and their devastating psychological effects on the people who went through them. His lectures, and the later book that resulted from them, can be understood as first attempts to approach the subject more broadly and publicly and to give insight into this part of the German past. The strong reaction that Sebald's lectures caused both in the press and among the population illustrates that Germans today also feel a need to explore the experiences of the bombings and their effects in more depth.

This new interest in the air war was again confirmed by the overwhelming success of Jörg Friedrich's history of the bombings, *Der Brand*, when it was published in 2002. Friedrich impressively describes the technical aspects of large-area bombings and how city after city was destroyed, but also shows the difficult physical and psychological situation they caused for the civilians on the ground.

[9] "The memory of the bombing war and the expulsion was, with varying intensity, always present."

[10] See, for example, Bill Niven's study *Facing the Nazi Past* from 2002. As he states in the introduction: "For a long time, the main victims in the eyes of many West Germans were the Germans themselves, who had been 'forced' to serve in Hitler's army, bombed by the Allies, treated unjustly in Soviet camps during and after the war, or expelled from their homes by the Czechs and Poles in 1945" (3).

However, Friedrich's approach is also not free of controversy. By divorcing the bombings completely from the Holocaust, which he hardly mentions, the picture he paints is somewhat one-dimensional and appears hollow and incomplete. Even over half a century after the end of the war, questions of German guilt cannot be ignored when approaching such sensitive issues as the bombings, where established parameters surrounding perpetrators and victims cannot be easily applied. The bombings did not simply occur independently of the historical situation, but were a response to the war that Germany had started, both against other countries and inside its own. When trying to understand the experience of the air war and its role in postwar Germany, it is thus necessary to define an approach that analyzes objectively the psychological effects of the air raids while concurrently allowing the proper cultural, societal, and moral contextualization of the consequences.

A similar approach is needed when evaluating the attention the air war has, or, according to Sebald, has not received in German literature. Authors who wanted to write about the bombings were subject to both inner psychological forces stemming from their experiences and also to cultural and historical pressures from their surroundings. Trauma of such magnitude can have devastating effects on the people who live through it, resulting in a variety of symptoms that make dealing with the experience inherently challenging, and color all attempts to come to grips with it. Using psychiatric theory, specifically diagnoses of acute and posttraumatic stress disorder, to analyze the available literature about the bombings, as presented in Chapter 2, can help shed light on the content and form of these works, the state of mind of the writers, and the general psychological toll air raids in war times can have on affected populations. Based on a clear set of criteria, it offers an objective approach independent of questions of morality or history. Yet, particularly in the case of the bombings, the traumatic experience cannot be treated in a vacuum. German writing about the war, and the critical evaluation of these texts, is intrinsically tied to questions of German responsibility and guilt during and after the Nazi era. The shame that Germans feel about their Nazi past also plays a role in the production and interpretation of such literature. How Germans relate to their past and their guilt, and how this complicated relationship has influenced and continues to influence the development of Germany and the behavior of its citizens is explored in Chapter 3.

Strangely, in the recent debate in Germany concerning the literature about the bombings, the available texts themselves have not been studied in great detail. Even though not dominating the literary landscape, the bombing theme actually features frequently in German literature after 1945, both in side-plots and also as the central focus of individual works. Chapter 4 examines some representative narratives about the bombings in German literature, such as Hans Erich Nossack's *Der Untergang* (*Doom and Destruction*), Wolfgang Borchert's poems and stories about the destruction of Hamburg, and Gert Ledig's recently rediscovered novel *Vergeltung* (*Payback*). In addition to these early representations, Chapter 4 also looks at two texts in the genre of documentary literature: Alexander Kluge's "Der Luftangriff auf Halberstadt am 8. April 1945" ("The Air Raid on Halberstadt on April 8, 1945") and Walter Kempowski's *Das Echolot: Fuga Furiosa* (*Sonar: Fuga Furiosa*). Finally, Dieter Forte's latest autobiographical novels *Der Junge mit den blutigen Schuhen* (*The Boy with the Bloody Shoes*) and *In der Erinnerung* (*In Memory*) are also examined. The texts are explored in the context of the psychological effects of the bombings both on the authors themselves and also on the characters depicted in the works, which helps to clarify the complicated relationships between the traumatic event, the writer who experienced it, and its depiction in literature. The works are further analyzed in terms of how they deal with the question of German guilt and responsibility, exploring both choices of avoidance and of inclusion, as well as what these methods disclose about the societal and personal pressures to which the authors were exposed. This approach allows a more critical look at the recent bombing literature debate. Taken together, the texts demonstrate the devastating psychological effects of the bombings as well as the difficulty of representing traumatic experiences in literary texts, particularly when they are set in conditions that might blur the categories of victims and perpetrators.

To illuminate further how deeply the air raids and their literary depictions are issues connected with German guilt and responsibility, several German-Jewish accounts of the bombings are presented in Chapter 5. This explores the description of an air raid in Victor Klemperer's diaries, a memoir by the physician Werner Schmidt, texts by Wolf Biermann about his experience of the Hamburg bombing in 1943, as well as the role of the air war in some of Günter Kunert's poems and his autobiography *Erwachsenenspiele* (*Adult Games*). Sadly, the number of available texts written from this unique perspective is extremely limited, because of the German persecution of its Jewish population, their deportation and murder. There were thus only very few Jewish citizens left in the cities when they were bombed. As in the German accounts, the Jewish narratives describe the air raids as extremely brutal events which can scar one for life, and yet they emphasize that despite their horror, the bombings were also welcome signals of freedom and the end of the war. By comparing the Jewish writers and their texts to the previously discussed works, the chapter investigates how this dual perception of the events influences authorial decisions on whether to write about the events at all, and the form of writing that is deemed appropriate if choosing to do so.

Interestingly, some of the most detailed and nuanced literary depictions of the bombings of German cities in World War II have been written by non-German authors. In Chapter 6 three such works about the bombing of Dresden, the American novel *Slaughterhouse-Five* by Kurt Vonnegut, the Dutch author Harry Mulisch's *Het stenen bruidsbed* (*The Stone Bridal Bed*), and finally the

French novel *L'Adieu à la femme sauvage* (*Farewell, Dresden*) by Henri Cou-longes are explored. Since the authors are not subject to the same issues of guilt and shame as their German counterparts, they appear to be able to approach the topic much more freely both in form and content. These texts, particularly the novels by Vonnegut and Mulisch, not only confirm how the bombings indeed can be the topic of literature but also, when compared to the German works, help to clarify the complex issues that are involved in the literary portrayal of the air raids by German authors.

Literature about the bombings offers a unique opportunity to gain insight both into the nature of the psychological effects of the bombings and also the short- and long-term reactions to these experiences by the people who lived through them. In this context, it is possible to understand better the difficulty of translating traumatic events into words, and what benefits might arise from this process, particularly when transformed into fiction. Furthermore, the texts clearly reveal the interdependence of the representation of the air raids on is-sues of German guilt and shame, unraveling the complexity of this controversial topic in Germany's past. Established critical theories and approaches to trauma theory in the humanities do not seem sufficient for grasping fully the intricacies of the topic. The application of psychiatric trauma theory to the texts offers new insight into the complicated relationships between traumatic event, author, fic-tional text, and audience, laying open the depth of the traumatic experience. In addition, by embedding this investigation in a historical context, by consider-ing the attitudes of Germans to their Nazi past and their perception of guilt and shame, a unique way of looking at Germany's recent past emerges. With this approach, it is possible to gain a better understanding of the ways that Germans deal with the bombings. It reveals the impact the air raids have had on writers' development as artists, without running the danger of being perceived as revi-sionist. Finally, it might help investigate the question of why a public discussion of the bombings, which was not addressed for so long in Germany, is suddenly coming to the surface over half a century after the war.

Chapter 2
Trauma and Its Consequences

2.1   A History of Trauma Psychology

While traumatic events and their consequences have been described for centuries, posttraumatic stress disorder (PTSD), has only been recognized as an independent psychiatric disorder since its inclusion in the 1980 edition of the *Diagnostic and Statistical Manual of Mental Disorders* (DSM-III). PTSD is the response to a catastrophic life event and has been explained by some as stemming from "an inadequate way of coping with extreme stress" (Kleber, Figley, and Gersons 234). The most recent edition of the *Manual*, DSM-IV-TR, defines PTSD as the result of a "person experienc[ing], witness[ing], or [being] confronted with an event or events that involved actual or threatened death or serious injury, or a threat to the physical integrity of self or others" (467) and to which he or she responds with "intense fear, helplessness, or horror" (467). Exposure to the trauma results in three groups of symptoms: intrusion, avoidance, and hyperarousal. Having faced a traumatic event, an individual persistently re-experiences it, and at the same time tries to avoid any stimuli that remind him or her of the trauma. The reaction is often accompanied by emotional numbing on the one hand and increased arousal on the other, which can impact such things as sleep behavior, concentration, and anger control. The inclusion of the diagnosis in DSM-III provided psychiatrists for the first time with both a name and operational criteria to assess the effects of traumatic experiences in an organized fashion. It opened the door to eliminating the multitude of diagnoses and labels used for different groups, such as abused women, concentration camp survivors, war veterans, and torture victims, who had experienced trauma and suffered from its effects, by emphasizing that different traumas lead to a final common pathway characterized by comparable symptoms. Appreciation of similarities in outcomes of different etiologies of trauma has led to vast interest in PTSD and increased study of the phenomenon.

Trauma research is complicated by the fact that the diagnosis of PTSD carries implications reaching far beyond the fields of psychology and psychiatry. PTSD has had a history of political and legal ramifications and overtones. The diagnosis (or the importance of considering the diagnosis of PTSD) came into existence after much political activism and debate about Vietnam Veterans who suffered from the effects of traumatizing war experiences, but who were denied official recognition of the symptoms themselves as well as the underlying causes. A diagnosis of PTSD finally sanctioned societal acceptance of the idea that the experience of trauma can make people sick. Partly because of this aspect of the diagnosis, some researchers, for example the anthropologist Allan Young in his work *The Harmony of Illusions: Inventing Post-Traumatic Stress Disorder*, describe PTSD as restricted to our time, as a construct that "is glued together by the practices, technologies, and narratives with which it is diagnosed, studied, treated, and represented and by the various interests, institutions, and moral arguments that mobilized these efforts and resources" (5). While it is true that the establishment of an official disorder and its inclusion in the DSM was partly politically motivated, it does not make the diagnosis a completely artificial construct or invalid. The symptoms caused by traumatic events are not invented or provoked through the establishment of PTSD, but posttraumatic stress disorder is a label for symptoms that have long been observed in trauma survivors and which are confirmed by research. As Sullivan and Gorman emphasize: "the accumulated phenomenologic, epidemiologic, biologic, and treatment evidence make it clear that PTSD stands alone as a unique psychiatric disorder" (463). Diagnosis plays an important role in identifying people who suffer from the effects of trauma and in establishing therapeutic methods.

Furthermore, the PTSD diagnosis itself is not perceived as a fixed entity, but rather will be modified as new research results become available from studies which test its validity, applicability, and value. For example, the operational criteria of the 1980 diagnosis have been changed in later editions of the DSM in order to define both the stressor itself and the reaction to the effects of trauma more precisely. However, it is true that the political side of PTSD may complicate the process of performing the necessary research. As the PTSD investigator Alexander C. McFarlane points out, "[a]s a consequence of this political backdrop, many of the uncertainties have not been openly discussed despite their importance in developing a better understanding of the effects of trauma" (32). While he thus cautions against lack of rigor and holding back from asking certain questions that would help to define PTSD more precisely (which would be signs of "poor science") he does not imply that posttraumatic stress disorder is purely a political invention. On the contrary, he is concerned rather that the influence of politics on PTSD research could be responsible for some continued skepticism in the field (32) about the effects of trauma, and he worries that certain circles such as "pension and compensation authorities that have an interest in limiting their liability" (51) could effect the studies. At this point, some of the newer research areas within the PTSD field suggest that McFarlane's warnings are becoming less pertinent. More controversial topics such as the relationship between personality and the occurrence of PTSD are now openly discussed. In addition, the inclusion of McFarlane's research and articles in several new collections of essential papers on PTSD show that Young's assertion that only "a small minority of people working in the PTSD field seem interested in [...] McFarlane's work"(139) – which deals with some of the "uncertainties" of the diagnosis that still need to be explored – is unfounded. Instead, it proves that Mc-Farlane and his concerns are very much part of the current scientific discourse on PTSD.[1]

Acceptance of the PTSD diagnosis is also not restricted to the American psychiatric establishment. Other countries, where political pressures are different and where Vietnam Veterans' advocates were not pushing for official recognition of the disorder, are also investigating PTSD. The World Health Organization's *International Classification of Diseases* (ICD) has acknowledged that disorders can arise as reactions to acute stress. Before 1993, it contained short term "acute reaction to stress" and longer term "adjustment reaction" diagnoses. In 1993, however, when the tenth edition of the ICD was published, it was changed to include a definition of PTSD. This definition contains some slight differences in emphasis from its American counterpart, but overall is very similar (Yule, Williams, and Joseph 5).[2] Indeed, studies on PTSD have spanned a variety of cultures and settings. For example, the effects of war and combat have been explored in European soldiers of the two World Wars, in Vietnam soldiers, in soldiers from Israel, several Arab countries, Sri Lanka, and the Soviet Union (de Silva and Marks 119-121). For other kinds of trauma, such as natural disasters, one finds a similar diversity of settings (de Silva and Marks 121-122). Certainly, there are differences that should be considered when looking at PTSD in various cultures. Cultural traditions and economic conditions are not independent of matters such as social support and the availability of professional care which can influence the way someone copes with the experience of trauma (de Silva 126-127).[3]Some might even respond to the experience within cultural belief systems, for example by believing to have been visited by dead spirits. However, while these differences should not be neglected, the general picture is one of international applicability and validity: "the vulnerability to PTSD is not culturally limited" (de Silva 125).

---

[1] Apart from Kleber, Figley, and Gersons' *Beyond Trauma*, which has been quoted here, McFarlane is also represented in Saigh and Bremner's *Posttraumatic Stress Disorder: A Comprehensive Text* (1999) and Horowitz' *Essential Papers on Posttraumatic Stress Disorder* (1999).

[2] Yule, Williams, and Joseph describe the main differences between the DSM and the ICD versions: "ICD requires the clinician to match an overall pattern of symptoms to the example given, whereas DSM provides somewhat more mechanistic guidelines and rules to follow" (5). In addition, ICD stresses the reexperiencing of the trauma as the major symptom of PTSD, but does not require numbing as a symptom for diagnosis while in DSM both are needed to diagnose PTSD (6).

[3] One example is the societal attitude towards rape victims. When rape is considered to shame the family, there is usually very little or no support for the victim, who is often ostracized. Clearly these views add significant psychological pressure and also make it nearly impossible to seek help after the trauma - conditions that can worsen the effects of the trauma on the individual (de Silva 127).

When PTSD was defined as an official diagnosis, it was not the first time that researchers had tried to describe stress reactions following trauma. Even though trauma research exploded towards the end of the 20th century, it attracted interest by scholars and therapists much before that time. Trauma and its psychological effects seem to have existed ever since humans have had to deal with death, abuse, torture, war, and disasters. For example, R. J. Daly noticed in *The Diary of Samuel Pepys*, in which Pepys describes his mental condition following the Great Fire of London in 1666, that Pepys' symptoms correspond to what we today would call PTSD. In one entry, for instance, over half a year after the fire, Pepys reports that "it is strange to think how to this very day I cannot sleep a-night without great terrors of fire; and this very night could not sleep till almost 2 in the morning through thoughts of fire" (734). Psychiatrists also like to point out literary depictions of the effects of traumatizing experiences to show the timelessness of the phenomenon. For example, in a passage of Shakespeare's *King Henry IV*, spoken by Lady Percy, the lines reveal some of the possible psychological consequences of war (Trimble 6-7; Weathers, Litz, and Keane 104):

> Tell me, sweet lord, what is't that takes from thee
> Thy stomach, pleasure, and thy golden sleep?
> Why dost thou bend thine eyes upon the earth,
> And start so often when thou sit'st alone?
> Why hast thou lost the fresh blood in thy cheeks
> And given my treasures and my rights of thee
> To thick-ey'd musing and curst melancholy?
> In thy faint slumbers I by thee have watch'd,
> And heard thee murmur tales of iron wars,
> Speak terms of manage to thy bounding steed,
> Cry "Courage! to the field!"
> [...]
> Thy spirit within thee hath been so at war,
> And thus hath so bestirr'd thee in thy sleep,
> That beads of sweat have stood upon thy brow (857)

Scientific interest in trauma arose in the 1860s when John Erichsen studied the distress suffered by victims of railroad accidents. He thought these problems stemmed from a physical cause, namely a damaging of the nervous system through a concussion of the spine during the accident, which became known as the "railway spine" (Erichsen 8). Around the same time, the American Civil War left some soldiers who had been exposed to combat with lasting symptoms such as increased arousal, irritability, and an elevated heart rate. This set of symptoms was called "Irritable Heart" or "DaCosta's Syndrome" named after the American physician DaCosta who first described it. He thought it to be a physiological reaction to the exposure to combat stress. Another term used during the Civil

War to describe soldiers' suffering from severe depression and loneliness was "nostalgia," since the symptoms were attributed to the men's long absence from their homes.

From this point on, war repeatedly drew attention to the study of trauma. With the expansion of the war machinery in World War I, the number of mental casualties also increased, making it necessary to readdress the issue of war trauma. Again, the psychological problems of the soldiers were at first seen as caused by purely physical symptoms. It was argued that exploding shells caused injuries to the brain, which were too small to observe, a phenomenon then termed "shell shock." However, as the war went on, the need for additional explanation started to emerge when the same symptoms were observed in soldiers who had not been shelled. Some physicians thus embraced the idea that behavioral disorders could arise through traumatic experiences and the strong emotions associated with them, which is largely in agreement with today's understanding. Others believed Joseph Babinski's concept of the importance of suggestion. His position was that a soldier learned to play the role of a sufferer of psychological symptoms either by suggestion from their therapist during treatment or by auto-suggestion (Babinski and Froment 44-45). Babinski was the successor at the Sorbonne of the influential French neurologist Jean-Martin Charcot who had been responsible for making hysteria a scientifically acceptable disorder at the time. He had compiled detailed descriptions of the symptoms of hysteria and emphasized that they were psychological in etiology and not due to physiological causes. Another group of doctors during World War I looked towards psychoanalysis for explanations. They embraced Freud's ideas about the war neurosis which is to be regarded as a traumatic neurosis whose occurrence has been made possible or promoted by a conflict in the ego. As he states in the "Einleitung zur Psychoanalyse der Kriegsneurosen" ("Introduction to Psycho-Analysis and the War Neurosis"):

[Der Ichkonflikt] spielt sich zwischen dem alten friedlichen und dem neuen kriegerischen Ich des Soldaten ab, und wird akut, sobald dem Friedens-Ich vor Augen gerückt wird, wie sehr es Gefahr läuft, durch die Wagnisse seines neugebildeten parasitischen Doppelgängers ums Leben gebracht zu werden. Man kann ebensowohl sagen, das alte Ich schütze sich durch die Flucht in die traumatische Neurose gegen die Lebensgefahr, wie es erwehre sich des neuen Ichs, das es als bedrohlich für sein Leben erkennt. (*Gesammelte Werke* V. 12 323)[4]

This definition allowed Freud and his followers to treat war neuroses as symptoms of regressions to an earlier stage of ego development.

---

[4] "The conflict is between the soldier's old peaceful ego and his new warlike one, and it becomes acute as soon as the peace-ego realizes what danger it runs of losing its life owing to the rashness of its newly formed, parasitic double. It would be equally true to say that the old ego is protecting itself from a mortal danger by taking flight into a traumatic neurosis or to say that it is defending itself against the new ego which it sees is threatening its life" (trans. 101).

This was not the first time that Freud had dealt with the effects of trauma. He had worked with Charcot at the Salpêtrière mental hospital in France in the 1880s and had become interested in trying to find the origin of hysteria instead of purely the description that Charcot had provided in his case studies. In collaboration with Joseph Breuer, Freud concluded in the 1890s that hysteria was caused by psychological trauma. Based on the revelations of his female patients, he claimed in *Zur Ätiologie einer Hysterie* (*The Aetiology of Hysteria*): "Ich stelle also die Behauptung auf, zugrunde jedes Falles von Hysterie befinden sich [...] *ein oder mehrere Erlebnisse von vorzeitiger sexueller Erfahrung*, die der frühesten Jugend angehören" (*Studienausgabe* V. 6 64).[5] However, Freud then revised his thesis by moving the trauma from a concrete and real childhood sexual encounter to the realm of fantasies and drives thus formulating the foundation of psychoanalysis – a development some feminists today find unforgivable.[6]

In this context Freud's colleague at the Salpêtrière, Pierre Janet, needs to be mentioned as well. Like Freud, Janet was interested in the origins of hysteria and also concluded that it was caused by psychological trauma. Similar to Freud's initial hypothesis, he believed that traumatic experiences could produce an altered state of consciousness which was then responsible for the symptoms associated with hysteria. The symptoms were thus recurring veiled representations of the traumatic events whose memory the sufferer suppressed. Janet called this altered state of consciousness "dissociation" (331). Breuer and Freud describe the phenomenon in similar terms in their *Studies on Hysteria* in 1895 (9). Freud and Janet's ideas about hysteria thus at first resembled each other, but Janet did not follow Freud's move of replacing the real trauma as the cause of hysteria with an explanation focusing on sexual drives and desires. This seems to explain why Janet has become popular with some trauma researchers today who see him as a key founder of trauma studies. However, one should keep in mind that not everyone supports the idea of Janet occupying such an important position in the history of the field.[7]

While not completely forgotten, trauma research did slow down after World War I. However, peacetime made it possible to shift the study of the psychological effects of trauma away from war back to other traumatic experiences such as sexual abuse, natural disasters or accidents.[8] During World War II, in-

---

[5] "I therefore put forward the thesis that at the bottom of every case of hysteria there are *one or more occurences of premature sexual experience*, occurrences which belong to the earliest years of childhood" (trans. 203).

[6] Trauma researcher and feminist Judith Herman, for example, states: "Out of the ruins of the traumatic theory of hysteria, Freud created psychoanalysis. The dominant psychological theory of the next century was founded in the denial of women's reality" (14).

[7] For a discussion of Janet's shortcomings and inconsistencies see chapter three in Ruth Leys' *Trauma: a Genealogy*.

[8] See, for example, Prasad's study of the great Indian earthquake in 1934 or Bender and Blau's work on the effects of sexual abuse on children.

creased attention was again paid to the psychological effects of war. The most prominent terms of the Second World War concerning these effects were "battle exhaustion" or "combat exhaustion," yet the symptoms were the same ones observed in the previous war and in hysteria diagnosis. What was new was the, albeit rather limited, study of the traumatization of civilians in war. With the use of large area bombings, civilian places turned into battlefields. For example, in England, Frank Bodman conducted a study of the effects of the bombings on the mental health of children in Bristol. While he concluded that "[t]he most striking finding of this survey is the extraordinary toughness of the child" (488), the children still suffered from a variety of symptoms comparable to some of the PTSD symptoms of today such as "general nervousness, trembling, crying, and aggressive behaviour," as well as "night terrors" (486).

The investigation of survivors of concentration camps after the war led to the description of "concentration camp syndrome," which entails "symptoms of anxiety, motor restlessness, hyperapprehensiveness, difficulty in sleeping, night terrors, fatigue, phobic reactions, and a constant preoccupation with recollections of persecutory experiences" (Kaplan and Sadock 128). The studies also show that these kinds of effects are long-lasting. When Leo Eitinger examined one hundred Norwegian concentration camp survivors in the early 1960s, eighty-five of them still reported symptoms of "chronic fatigue," seventy-eight "impaired concentration, restlessness and irritability" (375). Eitinger also found that most of his subjects suffered from "painful associations" that could occur in "any connection whatsoever, from seeing a person stretching their arms and associating this with his fellow prisoners hung up by their arms under torture, to seeing an avenue of trees and visualizing long rows of gallows with swinging corpses" (378).

Other important research after World War II dealt again with the psychological condition of people who had survived a natural or industrial disaster, such as tornadoes, ships sinking, earthquakes, mudslides, nuclear accidents, or explosions. A lot of the increased attention to these types of trauma experiences during peace time, and the research funding provided by the National Academy of Sciences, can also be explained by the idea that the information corresponding to the consequences of these disasters would be able to predict the psychiatric effects of events occurring during war time (for example during nuclear explosions). Another branch of trauma literature started to look at the effects of rape on women, leading to the term "rape trauma syndrome" in 1974. Again, the symptoms displayed by rape victims, such as nightmares and thoughts related to the rape, avoidance behavior, fear, and anger (Saigh and Bremner 4), resembled those of other survivors of traumatic experience. While it emerged that the effects of different traumas on the people who experienced them could be strikingly similar, it was ultimately the struggle for acknowledgment of the psychological effects of combat on soldiers during and after the Vietnam War that led to the specification and clarification of the diagnostic criteria of PTSD, thus providing a framework for the field of trauma research and finally causing the acceptance of PTSD as a valid diagnostic category.

As the history of PTSD shows, it is not surprising that the introduction of its diagnosis in 1980 cannot be completely separated from the political and legal arena. Many kinds of trauma occur in contexts that necessarily involve political, social, and legal issues. As early as the time when Erichsen was studying the so-called "railway spine," compensation concerns were part of the discourse developing around the topic of industrial accidents and their consequences. Similarly, the view of hysteria as a solely female ailment, and later Freud's disbelief concerning the sexual abuse of women as children have always had consequences beyond the psychiatric discipline. Sexual abuse, rape, and other violent crimes are often involved in litigation. Symptoms and complaints of psychological suffering among soldiers were, and still are, often suspected of being mere malingering, an opinion which may be sanctioned by the governments involved who are mainly interested in retaining their fighting power.

Due to these implications, it is unlikely that PTSD will ever be completely free of the suggestion by some that it is only a political construct of our time. However, the history of trauma also proves that this diagnosis is more than just a post-Vietnam era politico-social phenomenon. Numerous groups at different times studying various kinds of traumas repeatedly document comparable symptoms. This route to the understanding of trauma is slow and might not always reveal what we would like it to, but only when clearly defined, explored and understood, can PTSD be validated. As such, PTSD should be solely based on the symptoms, independent from moral or ethical beliefs we try to attach to the diagnosis. Scientific investigation thus seems particularly well suited to approach trauma and its manifold effects.

2.2   Trauma Studies in the Humanities

The emphasis of this chapter on the importance of the scientific exploration of trauma is also a response to the ways trauma studies are often conducted in the humanities. In the last decades, trauma has become a popular topic in non-scientific disciplines, especially in relation to the Holocaust and the sexual abuse of women. Unfortunately, the approach utilized by a surprisingly large number of these studies, including some of the most influential ones, is problematic. While the following treatment of trauma literature in the humanities is not a complete review of *all* the works produced on the subject, it attempts to illustrate some of the major worrisome tendencies in the field and their consequences.

One of the most striking paradoxes in much of the literature on trauma concerns the definition of "trauma" and "posttraumatic." Many scholars both grossly exaggerate and, at the same time, limit the applicability of the terms. The experience of trauma is expanded to involve not only the individual, but our whole culture. According to these works, trauma, "whether conscious or not" (Felman and Laub xiv), defines all of our lives and the way we see and interpret the world, even if we have never suffered any trauma ourselves. We are thus part of a *Post-traumatic Culture*, as the title of a work of literary criticism reveals. Shoshana Felman, who together with the psychoanalyst Dori Laub published the influential study on trauma and the Holocaust, *Testimony*, also reminds the reader twice on the first page that we all live "in a post-traumatic century" (1). The book repeatedly expands trauma to apply to more than just the person who experienced it. Laub emphasizes the importance of testimony when dealing with trauma, since before it has been shared with a listener, "the trauma - as a known event and not simply as an overwhelming shock - has not been truly witnessed yet." For Laub, the therapist thus takes on an important role because it is only through the therapist that the traumatic experience can be fully known. Yet Laub does not stop here. In his eyes, the therapist is not only a facilitator in helping a traumatized individual to create a narrative of the trauma, but "[b]y extension, the listener to trauma comes to be a participant and a co-owner of the traumatic event: through his very listening, he comes to partially experience trauma in himself" (57).

Another important scholar in this area, Cathy Caruth, expands the meaning of trauma even further. She is the editor of *Trauma: Explorations in Memory* and the author of *Unclaimed Experience: Trauma, Narrative, and History*, which are both extensively referenced in the literature. There are obvious similarities between her approach and that of Felman and Laub.[9] Caruth emphasizes the importance of trauma "in our catastrophic era" (*Unclaimed Experience* 56) in which history is only accessible through the effects of traumatic events. Again, trauma is seen as something that is not consciously experienced when it happens. Trauma is also not an individual experience, but it is, like history, "never simply one's own" (*Unclaimed Experience* 24). Instead, Caruth asserts that "we are implicated in each other's traumas" (*Unclaimed Experience* 24). Only through this 'contagious' nature of trauma, can we gain some knowledge of the trauma and access to the history of our recent traumatic past. This means that, according to Caruth, we are all marked by the traumas suffered in the past, and become witnesses to them. Traumatic experiences are not any longer particular incidents happening to individuals, but are unlocatable, shared, and influence all of us.

To characterize us and our era through the catchy term "posttraumatic" creates several problems. While it is true that the twentieth century has been particularly marked by mass violence, especially because of the availability of new

---

[9] Not surprisingly, Caruth is acknowledged by Felman and Laub in *Testimony*, as are they in Caruth's *Unclaimed Experience*. Furthermore, Caruth includes essays by both authors in her collection on trauma.

technologies, it clearly trivializes the experience and the often tremendous personal suffering of individuals, who actually went through a trauma, to see us all as traumatized simply because we live during post-World Wars, post-Holocaust, post-Hiroshima times. The idea that trauma only truly arises when it is shared, leads to a shift in emphasis from individuals and the trauma they suffered to that of a listener who is now the actual witness of the trauma and consequently, according to this approach, a fellow sufferer. The actual traumatized person is thus accorded less importance in favor of a diffuse form of shared trauma experience that suddenly puts the therapist or critic, who interprets the trauma for us, in the center. In addition, this approach deemphasizes the externality of trauma. Instead, trauma is now vaguely defined as being located somewhere in the transmission from one person to the next. In the extreme case of Caruth, the trauma itself never even surfaces any longer, but is only an unspeakable undercurrent spreading through and defining a culture.

Paradoxically, many of the critics who expand "posttraumatic" as a characterization of our current culture, at the same time limit its definition by attaching ethical standards to it. A person experiencing trauma is often automatically equated with a victim. For many of these critics, being a "survivor" is more than someone who made it out of a life-threatening situation alive; he is a victim that is given a special status and high moral authority.[10] However, this formula fails with some trauma "victims." Soldiers in wartime are under constant threat of losing their lives and clearly can suffer trauma, yet soldiers also take the lives of others. Some of the SS-officers overseeing concentration camps suffered from chronic headaches, stomach cramps, or nightmares, yet one can hardly describe these perpetrators as victims. These issues surrounding the equating of trauma experiences with victimhood have prompted some writers to address this misguided notion. For example, Dominick LaCapra concludes that " '[v]ictim' is not a psychological category" and that "not everyone traumatized by events is a victim" ("Trauma, Absence, Loss" 723). Unfortunately, these voices of reason are usually drowned out. Instead of dealing with the issue, discussions of trauma in cases where the victim-perpetrator division is not clearly defined are often excluded. To avoid conflicts, the literature mainly focuses on Holocaust survivors or abused women. In other cases, authors attempt to characterize the traumatized individuals they write about as solely victims even if this categorization is not always appropriate (for example in the case of the Vietnam soldier).[11]

---

[10] For an interesting discussion on victimhood, survivor status and moral authority see Marita Sturkel's "Narratives of Recovery: Repressed Memory as Cultural Memory."

[11] The feminist critic Kali Tal has expressed her dissatisfaction with this tendency. In reference to Vietnam soldiers, she notes: "Much recent literature [...] places the combat soldier simply in the victim's role; helpless in the face of war, and then helpless to readjust from the war experience upon his return home. Feminist critics should be quick to voice their disapproval of an interpretation so drastically at odds with reality. The soldier in combat is both victim and victimizer; dealing death as well as risking it. These soldiers carry guns; they point them at people and shoot

The tendency to define the traumatized individual as a victim and to assign him or her special moral authority is in accordance with some additional underlying goals often pursued by trauma theory in the humanities. Many of the writers are not only interested in engaging in scholarship, but they actively intend to convey moral and political messages and provide a testimony. By embracing the idea that one can partake in the trauma one writes about and analyzes, critics in their works try to take on both the role of witness to the trauma, and the moral authority they associate with witnessing - a process that has been called "narrative witnessing" (Kacandes 55).

Another way to mix scholarship with witnessing is to refer repeatedly to one's own experience of trauma. Since the authority of the text is based on claims deduced from a trauma that the author had previously suffered, the distance between the critic and the object of study is completely erased. This loss of distance, however, is not seen as problematic. There is also no consideration of the fact that individuals react differently to trauma. Instead there is an implication that one needs to suffer through trauma in order to be able to study it. For example, Roberta Culbertson, who was sexually abused as a child, uses her own experiences to give authority to her general statements about childhood memories of trauma: "I refer to particular childhood memories here because they are my own, *allowing me* to speak about them and their presence, and the process of deconstructing/reconstructing them" (181, emphasis added). These works are thus actually self-testimonies, ways to share what has happened in order to heal. Some statements of Susan J. Brison for example, who had been attacked by a man, raped and nearly murdered, also reveal indirectly that her article is another way of once again bearing witness to her own trauma. Brison explains that when she was forced to recount to the police what happened right after being attacked, it was painful but also healing to tell the story:

> [I]t was, even at that early stage, therapeutic to bear witness in the presence of others who heard and believed what I told them. Two and a half years later, I found it healing to give my testimony in public and to have it confirmed by the police, prosecutors, my lawyer, and, ultimately, the jury, who found my assailant guilty of rape and attempted murder. How might we account for this process of 'mastering the trauma' through the *repeated telling* of one's story? (46, emphasis added)

While there is nothing wrong with giving an account of one's own trauma, these testimonials should not be classified as scholarship or claim special authority for the understanding of all trauma.

Another puzzling characteristic of trauma studies in the humanities is its isolation from research conducted on trauma in other disciplines. When interpreting a text, claims about its meaning have to be backed up with evidence in order to

---

to kill. Members of oppressed groups, by contrast, almost never control the tools of violence" (10).

view the analysis as valid and convincing. When talking about trauma, the same
caution and rigor should be applied. This means that evidence collected concerning the manifestations of the effects of trauma and its causes has to be taken
into consideration. Unfortunately, some critics mainly rely on quoting each other
in backing up their claims, without seriously consulting research conducted in
other fields such as the sciences. Others refer to scientific and medical studies,
yet their references are often vague or incomplete. For example, Cathy Caruth is
frequently hailed for bringing scientific research about PTSD to trauma studies
in the humanities, especially with her collection of essays: *Trauma: Explorations
in Memory*. While it is an interesting anthology offering views from different
disciplines, it does not contain a thorough overview of scientific opinion about
trauma. It is troubling to see that, for many critics, this is the only source of
scientific knowledge about PTSD.

Bibliographies reveal an overwhelming tendency to quote Bessel van der
Kolk, a neurobiological researcher on PTSD who is included in Caruth's collection. Even though he is a known PTSD researcher, he is certainly not the
only authority on the subject in the scientific community. His dominance in the
works-cited pages of many literary critics would thus be puzzling if one ignored
the fact that they almost exclusively quote the article contained in Caruth's essay collection.[12] Van der Kolk's psychobiological model partially agrees with
Caruth's understanding in that intrusion symptoms after traumatic experiences
can be characterized as the return of exact, unchanged moments of what has happened because they were stored completely separately in the brain, unavailable
to normal processing and not influenced by personality.

However, van der Kolk's rather speculative conclusions about the unchange-
ability of traumatic experiences is by no means shared by the majority of the
PTSD research community. In fact, his psychobiological model is not uniformly
accepted, as it has been seen by some as not accounting for the complexity of the
memory process.[13] Van der Kolk only describes one of many different models
of trauma, and apart from other psychobiological models, there are also psy-
chodynamic and cognitive approaches available to explain what happens when
a person experiences trauma. Based on some degree of empirical evidence, it
is important to remember that these models are hypotheses; they are theoretical
constructs that help explain the available data and can assist in conceiving of
future studies, but they may turn out to be invalid when more data become available. It is thus misleading to limit one's point of view to van der Kolk's model
and present it as fact, or even to use it to prove one's assumptions, and doing so
constitutes a danger of ignoring other important findings.

---

[12] A good example is the anthology *Acts of Memory*, edited by Bal, Crewe, and Spitzer. Here, the
van der Kolk essay published in Caruth's work appears in nearly every bibliography and is often
either the only scientific source, or one of a very small number. Van der Kolk's important role in
trauma studies in the humanities has also not gone unnoticed in the field. Ruth Leys' commentary
on van der Kolk and his research will be discussed later on in this chapter.

[13] See, for example, Craig C. Piers, "Remembering Trauma: a Characterological Perspective."

Interestingly, contrary to common belief, Caruth herself does not actually integrate much scientific research in her own work, but rather presents a set theory, which she tries to justify through science after the fact. This becomes evident in her interview with Robert J. Lifton, a psychiatrist who has done much work with survivors from Hiroshima and also with Vietnam veterans (published in her *Trauma* collection). Here, Caruth attempts to get confirmation from Lifton for her assumption that trauma can never be experienced or known when it actually occurs, that it is afterwards always incomprehensible and only present as a wound - an idea which is central to her work *Unclaimed Experience* published a year after this collection. However, Lifton does not directly agree with Caruth's theory. While he confirms that at first it is difficult for individuals to comprehend experiences like Hiroshima because of the lack of appropriate imagery to describe them, they eventually do take them in since "there was the capacity to enlarge on their own inner imagery, enlarge on their life experience" (Lifton and Caruth 135). Caruth tries to get Lifton to agree with her three times – yet she never receives the concrete answer that she is looking for (134, 136, 141). In *Unclaimed Experience*, her science references are often vague and she gives no sources or only incomplete references for her generalizing statements about the scientific view of trauma.[14] While PTSD is mentioned, it is done so in passing and is not fully defined (11, 57-58). For example, the effects of trauma are only characterized as intrusive repetition, whereas other major reactions to trauma, avoidance and numbing, are hardly mentioned. For most of her arguments, Caruth does not rely on the research results of contemporary trauma science at all, but rather draws on Freud, de Man, and Lacan.

Recently, some discontent has been expressed with the direction that trauma studies have taken in the humanities. In *Trauma: a Genealogy*, Ruth Leys vehemently criticizes Caruth's approach and also that of Bessel van der Kolk, whom she sees as presenting an "alliance of a certain version of deconstructive criticism with empirical neuroscience" (17). Overall, Leys' criticism of the discipline in general and of Caruth in particular is convincing. Leys points to many weaknesses in Caruth's thinking; however, she fails to discuss one of the main reason why Caruth's approach is so troubling. Caruth does not back up her strong claims and sweeping conclusions with studies conducted on PTSD (and often not even with convincing textual evidence from the literature she studies), but at most with vague references to modern science. It could be that Leys overlooks this point because of her own uneasiness with connecting the biological phenomena to trauma. It is not clear why Leys is so vehemently opposed to biological research about trauma, but the fear of the physical involved with

---

[14] To give just one example from her work: "In modern trauma theory as well, there is an emphatic tendency to focus on the destructive repetition of the trauma that governs a person's life. As modern neurobiologists point out, the repetition of the traumatic experience in the flashback can itself be retraumatizing; if not life-threatening, it is at least threatening to the chemical structure of the brain and can ultimately lead to deterioration" (63).

the psychological and psychological illness shimmers through the texts of some other scholars as well. All appear to feel threatened by the thought that our mind might not be as independent of purely physical, out-of-our-control processes in the brain as many would like to assume. Leys thus cautions against neurobiological researchers such as Bessel van der Kolk and the, according to her, misguided trend to see these ideas as "represent[ing] an important approach to trauma in our present culture, especially in the United States, where biological paradigms are in the ascendant in psychiatry" (16). In her attempt to keep biology out of trauma, or, in using her own words, to shift from the body back to the mind, she overestimates van der Kolk's position in the research world, thus repeating the same mistake as other scholars who consider him alone as sufficient to represent all scientific research in trauma. Leys describes his research as "serv[ing] as a blueprint for much current research in the field" (6). However, he only offers one possible model of PTSD, which coexists with a multitude of other models of many other areas in PTSD research and he does not represent the central focus of PTSD study. Empirical PTSD research is still in its early stages and it remains to be seen whether the currently proposed models can accommodate the results of future study.

In *Writing History, Writing Trauma*, the historian Dominick LaCapra also points to problems with recent theoretical approaches to trauma in the humanities. He is particularly interested in the relationship between trauma and history, specifically historians writing about trauma. In his work, he correctly calls attention to the dangers of completely equating history with trauma, warns against the tendency to correlate, without distinction, victim position and trauma experience, and the problems with losing critical distance by identifying too much with one's object of study. LaCapra suggests an approach that does not give up on historical objectivity, but is coupled with expressions of what he calls "emphatic unsettlement" (41) in order to give credit to the special position that trauma takes on in people's lives. Yet does such an approach really safeguard against the overidentification between critic and trauma sufferer that LaCapra himself rejects, particularly since it is again a style that is only appropriate for writing about those experiencing trauma who were innocent victims? LaCapra understands the difficulty of applying this approach to trauma to those who are less easily categorized, or to perpetrator trauma, but brushes aside these intrinsic objections with a few vague comments in parenthesis.[15] In his search for a historical approach that could help provide this new style of objectivity and empathy,

---

[15] "(With respect to perpetrators, who may also be traumatized by their experience, I would argue that the historian should attempt to understand and explain such behavior and experience as far as possible – even recognize the unsettling possibility of such behavior and experience it in himor herself – but obviously attempt to counteract the realization of even its reduced analogues)" (41). It is unclear how this kind of approach would play out stylistically and how one would be sure not to fall into the trap of the "middle voice" which LaCapra finds unfit for the presentation of perpetrator trauma (199).

LaCapra suggests a need to go beyond one's own disciplinary limitations in order to understand trauma and its effects. Surprisingly though, medical science does not play an important role in his vision of an interdisciplinary approach despite its crucial place in trauma research; it is rather an afterthought, revealing a diffuse understanding of the area of study and included without explanation. The examples he offers for possible breakdowns of departmental limitations and disciplinary boundaries are thus only crossings within the humanities.[16] Yet it is precisely a linking of history and science that could provide the appropriate measure of objectivity any approach to trauma should have. While LaCapra is adamant in demanding that a degree of objectivity cannot be lost in historical writing, he uncritically embraces the idea of the trauma experience as illegible and unexplainable, a situation ungraspable with objective measures. However, trauma studies in psychiatry show us that a measure of objectivity in describing trauma is possible. LaCapra is correct in pointing out that historiography should not completely dismiss objectivity. There is no reason why psychological study should not adhere to the same standard.

It is necessary to redefine trauma studies for the humanities. The terminology has to be more precise, particularly concerning "trauma" and the "posttraumatic." While ethical questions obviously have to be addressed, they must be treated separately from the actual description of the reaction to trauma. Trauma research should not be limited to those individuals who, in the eyes of the scholar, qualify as victims since this approach hinders gaining an understanding of the whole spectrum of trauma and its effects. Scientific knowledge about trauma also has to play a larger role in the way research is conducted. There must be more than vague references to, or a brief mention of, PTSD to imply a scientific touch. Instead, the implications of trauma theories have to be checked against the results of studies in other fields. Similar to scientific models, if these theories do not agree with the results, they have to be modified or discarded (and not vice versa). Leys, LaCapra, and some other critics are taking steps in the right direction to reform trauma studies in the humanities. However, only when the critics free themselves from their uneasiness towards scientific research and do not see it as a threat to their discipline but as a partner that can help enlighten the subject, can trauma studies in the humanities be taken seriously.

2.3 What Is Trauma?

As the history of trauma research illustrates, for a long time trauma and the symptoms it causes were not clearly defined. With the introduction of the diag-

---

[16] LaCapra asks in his conclusions: "What is the role of the social sciences or *even* the natural sciences, including neuroscience, in relation to more interpretive approaches", yet then goes on to reflect on the question whether historians should look at art or read literary texts (*Writing History* 205-206, emphasis added).

nosis of posttraumatic stress disorder (PTSD) in 1980, to which the diagnosis of acute stress disorder (ASD) was added in 1994, the field of trauma studies finally gained a more uniform understanding of both trauma and its effects. The term "trauma" does not refer to the reactions to the event, which is a now out-dated view of formulating psychological stress, but to the actual event whose nature is traumatic (Yule, Williams, and Joseph 10). In 1980, such a traumatic event was defined as "outside the range of usual human experience," yet it soon became clear that this description was too general in its approach. In order to avoid having to decide what is "usual human experience" and what is not (for example, can the death of a loved one be classified as being "outside the range of usual human experience"?), DSM-IV introduced a more specific definition in 1994 which involved both a characterization of the stressor and of the reaction of the individual. DSM-IV and its follow-up edition DSM-IV-TR thus account for both objective and subjective elements of trauma. The traumatic event has to be of considerable severity posing a threat to one's life or that of others, involve actual death or serious injury or threaten one's physical integrity or that of oth-ers. It can be either experienced or witnessed by the individual. The severity of the stressor is linked with the likelihood of developing PTSD (464) so that the intensity of the event and the physical proximity to it can be predictive of the arising of later symptoms. For example, a study of a factory explosion disaster, where mortality and injury were dependent on the distance from the explosion, confirmed that workers closer to it were more likely to develop posttraumatic stress disorder (McFarlane and Potts 99). Yet not everyone experiencing a trau-matic event actually ends up developing PTSD. While one needs to remember that "[t]he origin of the individual's problems is found in an external factor, something outside the person" (Kleber, Figley, and Gersons 11), the reaction of the individual to the situation is also of importance and contributes to whether or not someone develops the disorder. DSM-IV-TR thus requires the subjective re-sponse to the trauma to involve feelings of "intense fear, helplessness, or horror" (467).

While the symptoms of acute stress often become visible very soon after the events, in many cases they disappear in a few days or weeks. In order to study these shorter episodes more completely, DSM-IV introduced, and DSM-IV-TR continues to include, acute stress disorder (ASD) as a diagnosis which is applied to cases that last a minimum of two days and a maximum of four weeks and oc-cur within four weeks of the traumatic event (471). In contrast, the diagnosis of posttraumatic stress disorder is used when an individual displays symptoms for more than one month. This means that one can have ASD, but after four weeks of persistent problems be considered to have PTSD. Consequently, the crite-ria are very similar, except that ASD focuses on dissociative symptoms which occur during or after the event in order to justify the diagnosis. These can be understood as symptoms of a disruption in the regularly "integrated functions of consciousness, memory, identity, or perception of the environment" (822). For example, the individual often experiences the events as dreamlike and unreal or as "being in a daze" (471). In addition, emotional reactions such as terror and fear may be so strong that one cannot recall parts or all of the trauma. Sufferers of this dissociative amnesia often state such things as: "I cannot remember anything. It was just horrible" or they might refuse to acknowledge the need for medical help despite obvious injuries (Malt 107). According to DSM-IV-TR, one may also have to deal with "a subjective sense of numbing, detachment, or absence of emotional responsiveness" (471), which can manifest itself as the so-called "psychic closing-off" (Lifton 127). For example, an officer doing rescue work after the atomic bomb hit Hiroshima reports that " 'After a while they [the bodies] became just like objects or goods that we handled in a very businesslike way. [...] We had no emotions.... Because of the succession of experiences I had been through I was temporarily without feeling' " (quoted in Lifton 126). This blunting of emotional responsiveness can also lead to an inability to experience pleasure and may be associated with a feeling of detachment from one's body (DSM-IV-TR 468). Frequently, trauma also causes an alteration in the perception of time and in cognitive ability: "Long-term thinking is reduced and priority is given to short-term thinking. The sense of time passing may be expanded or shortened, and the ability to think analytically is reduced" (Weisaeth 82). Sleep disturbances, somatic changes, and difficulty concentrating, as well as feelings of "hopelessness" and "survival guilt" are also common reactions to trauma (Kaplan and Sadock 1229).

The other symptoms of acute stress disorder correspond to the three major symptom-clusters that define posttraumatic stress disorder, which are intrusion, avoidance, and hyperarousal. Intrusion refers to persistent reexperiencing of the traumatic event "in the form of distressing images, thoughts, perceptions, dreams, or reliving" (Kaplan and Sadock 1227). These cognitive processes are not voluntary, but simply "*happe[n]* to the person" (de Silva and Marks 163). They are often triggered by internal or external cues that are reminescent of an aspect of the trauma and are ususally "specific sensory phenomena, such as sights, sounds, and smells that are circumstantially related to the traumatic event" (Miller 18). Symptoms of intrusion can be psychological as well as physiological. For example, a 12-year-old girl who had been sexually assaulted by her uncle, experienced rape-related thoughts and images every time she heard the music that had been playing during her assault. She also developed nightmares about the rape and often woke up from them perspiring and breathing heavily (Saigh and Bremner 12). The most common intrusive phenomena in PTSD are images and thoughts, which are actually far more common than dreams or flashbacks (feeling or acting as if the trauma was recurring) (de Silva and Marks 165). Even though research often does not distinguish between images and thoughts, it appears that intrusive recollections in visual form are more common than in verbal form since many individuals describe them as "pictures that pop into my mind" (de Silva and Marks 166). Although less common than visual images, intrusions can also be auditory, tactile, olfactory, and gustatory. For example, patients with war trauma often "hear" explosions, gunfire, or other war-related noises or a car accident victim might experience the smell and taste of oil or gas (de Silva and Marks 166-167). Frequently, an individual may ruminate on unanswerable questions, for example, "Could I have prevented what happened?," "Did it have to happen this way?," "Why did it have to happen?" While these intrusive thoughts are not recollections of the trauma, they are still extremely distressing to the individual and can cause considerable impairment in normal functioning (de Silva and Marks 168-169).

Symptoms of intrusion are inherently linked to those of avoidance. Thoughts about the trauma are so disturbing that an individual might exert considerable effort to avoid "thoughts, feelings or conversations associated with the trauma" as well as "activities, places, or people that arouse recollections" (DSM-IV-TR 468). Studies of prisoners of war report that many of them never discuss their experiences with anyone (Herman 89) and it has been shown that victims of natural disasters often have a strong desire to move away from the area where the event occurred (Lifton and Olson 221). Not surprisingly, the symptom-cluster of avoidance can contain some of the dissociative symptoms described earlier for ASD, such as amnesia about one or several important aspects of the trauma and diminished interest in, or an estrangement from, the world around one, both concerning activities or other people, as well as a reduced ability to feel emotions (DSM-IV-TR 464). Some individuals also have a sense of a foreshortened future and do not expect to have a career, a family, or a normal life span (DSM-IV-TR 464). For example, in a study of children in war situations in Uganda, the children showed much uncertainty about their future. This uncertainty is reflected in their comments: " 'If I am not a bunch of bones in my grave, I will be a businessman' " or " 'If I reach 2000 and I am still alive ...' " (quoted in Macksoud, Dyregrov, and Raundalen 629).

However, avoidance cannot completely shut out the traumatic experience and intrusions continually break through the memory barriers, causing stress for the person and again reenforcing the attempts at avoidance. It is not yet clear which symptoms arise first.[17] It is commonly accepted, however, that the symptom-clusters of avoidance and intrusion reenforce each other. Evidence suggests that the more a person tries to suppress the intrusions, the more frequently they occur and the more uncomfortable they are found to be (Trindler and Salkovskis 833). This combination of avoidance and intrusion thus "further exacerbates the trau-

---

[17] According to Mardi J. Horowitz, whose work on stress was instrumental in the formulation of PTSD, after an outcry period right after the event takes place, a phase of denial follows, which then gives rise to intrusion (Horowitz 6). In contrast, another important model by Mark Creamer et al. understands avoidance as a coping mechanism to deal with the intrusions that arise first due to stimuli in the environment (Creamer, Burgess, and Pattison 452).

matized person's sense of unpredictability and helplessness" and "is therefore potentially self-perpetuating" (Herman 47).

The third symptom-cluster noted in both ASD and PTSD concerns increased arousal and anxiety. According to DSM-IV-TR, hyperarousal can manifest itself through such problems as difficulty sleeping (often because of recurring nightmares during which the individual relives the trauma), hypervigilance, an exaggerated startle response, an inability to relax, and feeling on the edge or constantly on guard. The smallest things might lead to extreme anxiety. Some individuals have difficulty concentrating. Others become easily irritable or exhibit outbursts of anger which can lead to violent behavior.

For the diagnosis of PTSD, DSM-IV-TR requires that, from these three symptom-clusters, the individual displays at least one symptom of intrusion, three symptoms of avoidance and numbing, and two of increased arousal. In practice, however, there are situations where an individual does not meet the diagnostic criteria for PTSD but exhibits significant problems due to traumatic stress. Some trauma researchers have suggested that it might be more useful to see PTSD as occurring "along a continuity of normal to abnormal stress reactions, rather than to view it as a dichotomous variable which is either diagnosed or not" (Yule, Williams, and Joseph 16). This view allows classifications such as "partial PTSD" or "sub-threshold PTSD" for people who develop not the full range of symptoms, but still suffer considerable impairment in functioning and might benefit from the same therapy strategies as individuals who suffer from PTSD (Yule, Williams, and Joseph 16). This approach also offers more flexibility when dealing with the fact that not everyone has an identical stress reaction to the same traumatic event. It is this range in responses that has become central to more recent research in PTSD which is starting to ask questions about how and why PTSD occurs.

While there has been empirical research on what factors play a role in the various reactions people display after going through the same trauma, focusing on such issues as personality and previous trauma experiences as well as coping techniques and social support networks after the event, these studies are still in their beginning stages and are not yet able to provide a complete explanation for the coming-about and symptom manifestation of PTSD. It is thus necessary at this time to develop theoretical models of the processes at work during and after experiencing trauma. As mentioned previously, there are models available in several research areas, addressing the issues from various angles and viewpoints.

There has been much interest in neurobiological models of PTSD. Scholars have explored the biological effects of trauma on memory, on neural information processing, hormonal activation, autonomic nervous system activation, and pain sensation, to name but a few foci of research.[18] This branch of research offers biological explanations for the response PTSD sufferers have to trauma.

Another approach for undestanding trauma is that of the cognitive models. Tim Dalgleish, a trauma researcher, asserts that "it is probably the cognitive approach which is the most fully developed and which provides the most coherent and successful attempts at accounting for the range of factors implicated in PTSD" (Dalgleish 194). Since it is beyond the scope of this work to discuss each cognitive model in detail, this section will focus on the characteristics which all of them share.[19] According to cognitive theories, an individual has sets of pre-existing beliefs and models of the world, of others, and of themselves, which are products of prior experiences. When one encounters new experiences, non-salient information is usually ignored, while that compatible with one's meaning-structures is easily absorbed. However, when a traumatic event occurs, an individual is suddenly faced with a very prominent experience, but one which is incompatible with the person's established beliefs and models. Consequently, the information cannot be neglected and yet it cannot easily be added either. It thus stays in what Horowitz terms "active memory" (262). The unsuccessful attempt to integrate the trauma-related information into preexisting beliefs and constructs prevents a "completion" of processing and leads to both trying to suppress the new information (avoidance) and experiencing its repeated reoccurrence (intrusion). One way an individual can resolve this problematic inclusion process successfully is to change the pre-existing models in ways that can accommodate the trauma experience. Incomplete resolution, however, will lead to PTSD. This theoretical model thus has practical implications. Based on this approach, therapy for PTSD has to focus on the successful processing of the trauma, so that the trauma experience "can be integrated into the survivor's life story" (Herman 175). It does not aim at forgetting the memories of the event, but at making them a part of one's past that can be more easily controlled.

2.4   Literary Production and Trauma Therapy

Apart from pharmacological treatments, there are two dominant therapeutic approaches to PTSD that, alone and combined, have proven successful: cognitive restructuring and exposure (Richards and Lovell 241). Cognitive restructuring aims at teaching an individual to identify dysfunctional thoughts (which can

---

[18] For excellent reviews of the psychobiology and neurobiology of trauma, the reader is referred to articles by Golier and Yehuda; McFarlane; Orr, Metzger and Pitman; Rabois, Batten and Keane; Sullivan and Gorman; Wong; McCewan; and Golier and Yehuda. These were published in a large series of review articles on PTSD in the June 2002 issue of *Psychiatric Clinics of North America*.

[19] The following description of the commonalities of cognitive theories is based on Dalgleish's review article "Cognitive Theories of Post-traumatic Stress Disorder." Dalgleish also offers detailed descriptions and evaluations of the individual approaches.

cause negative emotional states such as fear or anger) and then evaluate them for their validity. The therapist can assist in replacing erroneous or unhelpful thoughts (for example, every time I hear a noise at night in my house, I immediately think that there is an intruder) with more beneficial ones (there are many sources of noises in my house ...) (Meadows and Foa 381). In exposure therapy, reduction of fear occurs with repeated and prolonged exposure to images or thoughts of the trauma. Patients realize that the traumatic event is over and that they no longer feel fear and anxiety because of it. In addition, exposure to the trauma can help to achieve cognitive changes in the way the trauma is perceived, and foster the emotional processing of the experience (Meadows and Foa 376-77). Consequently, exposure and cognitive restructuring are not mutually exclusive but can compliment each other productively. It is thus advisable "to take a both/and, rather than an either/or stance" when dealing with a PTSD patient (Horowitz 327).

One way to expose patients to their traumas is to have them replay the event in their head and recount it out loud to the therapist ("imaginal exposure") (Meadows and Foa 378). Imaginal exposure thus relies on the development of a verbal account during the therapy session. This process is complicated not only by the symptoms of PTSD, but also by the nature of the traumatic memories. They are predominantly visual images instead of verbal constructs. The presence of strong avoidance symptoms makes it even more difficult for the patient to face the details of the trauma. It has been suggested that this telling of the story of the trauma, this putting the experience into words, is the first step in processing the trauma information in such a way that it can finally be viewed as a part of one's past and be properly included in one's memory structures (Herman 176-181).

The construction of a story is not limited to the oral arena of the therapy session. Research indicates that writing the story down can have similar effects if the patient fully engages in the task (Richards and Lovell 243, 250). Richard Pennebaker's studies are particularly important in the development of this position. Pennebaker was initially interested in the use of writing as a way to influence people's physical health (Pennebaker "Telling Stories" 3). One of his early studies investigated whether freshman college students would benefit from writing about their experiences of being in college during this stressful time of their lives. One group of students was asked to write for twenty minutes on three consecutive days on their "very deepest thoughts and feelings about coming to college," while another one was asked to "describe in detail what you have done since you woke up this morning." This group was also told not to mention their "own emotions, feelings, or opinions" and to "be as objective as possible" (Pennebaker, Colder, and Sharp 531). The investigators then counted the number of visits to the health center in the months following the experiment by both the experimental and the control group, finding that the number of visits dropped for the students who wrote about their emotional experiences. Similar studies have since been conducted with diverse groups who went through traumas and stress of different severity, such as inmates of maximum security prisons, distressed crime victims, medical students, women after the birth of their first child, and men laid off from their job. All of them indicate positive health and behavioral effects through writing about themselves and their situation (Pennebaker "Telling Stories" 5). The 1999 study by Joshua M. Smyth *et al.* on "The Effects of Writing about Stressful Experiences on Symptom Reduction in Patients with Asthma or Rheumatoid Arthritis" looked for the first time at the question of whether the benefits of writing also apply to people who are not physically healthy. Earlier research results were indeed confirmed. Interestingly, even though the patients did not necessarily write on events that were related to their illness, but were asked to focus on emotionally traumatic experiences, such as the death of a loved one, their state of health improved (1308).

Apart from objective health changes, these studies also suggest that writing has positive psychological effects. Participants in all the studies have indicated that they experienced the writing exercise as "a valuable and meaningful experience" and "routinely report that the study caused them to think differently about the trauma" (Pennebaker and Francis 602). Writing has thus shown itself to be a powerful tool in dealing with stressful events and can help to improve both physical and psychological health. Although the amount of research regarding people who have experienced serious trauma or have PTSD has not been vast up to this point, theoretical-based case examples and empirical studies do suggest that writing is helpful for these groups. It has been noted by Gidron et al. that a particularly severe trauma might require a longer period of writing about the trauma experience and its effects than has been used in previous experiments (506).

When trying to find out why and how writing can have these positive health effects, it is helpful to think of the cognitive models discussed previously. According to these models, improvement occurs when memories of the traumatic experience can be included in the memory structures of the individual. A translation of the trauma and its effects into words can help facilitate this process. However, it has been shown that exposure through disclosing the facts about the trauma is not enough. When three groups of students were asked to write about a traumatic event by either focusing only on the facts of the trauma, or on the emotional response, or combining both, it was only the last group that exhibited positive long-term health effects. The verbal accounts thus should be a combination of both facts and emotions (Pennebaker and Francis 603). Yet a recent study looking at both optimists and pessimists expressing their stressful experiences has shown that even if the individual does express emotions, health benefits also depend on one's outlook on the world (Cameron and Nicholls 84). With pessimists, for example, these accounts can become unhelpful dwellings on the negative aspects of the trauma. In contrast, the study concluded that students who were asked to combine an exploration of the feelings and emotions they experience about the event with reflections on how they plan to cope with the events benefited more from the task. The positive effects of including cognitive processes in the texts are also confirmed by other findings. When doing word analysis of the written accounts that emerge during these types of experiments, it was discovered that the individuals who benefitted most from the writing task were those who used an increasingly large number of insight-related and causal words in the course of the exercise (Pennebaker and Francis 603). Furthermore, subjects who improved in health also improved the overall organization of their writing over time (Pennebaker "Putting Stress into Words" 543). These findings regarding the written accounts agree with the kind of story Herman believes needs to be constructed orally in therapy sessions with trauma sufferers:

> Out of the fragmented components of frozen imagery and sensation, patient and therapist slowly reassemble an organized, detailed, verbal account, oriented in time and historical context. [...] At each point in the narrative, [...] the patient must reconstruct not only what happened but also what she felt. The description of emotional states must be as painstakingly detailed as the description of facts. [...] Reconstructing the trauma story also includes a systematic review of the meaning of the event, both to the patient and to the important people in her life. (177-178).

All these findings suggest that it is not the story itself that is beneficial when telling or writing down one's trauma account, but the very process of composition which combines the exposure to the trauma and its effects together with a cognitive evaluation of the event (Pennebaker "Putting Stress into Words" 546). The process of composing an account about the trauma and its consequences is thus a way to process traumatic experiences so that they can be successfully moved out of active memory into one's more inclusive memory structures and belief systems.

Account-making about the trauma does not necessarily involve a therapist, especially when it is done in written form. Instead, it is suggested in the literature that many people can direct their own therapy. Without instructions or feedback, a patient can achieve better health through the process of writing because it fosters in the course of the exercise both a heightened ability to expose oneself to details of the trauma and the cognitive processing needed to deal with the event and its effects (Pennebaker "Putting Stress into Words" 546). The final story, however, is much less detailed than the raw data used to create it. One consequence of making a coherent, organized account out of the images and fragments of the traumatic memory is that in the end it is never completely accurate:

> The net effect of constructing a good narrative is that our recollection of emotional events is efficient - we have a relatively short, compact story - and undoubtedly biased. [...] Ironically, then, good narratives can be beneficial in making our complex

experiences simpler and more understandable but, at the same time, they distort our
recollection of them. Translating distress into language ultimately allows us to [...]
move beyond the experience. (Pennebaker "Telling Stories" 13)

In fact, there is evidence that the trauma story does not even necessarily have
to be one's own experience in order to have positive physiological and psychological health effects. In a recent experiment, college women who had experienced trauma in the past were divided into three groups. The members of group
one, the so-called "real-trauma group," were asked to write about their own
traumas and their emotional reactions to it, recreating "this memory as vividly
and fully as [they] can" (Greenberg, Wortman, and Stone 590). Group two, the
"imaginary-trauma group" wrote about imaginary traumas they had not previously experienced with the instructions to "[d]escribe as vividly and fully as possible all of the thoughts and feelings" they had when imagining the event (590).
Group three was the control group and wrote about trivial and non-emotional
events. Not only were the resulting texts of group one and two different from
those of the control group, but they were also different from each other. Overall,
the real-trauma stories sounded more personal and emotionally truthful and were
richer in sensory images. Imaginary trauma essays contained more cognitive elements (questions such as 'why me' ...) and some seemed more contrived or
melodramatic. However, when counting the number of health center visits in the
months after the event, members of *both* groups had significantly lower visits
to the center than the control group. Thus, contrary to some earlier speculation,
the results of the study show "that event-specific emotional disinhibition is not
necessary for the production of health effects following emotional disclosure"
(598). In contrast, it can be even more beneficial for a person who experienced
trauma in the past, not to disclose his or her own trauma, but an imagined one,
since self-exposure can increase the negative psychological effects caused by
the trauma. Real trauma participants reported more fatigue and greater avoidance than did participants in the other two groups. Consequently, members of
the imagined trauma group experienced no such reaction while having the same
decrease in health center visits. The study suggests that the imaginary context
can help to counteract the depressive influence of distressing materials such as
the traumatic scene, while at the same time helping to cope with one's own
trauma experience and other life stressors (599-600). The imaginary context allows one to become emotionally immersed in the imaginary trauma while at the
same time still being distanced from it through the fictional character of the experience. The emotional reaction to it can thus be modulated and limited to a
less distressing level.

It follows from these studies that the autobiographical eye-witness account
is not the only way one can write about trauma and still start healing from past
traumatic experiences. Trying to describe one's experience in complete detail
just as it happened is bound to fail since the report will never be completely

factually true because of the sheer necessity of translating the fragmented visual memory into a coherent verbal construct. Instead, it seems easier to face one's own trauma through the lens of another traumatic experience, not one's own, or transplant one's own onto someone else. Fiction can thus become a powerful tool in promoting the processing of a traumatic event and the emotional reactions it produces. The psychiatrist Lenore Terr sees a strong connection between (childhood) trauma and artistic production. She suggests that "[c]reative work may be inspired by external events that overwhelm and overpower the young psyche, forcing repeated attempts to discharge the 'traumatic anxiety' that was originally stirred up" ("Terror Writings" 372). Even if writers do not directly reflect on their own trauma, their works are "re-creations of the artist's experience" and reflect the "tone of trauma - of helplessness, confinement, and panic" ("Childhood Trauma" 546). Terr's focus is on terror literature, tracing to Edgar Allen Poe's childhood, for example, his imagery and tone in horror stories. When he was only three years old, Poe witnessed the death of his mother while alone with his younger sister and Terr understands this incident as the source for Poe's later style ("Childhood Trauma" 548-550). While Terr restricts herself to horror writers, her observations are applicable to many artists. As David Aberbach suggests, "through creativity, the artist may confront and attempt to master the trauma on his own terms" (3). Creative writing is a form of self-therapy containing both exposure and cognitive reevaluation, but facilitating the process of working through the trauma by interjecting the fictional plane between the individual (the writer) and his or her own traumatic experience.

However, talking about one's trauma, even if done indirectly through fictional means, is not easy. The emotional numbing caused by the experience and the vast array of avoidance techniques employed by the trauma survivor to protect him- or herself against the memories of the event can "far from opening the wellsprings of creativity, [...] in fact destroy the survivor's power to fantasize" (Aberbach 2). In addition, writers also find it extremely difficult to translate the experiences into language. Several authors have commented on how challenging the process can be and these problems are reflected in the works themselves. Greenberg, Wortman and Stone's experiment on the production of imaginary-trauma accounts versus real-trauma accounts in fact helps illuminate further why authors have such difficulty with finding words for their experiences. Even though the participants reported no trouble with articulating imaginary trauma stories, which were just as beneficial or even more so than the real trauma narratives, the texts appeared contrived or melodramatic. Part of the difficulty of fictionalizing trauma is thus also the problem of finding the fitting language and style to represent the experience in a way that the story still comes across as truthful and real. A trauma usually lies outside of the normal range of events that humans face. Therefore, traditional story telling and established literary patterns are not necessarily appropriate to capture the full experience.

The processes writers have to go through in order to create a story of the trauma can be compared to the ones described in cognitive PTSD models. Just as individuals have certain sets of beliefs about the world and people around them before they are confronted with the trauma, so are writers part of literary traditions and writing styles developed to describe these schemata. When the individual goes through an experience outside of his or her models of how the world behaves, it cannot be properly processed and included without changing these very belief structures. Writers face a similar problem. In order to capture the events, new ways of writing have to be explored, a new language and style needs to be developed to achieve a successful representation of the trauma and its aftermath. Completing a fictional piece about the trauma, one that works and is convincing in its representation, is thus comparable to processing the trauma and including it in one's memory structure, the most important step in therapy.

However, the consequences of literary production about trauma by writers go beyond the personal effects on the author. While writing as therapy can be a completely private matter,[20] authors usually publish their works, which means that they anticipate an audience when constructing their stories. It has been suggested that artists are uniquely fit to take on the role of witness to traumatic events because they allow their audience to understand better the traumatic experience and its effects because of their special skills:

> Much of [clinical literature] is empty of relevant accounts; and, even when a clinician recognizes the need to record the world his patient lives in, too frequently the pen is not equal to the task. This is where the artist scores. As a person whose primary task it is to describe what it feels like to be in some carefully defined human situation, he has both the time and the skill to recreate the situation and to tell us how one person was affected by it - how he thought and felt at the time, how he acted, how he extricated himself or failed to extricate himself, and how perhaps it permanently altered his ways of thinking and feeling about other people. (Bowlby vi)

With its publication, the text becomes part of the network of social, political, and moral currents that define both society and its culture and will be evaluated in accordance with their values and opinions. This issue is less pertinent with trauma stories about people who can be clearly identified as victims, for example texts about victims of the Holocaust, child abuse, or rape. The writer still faces the difficult task and heavy burden of creating the trauma in a way that it is accessible to the audience and accurately conveys the horror of the experience, but the author can feel relatively safe from being accused of trying to rewrite history. However, how does one deal with traumatic experiences which were extremely influential on the psychological make-up of people, but at the same time did not

---

[20] In some experiments, for example, participants could keep their writing samples, or write on a child's magic pad from which the story could be immediately erased. The results did not reveal any adverse effects stemming from these methods (Pennebaker "Telling Stories" 6).

happen to the innocent? Can these experiences be represented without distorting historical truths? Should they be shared or should they be simply forgotten? These are questions German writers necessarily faced when contemplating describing and fictionalizing the bombings of German cities during World War II. The texts that finally did emerge about the topic reveal the full complexity of the issue of the bombings in German society and bear witness to the authors' difficulty in presenting the interrelation between the effects of personal trauma experiences and German guilt without having available adequate literary patterns or language to talk about the events. Critics also need to use caution when analyzing these literary accounts and make sure that they do not misrepresent the reality of German responsibility for the suffering during World War II. Reading the narratives in the larger context of trauma literature and applying psychiatric criteria while at the same time studying the German guilt question might be one way to explore the issues in a manner sensitive to these concerns.

Chapter 3
Confronting the Past? The Role of Guilt and Shame in Postwar Germany

3.1   The End of the War: Facing Complete Destruction

For Nazi Germany, the war ended in 1945 in complete defeat. The whole country was occupied and split into four separate zones each ruled by one of the Allied forces. Most cities were reduced to heaps of rubble and there was hardly any food available to sustain the population. Families were broken up and refugees were desperately trying to find places where they could settle down. The ideology that Germans had readily embraced for the past twelve years suddenly had to be refuted, at least outwardly. This break with the past was exemplified by the removal and burning of the pictures of Hitler, which had been on display in many German living rooms, shortly before the Allies appeared at people's doors.[1] Germans were finally forced to face the terrible crimes they had committed against millions of people during the Nazi era. Yet did they really confront what had happened? Texts dealing with the period between 1945 and 1948 emphasize the refusal to believe in, or admit to, German atrocities when the population was faced with the horror of concentration camps in pictures, films, and reports. Günter Grass (born in 1927), for example, relates how he himself could not find any other reaction than complete denial in the face of the crimes:

> [A]ls ich mit vielen meiner Generation [mit] den Ergebnissen von Verbrechen konfrontiert wurde, die Deutsche zu verantworten hatten und die seitdem unter dem Be-

---

[1] In *Erwachsenenspiele*, Günter Kunert memorably describes this last-minute "denazification" which he observed hours before the Russian troops arrived in Berlin: " 'Im Heizungskeller ist ein Feuer angezündet worden! Wer etwas verbrennen möchte ...!' [...] Getümmel setzt ein. Papiere werden hervorgezerrt, Dokumente, Ausweise, Fotos, Indizien für die eigene Schuld, für die Mitverantwortung an dem Komplex 'Drittes Reich.' Ab ins Fegefeuer mit dem belastenden Material, auf daß man selber gereinigt und geläutert aus dem Keller in eine neue Zeit hervorgehe. [...] Morgen früh werde ich mich unter lauter Opfern des Faschismus befinden" (85). (" 'A fire has been lit in the boiler room! Whoever wants to burn something ...!' [...] Turmoil ensued. Papers were produced, documents, I.D.s, pictures, indicators of one's own guilt, of the shared responsibility of the Third Reich complex. Straight into the fires of Purgatory with the accusing material, so that one can climb out of the cellar into a new era cleansed and free of sin. [...] Tomorrow morning I will be only among victims of fascism.")

griff Auschwitz summiert sind, sagte ich: Niemals. Ich sagte mir und anderen, andere sagten sich und mir: Niemals würden Deutsche so etwas tun. (*Schreiben nach
Auschwitz* 8)[2]

This initial vocal denial later gave way to complete passivity among the majority
of the German population, making them "die Volksgemeinschaft der Schlafwan-
dler" (Scheer 219)[3], as a journalist fittingly described them. Thought was directed mainly toward obtaining food, coal, and shelter. The population followed
the rules set forth by the occupation forces, in some ways continuing what they
had done before; taking and executing orders, and there were few signs that this
outer shift of political direction caused many changes in thinking at this time.
Stig Dagerman, a Swedish journalist who visited Germany in the fall of 1946,
points to the extreme living conditions as one reason why Germans seemed unable to reflect on their recent past:

> People demanded of those who were suffering their way through this German autumn
> that they should learn from their misfortune. No one thought that hunger is a very bad
> teacher. Anyone who is properly hungry, and helplessly so, does not upbraid himself
> for his own hunger: instead, he upbraids those from whom he thinks he could have
> expected help. Nor does hunger encourage investigation into the web of causes [...].
> (13)

Dagerman does not excuse the Germans' lack of self-reflection and disapproves
of their behavior, but also does not see much chance for change before the living
conditions improve (16-17). Other commentators are more critical of the behavior of the Germans, fearing that hunger is also used as another excuse to hinder
an inner regeneration, to allow a "Flucht aus dem Denken" (Scheer 215),[4] and
to blame others for one's own misery (Scheer 213).

Officially, of course, Germans were forced to face their own and Germany's
guilt through the Allies' Nurenberg and other trials and the attempts at denazification of the population. While one would expect that there would have been
a strong reaction to the Nurenberg Trial, after all some of the most important
"leaders" of the past twelve years were facing prosecution, Germans remained
mainly indifferent to the event. Most Germans wanted to engage in as little discussion as possible, even wishing the Allies would resolve the issue quickly by
simply hanging all twenty defendants to get the story over with (Süskind 308).
Despite this, the criminals were tried and punished in Nurenberg according to
the standards established by the Allies. The vast project of evaluating everyone's

---

[2] "When I and many others of my generation [...] were confronted with the consequences of the
crimes that Germans were responsible for and that today are summed up by the term Auschwitz,
I said: never. I said to myself and to others, others said to themselves and to me: never would
Germans do such things."

[3] "A nation of sleepwalkers"

[4] "escape from thinking"

level of involvement with questionnaires and denazification trials, however, was not always successful in identifying the worst culprits and even less so in bringing about inner change. Soon, the questionnaires and proceedings were ridiculed and thus dismissed by the population because of the inability of the bodies carrying out the proceedings to apply uniform standards and to combat widespread corruption (Glaser 343). An additional consequence of the denazification movement was the idea of many Germans that once officially denazified, they were free of any responsibility for the past. They saw themselves as rehabilitated, rejecting or suppressing any moral guilt (Dürr 5).

However, not all Germans followed this trend of avoidance and suppression. Especially among intellectuals, a discussion of German guilt and responsibility did start to take place very soon after the Nazi regime had fallen. Yet the literary field was going through some degree of turmoil at the time. Established literary figures were caught up in a struggle between those who had gone into exile during the Nazi years and those who had decided to stay in Germany in a state of so-called "inner emigration," and young literary talents were still in the process of defining themselves and their future direction. It were thus historians and philosophers who were the first to tackle the question of German guilt. In *Die deutsche Katastrophe* (*The German Catastrophe*), for example, the historian Friedrich Meinecke tries to analyze the rise of Hitler-Germany in a larger historical context. Starting at the end of the 18th century, he outlines how German history led to Nazism because of both the influence of Prussian militarism with its unconditional and unquestionable devotion to duty, following of orders, and the move towards a nationalism that embraced a Machiavellian, amoral stand. By looking at the past two hundred years of German history through the lens of what had happened between 1933 and 1945, Meinecke was beginning to change established positions of German historiography. His new ideas and his firm stance on the influence of Prussian militarist thinking still earns him praise today by other historians.[5] Yet while Meinecke offers some sound historical insights and is at times quite progressive, his solutions to the German guilt question seem highly idealistic and naive. Meinecke emphasizes the idea of the two Germanies, the corrupt bad (Nazi) Germany and the good and true Germany, the country of high culture, of poets and thinkers. Hitler can thus be explained as "eine innere Fremdherrschaft" (152) so that his ideas are not really a part of the German character or spirit.[6] In order for Germans to fulfill their duty to "sich selber nunmehr zu reinigen von erlebtem Graus" (142), [7] Meinecke wants to reawaken the true German spirit by exposing everyone to German high culture:

> In jeder deutschen Stadt und größeren Ortschaft wünschen wir uns also künftig eine Gemeinschaft gleichgerichteter Kulturfreunde, der ich am liebsten den Namen einer

---

[5] Wolfgang J. Mommson, for example, calls Meinecke's work a "courageous book" (258).

[6] "an inner foreign rule" (trans. 103)

[7] "to cleanse themselves of the horror which they have undergone" (trans. 96)

"Goethegemeinde" geben möchte. [...] Den "Goethegemeinden" würde die Aufgabe
zufallen, die lebendigsten Zeugnisse des großen deutschen Geistes durch den Klang
der Stimme den Hörern ins Herz zu tragen, – edelste deutsche Musik und Poesie
zugleich ihnen immer zu bieten. (174)[8]

By making Hitler the "foreign rule" that had invaded the German spirit which is
pure and true, Meinecke unconsciously seems to try to lessen some of the guilt
and to foster escapism and suppression of the past. It contradicts some of his
earlier endeavors and bolder statements about the causes leading to the Third
Reich, since not surprisingly, the conservativeness of Meinecke's wishful ideas
based on the 'good Germany' echoed the views of many whom he had earlier in
his work criticized for their lack of initiative – Germans who had been raised in
the Prussian military tradition.[9]

One of the most important and most complete treatments of the German situation after the war is Karl Jaspers' *Die Schuldfrage* (*The Question of German
Guilt*) from 1946 which is based on parts of a lecture series the philosopher held
at Heidelberg University in the winter semester of 1945/46. Here, Jaspers explores in detail both guilt in general and the German situation in particular. He
defines different guilt concepts so that the term "guilt" is less vague and can
be applied more specifically. In addition, one by one, Jaspers refutes and cor-
rects false assumptions and excuses with which Germans consciously or unconsciously attempt to cover up their guilt. By analyzing guilt thoroughly, Jaspers
tries to avoid the temptation to evade or suppress guilt and offers a basis for a
true exploration of individual and German responsibilities, since "wir Deutschen
ohne Ausnahme verpflichtet [sind], in der Frage unserer Schuld klar zu sehen
und die Folgerungen zu ziehen" (15).[10] As another goal, Jaspers wants to pre-

---

[8] "In every German city and larger village, therefore, we should like to see in the future a community of like-minded friends of culture which I should like best to call Goethe Communities.
[...] To the Goethe Communities would fall the task of conveying into the heart of the listeners
through sound the most vital evidence of the great German spirit, always offering the noblest
music and poetry together" (trans. 119-120).

[9] For example, in his autobiography *Requiem for a German Past* from 1999, Jurgen Herbst, who
had been raised to be a professional soldier and who throughout his book shows the military in
a very positive and completely uncritical light, describes how Meinecke's ideas served him and
his friends as guidance after the war: "For a time we became romantic idealists. We read and
embraced Friedrich Meinecke's *Die deutsche Katastrophe* with its fervent wish for a rebirth of
the spirit of Goethe. In Etzel's room we sought to realize for ourselves Meinecke's dream of
creating small reading circles throughout the land [...]. We gathered other friends around us and
read the German idealist poets and tried to lose ourselves in their world of friendship and love"
(Herbst 217). Even Herbst, however, who is not very critical about any of the German institutions
or traditions, describes that he realized the futility of these endeavors: "by immersing ourselves
in poetry and music and shutting our eyes to the world that surrounded us and turning our backs
on the past we had lived through, we could not come to terms with either our past or our present"
(Herbst 217).

[10] "we Germans are indeed obliged without exception to understand clearly the question of our
guilt, and to draw the conclusions" (trans. 28).

vent that the concept of collective guilt is applied to Germany as a whole, because it consists of unreflected generalizations (31). While he agrees that there is collective German *liability* (41), he emphasizes that one cannot make an individual out of a people: " Ein Volk kann nicht heroisch untergehen, nicht Verbrecher sein, nicht sittlich oder unsittlich handeln, sondern immer nur die Einzelnen aus ihm" (25).[11] However, this does not mean that Jaspers denies German guilt. He makes abundantly clear that he thinks, "dass jeder Deutsche in irgendeiner Weise schuldig ist" (49).[12]

In order to define guilt more clearly and also to have a better understanding of how Germans should and could deal with their past in a responsible manner, Jaspers distinguishes four kinds of guilt. *Criminal guilt* addresses crimes against specific laws, and jurisdiction lies with the courts (17). The Nurenberg Trials dealt with this kind of guilt, when individual criminals were persecuted for specific crimes (32-33). *Political guilt* refers to the deeds of the state. Everyone is responsible for the way that they are governed and the deeds committed in the name of the country (17). Jaspers stresses that there is no standing aside regarding politics in a modern state; an apolitical, passive stance leads to guilt (41-42). *Moral guilt* deals with the question that one has to ask oneself: "how am I guilty?" This is individual guilt, including the following of orders, and can only be judged by one's conscience (17). It also contains convenient self-deceptions like those of many intellectuals who were at first charmed by Nazism, then turned away to see themselves finally as victims of the Nazis (46), or those in the military who wanted to get rid of Hitler, but only after they had won the war (45). Moral guilt also arises through every failure to take action, or blindness to others' misfortunes (47). Finally, *metaphysical guilt* is entailed by violating one's responsibility for the world and the other human beings in it, by letting wrongs and injustices happen, especially when crimes are committed with one's knowledge. Metaphysical guilt can also arise as survival guilt when we do not give our own life in order to save that of another, or do not resist, even if we do not accomplish anything by such resistance and morally do not have the duty to do so (48).

According to Jaspers, when each individual - collective change is an illusion - reflects truthfully on both his or her own role in Nazi Germany, and without excuses, thus making his or her guilt conscious on all levels, an inner transformation or purification can begin to take place (70). Adopting this approach also means to distinguish between what is and is not relevant to the question of guilt. Jaspers points out that, while there is no doubt that Germans had to suffer during the war and continued to suffer under the terrible consequences of the bombings afterwards, this state of misery is completely unrelated to the question

---

[11] "A people cannot perish heroically, cannot be a criminal, cannot act morally or immorally; only its individuals can do so" (trans. 41).

[12] that all "Germans [...] are guilty in some way" (trans. 73).

of guilt. One's own suffering cannot atone for guilt and one should not expect to be praised or excused because of suffering (77-78). Since moral and meta-physical guilt never ceases, confronting one's guilt and striving for purification is a never-ending process lasting throughout one's life. In addition, already at this early point in time, Jaspers correctly states that guilt is not restricted to the generation that lived through the Nazi period:

> So fühlt der Deutsche [...] sich mitbetroffen von allem, was aus dem Deutschen erwächst. Nicht die Haftung des Staatsangehörigen, sondern die Mitbetroffenheit als zum deutschen geistigen und seelischen Leben gehörender Mensch, [...] wird hier Grund nicht einer greifbaren Schuld, aber eines Analogons von Mitschuld.
> Wir fühlen uns weiter beteiligt nicht nur an dem, was gegenwärtig getan wird, als mitschuldig am Tun der Zeitgenossen, sondern auch an dem Zusammenhang der Überlieferung. Wir müssen übernehmen die Schuld der Väter. (53)[13]

While Jaspers here refers to the connection between the rise of National So-cialism and the previous history of Germany similarly to that which Meinecke outlined in his work, he also already prognoses the future German condition which even in generations after 1945 has to bear the heritage of moral and meta-physical guilt from the Nazi past. Consequently, the need for purification, the honest facing of guilt, does not end with the generations involved directly, but continues into the future if a learning process is to be ensured. Germans will always have to bear the burden of this past and have to be sensitive and truthful about these issues if they want to look responsibly at their history.

Jaspers does not outline specific solutions or concrete political plans for the future or what consequences the spiritual involvement in the Nazi ideology should entail. For example, he does not comment on whether someone who was partially or wholly involved in Nazism should still be able to hold a political office or work for the government after 1945. Yet what Jaspers offers is both a sharp analysis of the situation concerning the guilt question after the war and a philosophical and spiritual basis for how Germans can go on in the future. In this sense, the historian Anson Rabinbach is correct when he sees Jaspers' work as "the secular variant" of "the efforts of Evangelical theologians and leaders like Martin Niemöller and Gustav Heinemann [...] in the *Stuttgarter Schuldbekennt-nis* of October 1945" (190).[14] The truthful evaluation of the past that Jaspers

---

[13] "Thus the German [...] feels concerned by everything growing from German roots. It is not the liability of a national but the concern of one who shares the life of the German spirit and soul [...] which here comes to cause, not as tangible guilt, but somehow analogous to co-responsibility. We further feel that we not only share in what is done at present - thus being co-responsible for the deeds of our contemporaries - but in the links of tradition. We have to bear the guilt of our fathers" (trans. 79).

[14] In this *Schuldbekenntnis*, the Protestant church blames itself for having made mistakes during the Nazi era, referring to the willingness of most of the church to collaborate officially with the Nazi state and its ideology. However, the suppression of guilt can also clearly be felt in the declaration: "Zwar bekannte man sich in Stuttgart dazu, nicht alles getan zu haben, was die Situ-

suggests in his essay can be a way to define oneself again as a German. Jaspers gives an answer to what it could now, after the Third Reich, mean to be a German who is acceptable to the world community - one who takes responsibility as an individual both for the past and for events in the future. Unfortunately, Jaspers' important call for purification and honesty when facing personal and political guilt remained without echo in most of the population. Instead, Germany headed into a period of restoration in its Western part and a time of official denial of any guilt in East Germany. Some historians have suggested that this period of suppression was needed in order to give the German population space for self-assertion in a world of complete insecurity (Mommsen 254), or have questioned whether it was even realistic or desirable to expect Germans to face and work through their guilt of these enormous crimes right after 1945:

> [W]ho is to say that this *Aufarbeitung* would have occurred in the "good" sense, that is, filled with remorse and comprehensive reeducation, which were to make the past the centerpiece of an ongoing and active process of self-evaluation in the public and private spheres? Could this really have occurred in a devastated country, populated by hungry and destitute people, confused about their fate, hateful of their predicament, and resenting their occupation? (Markovits 221)

Whether an unavoidable development or not, a consequence of this silence after the breakdown of the Nazi regime was that the new German countries were founded on avoidance and suppression. The influence of these circumstances was, and still is, considerable and makes the question of German guilt an important factor in the development of Germany in all respects – political, cultural, as well as social. Jaspers' definitions of guilt thus can still prove helpful to gain a more complete understanding of German progress and shortcomings in relation to the guilt question.

3.2   Constructing a Past and a Future: The Adenauer Era

In East Germany, the policy of denial of responsibility was officially orchestrated by the state. The party simply defined the state as based on antifascism, thus giving itself a founding myth. Good examples of this myth are the many literary narratives exploring the past by focusing on the antifascist father.[15] This process of legitimating oneself culminated in the idea that "the Party, its state,

---

ation jeweils erfordert hätte. Gleichzeitig jedoch wurde mit vier negierten Komparativen ('nicht mutiger bekannt, nicht treuer gebetet, nicht fröhlicher geglaubt und nicht brennender geliebt') der Eindruck erweckt, das Geleistete sei mutig und tapfer gewesen" (Glaser 327). Jaspers' request for complete admittance of guilt goes much further.

[15] Julia Hell lists a number of these texts in her article "History as Trauma, or, Turning to the Past Once Again: Germany 1949/1989," such as Anna Seghers' *Die Toten bleiben jung* or Willi Bredel's trilogy *Verwandte und Bekannte* (Hell 915).

and, later, its people were on the side of the 'victors' in the battle of history, that they were the victors of history" (Hell 918-919).[16] While responsibility was officially denied in East Germany, the situation in the West was somewhat more complex. It has been said that the ahistorical attitude of West Germans was independent of political policies, as "the authorities certainly supported historical research and teaching on these matters. [...] It was rather that the disinclination of the public to embark on a full discussion of Germany's most recent history had become of deep-seated attitude" (Mommsen 253-254). It is correct that there was considerable effort among (some) West German intellectuals to illuminate the past and its consequences. Also, Nazi trials were still being held and some political responsibility was accepted, as manifested in the restitution payments for Nazi victims, and in the fact that the democratic government engaged in some public discussions over questions of responsibility, particularly under the leadership of Theodor Heuss, the country's first President. However, the new West German government under Chancellor Adenauer also played an integral part in fostering the structures of silence in Germany. One of the major compromises Adenauer supported was that a large number of people who had been part of the Nazi regime were again allowed to enter into important government, political, and economic positions. Adenauer thought that concentrating on integration was vital for ensuring the functionality of the new democracy. With this attitude, he fostered an atmosphere that allowed one to erase past crimes from one's conscience. His views were widely supported by the general population of which, according to a survey conducted in 1951/52, only "four percent thought that all Germans 'bore a certain guilt for Germany's actions during the Third Reich,' and only twenty-one percent felt 'some responsibility for rectifying these wrongs' "(Herf 274).

These policies of silence, forgetting, and erasing the past were also felt in other areas. Instead of accepting the complex net of moral and metaphysical responsibility and working on inner renewal, as Jaspers had hoped, Germans invested all their mental and physical energy into rebuilding the cities and striving for economic recovery. Alexander and Margarete Mitscherlich emphasize in their influential psychoanalytic study *Die Unfähigkeit zu trauern* (*The Inability to Mourn*) from 1967 the importance of this phase. According to the Mitscherlichs, this immense collective effort of rebuilding, "das manische Ungeschehenmachen,"[17] constitutes one of the major ways of avoiding facing the burden of German guilt (40). Significantly, the rebuilding that took place was again symptomatic of the psychological situation in Germany. While the ruins had been ex-

---

[16] Obviously this stance by East Germany precluded a real attempt at facing the past and the guilt Germans had undoubtedly acquired also in the eastern part of the country. However, one should not forget that it was, of course, true that a much smaller number of the important figures in culture and politics in East Germany had associations with the Nazi era.

[17] "the manic 'unmaking' "

ternal reflections of the inner destruction of the people who, without orientation, existed among them, the approach taken to rebuilding the cities immediately after the war displayed the now deep seated suppression and denial of both the horror Germany had caused and the destruction of its cities which was one of its consequences.

Just as in history, philosophy, and literature, where scholars and writers were searching for new approaches, new methods, and new forms adequate for a new beginning, architects hoped for a distinct counter-movement to the building styles of the Nazi period. They were aiming at a simple clear style, one of 'democratic honesty' which would oppose the bombastic and overpowering tastelessness of the official NS-architecture (Glaser 141). Yet their wishes and hopes were deeply disappointed. These architects soon had to realize that their ideas went completely against the official policies of "Erhaltung, Wiederherstellung, bestenfalls vorsichtige[r] Korrektur" (Glaser 143).[18] Some of the urban planners from the Third Reich moved to different places and continued implementing their ideas developed under National Socialism for reconstructing the cities (Diefendorf 91). In many other instances, German city officials after 1945, with broad support from the population, tried to erase the traces of the war by rebuilding everything the way it had been before the air raids began. They were especially interested in looking further into the past and restoring and rebuilding historical landmarks as precisely as possible.

A good example of this trend of conservation and restoration can be found in Frankfurt. The conflict between which part of history is remembered and which is not becomes clear when one compares the different approaches applied. So, while there is no trace left of the old Frankfurt synagogue at Börneplatz,[19] the city immediately decided to restore the "Goethehaus" to its original state (Brockmann 69). In an air raid in 1944, Goethe's house of birth had been completely destroyed except for a small part of the front wall of the house, which later collapsed as well. Despite being nothing but a pile of rubble, its rebuilding started as early as 1947, though the whole surrounding area lay in ruins. At the time of its completion in 1951, newspaper pictures still show the newly reconstructed house amidst a field of rubble (Meier 187). The stark contrast between the rebuilt Goethehaus and the destruction surrounding it exemplifies the conflicts between different internal and external needs of the population and reveals the direction Germany was choosing in reestablishing itself. Finding inner stability by creating spaces in which one could resurrect one's cultural and national identity was seen as being at least as important as developing outer security by providing places to live and work. Rebuilding cultural landmarks immediately after the

---

[18] "upkeep, restoration, at the most careful corrections"

[19] In the 1980s, city council members were even pushing to put a monstrous administration building in its place (Boelich 62). However, the so-called 'Börneplatz controversy' that arose from these intentions finally led to the establishment of a second location of the Frankfurt Jewish Museum at Börneplatz, the 'Museum Judengasse,' in 1992.

war was thus a way to rebuild oneself; as the landmarks rose out of the ruins, so too did the Germans who saw themselves mirrored in their beauty. The ruins, reminders of Germany's downfall and guilt, were opposed by what many saw as icons of German culture and greatness. As the Goethehaus in its perfection could mask out the bleakness of its surroundings, so many Germans tried to redirect attention from a dark past to a happier one. Restoring cultural landmarks thus became also a symbol for the refusal to reflect on the recent past.

The large support for the Frankfurt Goethehaus project after 1945 confirms the fundamental importance of the rebuilding in terms of German self-definition. The historical "restoration" of the Goethehaus to its previous condition, even though it entailed a complete rebuilding, was possible because its appearance and structure had been extensively documented with drawings and photographs. In addition, its interior had been carried to safety shortly after the war had started, thus providing the original furnishings for the new structure.

Yet the cultural significance which was allotted to the building was even more important. Cultural identity is repeatedly linked to specific places and spaces and it is intrinsically tied in with the physical structures and the architectural design organizing this space. In *The Architecture of the City*, for example, the Italian architect and theorist Aldo Rossi emphasizes the strong interdependence of collective history and memory with objects and places. The city is here understood as "the collective memory of its people," a relationship that is responsible for the special significance an urban structure represents and what distinguishes it from others (130-131). At the same time, this interaction guarantees an expression of continuation and identity, a union between the past, when a building or monument was erected, and the future (131). In accordance with these ideas about the city and its collective, architect Donatella Mazzoleni has defined architecture as an extension of the human and societal body as well as a metaphor of this body (289). Buildings can be understood as locales for the expression of a certain (cultural) understanding, can function as signs with which the community shares its self-view, and can provide the space for the reassertion of one's identity in times of turmoil (290-291).

In the case of the Goethehaus, the building was seen as not only representing, but actually being Goethe and his spirit, the embodiment of German high culture. This connection was facilitated by the fact that the air raid which had destroyed the building had taken place on the anniversary of Goethe's death, March 22nd. In the words of a Frankfurt citizen:

> "[...] solange wir in den gleichen Räumen atmen, seine Treppenstufen emporsteigen, durch nämliche Fenster wie er auf Welt und Himmel schauen durften, konnten wir das Gefühl seiner unmittelbaren Nähe haben. Nun [...] hat sich eine Kluft aufgetan, unüberbrückbar. Es ist, als sei er nun wirklich gestorben." (quoted in Meier 185)[20]

---

[20] "[...] as long as we could breath in the same rooms, walk up his stairs, look as he did at the world through those windows, we could feel him close to us. Now an unsurpassable gap has opened up. It feels as if he were now truly dead."

For many, not reconstructing Goethe's house of birth speedily and in a historically accurate manner would have meant accepting the complete destruction of any notion of German national and cultural identity that was based on German history. Going back to Goethe or other historical sites allowed the recreation of a Germany one could still be proud of: Germany as the haven of culture. The more recent past with its barbarous and monstrous characteristics and the severe consequences it entailed was thus dismissed from consciousness as well as from the physical environment.

The significance of both the destruction and restoration of building structures as symbols for the inner psychological condition of the German population is further confirmed in Heinrich Böll's important work *Billiard um halbzehn* (*Billiards at Half-past Nine*). Here, even though the novel takes place on only one day in 1958, Böll analyzes the German postwar condition and in particular the inability of Germans to face their past by focusing on three generations of architects and the construction, destruction, and rebuilding of an Abbey with which they were involved. The Abbey St. Anton, around which the plot evolves, had been built by Heinrich Fähmel in 1907 and was then blown up by his son Robert during the Second World War. While he was under a military order by an insane superior officer to destroy the Abbey in order to clear the path for better shooting opportunities, his true reason was the wish to demolish Nazi structures, since even the monks of the Abbey had been supporters of Hitler, and to remember Nazi victims: "ein Denkmal aus Staub und Trümmern wollte er denen setzen, die keine kulturgeschichtlichen Denkmäler gewesen waren und die man nicht hatte schonen müssen" (184).[21] Finally, Robert Fähmel's son Joseph rebuilds the Abbey after the war as if it had never been blown up. The monks of the Abbey see the rebuilding of it as an act of reconciliation (227), but what it really entails is a negation of history and of the victims which the destroyed monastery was supposed to commemorate.

Joseph, however, does not understand the meaning behind the destruction of the Abbey. When he finds out that his father was the one who had destroyed it, he is outraged. His reaction is an example of the apolitical attitude to the past typical in the 1950s: he does not accept his father's motivation, as he strongly believes that culturally significant buildings need to be saved under any circumstances. Joseph is unable to understand the destruction as an act of defiance and he cannot comprehend the interrelation between the Abbey's destruction and the crimes committed against people under Nazism. Especially through the actions of Heinrich Fähmel's wife, Johanna, Böll connects the restoration of the Abbey with the rebuilding of old structures in the new state where successful Nazis can again gain political power. A patient in a mental hospital for many years, she is

---

[21] "He had wanted to erect a monument of dust and rubble for those who had not been historical monuments and whom no one had thought to spare" (trans. 156).

marginalized by society, but ironically sees most clearly the regaining of power by Nazi criminals in Germany:

> ich habe Angst, viel mehr als damals; ihr habt euch offenbar an die Gesichter schon gewöhnt, aber ich fange an, mich nach meinen harmlosen Irren zurückzusehnen; seid ihr denn blind? so leicht zu täuschen? Die werden euch für weniger als eine Hand-bewegung, für weniger als ein Butterbrot umbringen! Du brauchst nicht einmal mehr dunkelhaarig oder blond zu sein, brauchst nicht mehr den Taufschein deiner Groß-mutter. (293)[22]

Johanna is the only one who takes action against what she sees, albeit without long-term consequences, and shoots and wounds an important politician. She perceives him as the embodiment of those attitudes and values that deny her grandson Joseph and his generation the chance of developing into independent individuals (Ryan 90). In contrast, while Heinrich and Robert Fähmel are also disgusted by what they see around them, they do not act upon it. Again, their be-havior is tied in with the Abbey St. Anton. Earlier in the day, they both promise to attend the reconciliation speech that the Abbot will give at the Abbey's conse-cration, even though they do not want to support this type of reconciliation and thus actually do not want to go (Böll 227-228). In the last scene of the novel, the conflict between action and silence is accentuated even more when Heinrich Fähmel is presented with a birthday cake which is a perfect model of the Abbey he had designed:

> Der Alte lief rot an, er sprang auf das Kuchenmodell zu, hob seine Fäuste wie ein Trommler, der zu zornigem Takt seine Kräfte sammelt, und einen Augenblick schien es, als würde er das gezuckerte Backwerk zermalmen, aber er ließ seine erhobenen Fäuste wieder sinken, schlaff hingen die Hände zu seinen Seiten herab. (327-328)[23]

Striving to explain the passivity and suppression after the war, Böll explores the state of individuals in society. They reveal themselves as unable to deal with their memories of the past. While their thinking is ultimately ruled by memories and the guilt for the many who died, they suppress these memories in order to function in an outwardly normal fashion. They thus flee into a rigid routine, like Robert Fähmel, or into irony like his father Heinrich, but they are unable to act against the dangerous developments around them, so that those who held power during the Nazi era can again pull all the strings. The victims from yesterday

---

[22] "I'm scared, much more than I was then. Obviously, you're all quite used to the faces. But I'm beginning to wish I were back among my poor old harmless lunatics. Are you all blind, then? So easily fooled? Don't you see they'd kill you all for less than a sandwich? You needn't even be dark-haired or blond any more, or show your grandmother's birth certificate." (trans. 251).

[23] "The old man flushed deeply, sprang toward the cake model, raised his fists, like a drummer gathering strength for a furious beat, and it seemed for an instant as if he would smash the sugared edifice to smithereens, but he let his fist sink slowly, till his hands hung loose at his sides" (trans. 280).

are then again the victims of today, which Böll expresses through the (somewhat too rigid) division of society into lambs and beasts. Just as the Abbey could not be permanently destroyed, Germany failed to rid itself of the beasts who instead have again become the foundation of the new state.

The publication of *Billiard um halbzehn* in 1959 coincided with that of two other important works, Günter Grass' *Die Blechtrommel* (*The Tin Drum*), and Uwe Johnson's *Mutmaßungen über Jakob* (*Speculations about Jakob*). This sudden emergence of groundbreaking texts is usually seen as a turning point in the cultural development of Germany. It was the first time that literature actively tried to deal with the past and the Germans' reaction to it and actually reached a wider audience in doing so. It also opened up many different viewpoints, since each writer dealt differently with the topic. While there had been earlier attempts, for example by Wolfgang Koeppen, to explore the Nazi past and the postwar condition of Germany, the public had not responded to them. Despite critical acclaim and the importance of his topic, Koeppen's three novels, published between 1951 and 1954 thus went mainly unnoticed and had no significant impact on the population (Barnouw 228-229). In the mainstream, it was escapist 'schöne Literatur' as propagated and practised by Gottfried Benn that dominated the literary scene. The newly formed 'Gruppe 47' also kept mostly in the background on political issues during the 1950s. Despite their firm antifascist standpoint, they did not get actively involved in the politics of the Adenauer era. When Böll, Grass, and Johnson published their works in 1959, it was the first sign of the beginning of a much broader confrontation of (West) Germany with the past among intellectuals, politicians, and the general public.

3.3   Constructing a German Identity Before and After Unification

In the 1960s memories and questions of guilt emerged slowly outside small intellectual circles in the West. In politics, this became most obvious in the 1965 political debate over extending the statute of limitations on Nazi crimes. It had become increasingly clear that the jurisdiction in place had not done its job and many murderers remained unpunished. Criminal guilt, in the sense of Jaspers' terminology, had thus not been dealt with sufficiently. However, the debate did not stop with criminal guilt, but also addressed political and moral guilt. Several politicians, especially from the Social Democratic Party, warned against rejection of responsibility for the Third Reich and any attempt to deny the importance of remembering this past. According to the Social Democrat Adolf Arndt, for example, neither the Nazi crimes nor the German guilt can ever be subject to a statute of limitations, as a people never lives only in the present, but is always part of, and the result of, previous generations (Herf 339). When Willy

Brandt became chancellor in 1969, the Nazi past and its consequences became much more central to German politics than it had been before, as Brandt emphasized the importance of memory for a vital democracy. Brandt, the pioneer of reestablishing relations with the Eastern block, thought it essential in this new relationship to acknowledge responsibility publicly and express remorse for the German crimes during the Nazi era. He acted on this belief when he fell to his knees in front of the memorial for Jews killed in the Warsaw ghetto.

In addition, the second half of the 1960s were the time of student revolts in which questions of guilt were raised and specifically targeted at the generation that was responsible for Nazism. While the students somewhat diluted the issues by addressing all of their perceived enemies as fascists and only rarely used the term to refer to the actual Nazi period (Schneider 284), they were still instrumental in bringing the past into the open and in highlighting the issue of responsibility in German society. At the time of the student movements, the questions of German guilt and the failure to face German responsibility for Nazi crimes became increasingly central concerns in all areas of German culture. Alexander and Margarete Mitscherlich published *Die Unfähigkeit zu trauern* in 1967, where for the first time they make a complex attempt to describe in psychological terms the problematic relationship of Germans to their past and thus the condition of postwar Germany in general. In literature, books like Siegfried Lenz' *Die Deutschstunde* (*The German Lesson*) reminded the public that they had not yet learned the lessons of history. The true start of a nationwide discussion of the subject among the general population, however, only came about a decade later, towards the end of the 1970s with the American television series "Holocaust" from NBC. It seems unbelievable that a fictional television show achieved more than numerous documentaries shown previously, but it apparently struck a nerve within the German population because it gave the chance to get emotionally involved, to identify with the victims, and to share their sorrow (Buruma 90).

By the 1980s, Germany had come a long way in dealing with its past. Many now conceived of the idea of facing their history and talking about it as an integral part of being German. Younger generations also continued to ponder the involvement of older generations in National Socialism also in order to understand and define themselves better. In literature, for example, more and more autobiographical aspects entered the texts in which the authors tried to work through the past by thinking about their fathers and their generations, the so-called "Vaterliteratur," often after the parent's death. These searches usually ended without any clear answers, but helped in formulating the issues and in bringing them out into the open. However, breaking the silence nearly forty years after the Third Reich necessarily entailed new problems. While no one could escape the topic since the social atmosphere of the times was no longer based on suppression any longer, several generations of Germans who were thinking about National Socialism had not been directly involved in Nazism. Especially young Germans were thus caught in a dilemma, or in a conflict of desires. While on the one hand they wanted to find out the whole truth about their country's past and the moral involvement of their ancestors, on the other they also wished to ignore the burden of history and the difficult position it put them in (Brendler 250). The movement of discussing and exploring the Holocaust and National Socialism thus came with a flipside. Since the past was widely talked about now, some thought this to be the right point in time to make a conscious and open decision to retire the topic as worked through and done with, to understand it as part of history, but not of one's own life in the present. This attitude went hand in hand with the newly emerging wish for a different German national identity which saw itself, while acknowledging the past, as personally unaffected by it. Proponents of this new identity tried to distance themselves from the idea, as voiced by Jaspers early on and later by many others, that awareness and even responsibility of moral guilt are not limited to the people committing the crimes, but last beyond these generations.

The spokesperson for this new direction of German nationalism was Helmut Kohl, who saw himself as a man of a new era and as the representative of those generations that had not been involved directly. Being only fifteen at the end of the war and being part of what has been called the flak helpers' generation, Kohl did not consider that he needed to feel responsible for what had taken place in the twelve years of National Socialism or base his actions or the way he defined himself on this part of the German past. He emphasized his attitude during a visit to Israel in the early 1980s, when he talked about his 'grace of belated birth.' It was the beginning of a new direction of politics in which Kohl hoped for a rebuilding of a "healthy," more self-assured national identity for Germany not necessarily founded on the horrid memories of National Socialism. In order to achieve this goal more easily, Kohl also aimed at creating a new vision of the past and the consequences it had entailed. In 1985, these efforts led to the controversial Bitburg visit by Helmut Kohl and Ronald Reagan. As a sign of reconciliation, Reagan and Kohl, after visiting a concentration camp, went to the German military cemetery in Bitburg where they put down wreaths in order to commemorate dead German soldiers, despite the fact that SS officers were buried there as well. By choosing Bitburg as a site for the Reagan visit, Kohl tried to normalize the German past by portraying German soldiers like any other "boys" who had simply done their duty for their country and deserved to be honored. He was thus not only trying to separate the army from National Socialism, propagating the myth of the "clean" military, but also to equate the effects of World War II with those of other wars such as World War I so as to normalize the history of the Third Reich. While the plan backfired to a certain extent as it caused outrage both in Germany and abroad, Kohl still managed to show American support for his ideas about Germany's new role in the world, self-definition, and re-vision of the past.

Just as Adenauer's politics of integration were opposed by Heuss' clear words about the importance of memory, advocates for a more careful and aware way of dealing with the Nazi past and its crimes found their spokesperson in Germany's President Richard von Weizsäcker. Kohl was, of course, correct when he drew a distinction between those Germans who directly participated in National Socialism and those who were only children, or not even born, at the time. However, he misused the passage of time to reinterpret the past in a manner that not only placed Germany in a better light, but also allowed historical events to seem irrelevant to the present time. Weizsäcker's stance was clearly opposed to this treatment of National Socialism and its crimes. He expressed his sentiments in his famous speech given on May 8, 1985, forty years after the war ended:

> Der ganz überwiegende Teil unserer heutigen Bevölkerung war zur damaligen Zeit entweder im Kindesalter oder noch gar nicht geboren. Sie können nicht eine eigene Schuld bekennen für Taten, die sie gar nicht begangen haben. Kein fühlender Mensch erwartet von ihnen, ein Büßerhemd zu tragen, nur weil sie Deutsche sind. Aber die Vorfahren haben ihnen eine schwere Erbschaft hinterlassen.
>
> Wir alle, ob schuldig oder nicht, ob alt oder jung, müssen die Vergangenheit annehmen. Wir alle sind von ihren Folgen betroffen und für sie in Haftung genommen. Jüngere und Ältere müssen und können sich gegenseitig helfen, zu verstehen, warum es so lebenswichtig ist, die Erinnerung wachzuhalten.
>
> Es geht nicht darum, Vergangenheit zu bewältigen. Das kann man gar nicht. Sie läßt sich ja nicht nachträglich ändern oder ungeschehen machen. Wer aber vor der Vergangenheit die Augen verschließt, wird blind für die Gegenwart. (18)[24]

In his speech, Weizsäcker thus clearly emphasizes that Germans have to build their identity on the past of the Third Reich. They have to look at it truthfully and without trying to change it. According to Weizsäcker, the Federal Republic of Germany can remain a successful democracy only if the memory of the past is kept alive in order to avoid repeating the same mistakes.

These two directions, exemplified by the standpoints of Kohl and Weizsäcker, can also be observed in other disputes about the past that were taking place in the 1980s. In the so-called "Historikerstreit," or "historians' debate," the conflict of the meaning of the National Socialist past in the present-day and German identity was at the core of the discussion, that reached a wide audience.[25] The dispute focused on a number of conservative historians who suggested in one

---

[24] "The largest part of our population was back then either only a child or not yet born at all. They cannot take blame for deeds that they have not committed. No feeling human being expects them to wear a penitential robe simply because they are Germans. Yet their ancestors have left them with a difficult heritage. All of us, whether guilty or not, whether old or young, have to accept our past. We all are affected by its consequences and have to take responsibility for it. Young and old must and can help each other to understand why it is so fundamentally important to keep the memory alive. It is not the goal to overcome the past. This is not possible. One cannot change it in hindsight or change it as if it never happened. Whoever closes their eyes to the past becomes blind in the present."

[25] While this important debate can only be briefly touched upon here, for further reference the volume *"Historikerstreit:" Die Dokumentation der Kontroverse um die Einzigartigkeit der na-*

way or another that the period of National Socialism should be reevaluated. All of them aimed at a form of normalization of this part of German history by trying to make it not an exceptional event, but a normal twentieth century historical development. The Holocaust was thus compared to other twentieth century crimes such as those committed under Pol Pot or Stalin. However, it is not necessarily the comparisons themselves that make this attitude troublesome, but the intention to use them in order to lessen the horror and the magnitude of the Holocaust in Germany during National Socialism. For example, Ernst Nolte not only compared the Holocaust to crimes under Stalin, but tried to imply a direct connection between Bolshevism and the Holocaust under National Socialism. He thus portrayed the Holocaust mainly as a reaction of fear by Hitler to the destruction of the Russian class system so that it became simply a copy of the original, the Russian revolution and its consequences (Nolte 32). Another historian, Andreas Hillgruber, also participated in this effort to reinterpret the past. By pairing an essay about genocide with one about the defeat of the Hitler regime and publishing both under the heading *Zweierlei Untergang: die Zerschlagung des Deutschen Reiches und das Ende des europäschen Judentums*,[26] he implied the equivalence of both events, making the "German Reich" as much a victim as the Jewish people (Maier 39).

The questionable nature of the approach of these conservative historians involved in the dispute is obvious. Anti-communist sentiments and nationalism took precedence over historical evidence in the construction of their arguments. As has been correctly pointed out: "das *tu-quo que*-Argument, die fingerzeigende Behauptung 'auch du' birgt keinerlei ethische Entlastung; die Verbrechen der anderen entschuldigen nicht die eigenen" (Leicht 364).[27] The strong impact of the debate was thus not so much because of the historical nature of the dispute, the positions of the individual historians involved had been long known in the academic community, but rather because of its political implications. It received such a high degree of attention since it corresponded exactly to the situation of West Germany at the time. The new nationalism propagated under Kohl welcomed these conservative opinions as good opportunities to create a past that would be easier for Germans to embrace. With their approach, the historians repeated what Kohl had tried to do in Bitburg, namely to deemphasize the role of Germans as perpetrators and to attempt to lessen the responsibility by offsetting Germany's crimes with those of others. While, in time, the historians' debate quieted down, the two directions in the question of the role of memory in present Germany continued, and in some ways became even more pronounced after reunification.

---

tionalsozialistischen Judenvernichtung, published in the Serie Piper, offers a good selection of different articles and arguments connected with the dispute.

[26] *Two Sorts of Destruction: The Shattering of the German Reich and the End of European Jewry*

[27] "the *tu-quo que* argument, the blaming utterance of a 'you as well' does not make up for anything ethically; someone else's crimes do not excuse one's own."

The years 1989/90 formed the most important caesura in postwar German history. Suddenly, the German nation was no longer divided. Whether desired or not, the new state required the construction of a new definition of Germany and of what it meant to be German - a situation that has been compared to that of 1945 (Jarausch 22-23). However, 1989/90 might fit even less than 1945 did the nearly mystical idea of the "zero hour" of a completely new beginning. The search for a new identity was still largely tied up with questions of memory and followed the same two, diverging, directions the discussion had taken in West Germany previously. The division of the country had been a direct consequence of World War II and a constant reminder of Germany's complete defeat. Now, with unification and the abolishment of the German Democratic Republic, the situation had drastically changed. It gave a huge boost to voices supporting a "normalization" of the view of the German past, since one of the most obvious reminders of the consequences of Nazism and war for Germany as a country had been eliminated. Yet opposition to this redefinition of Germany and its history also gained momentum after unification. While the length of time that had passed and the disappearance of direct reminders of the lost war required a re-thinking of how best to remember Germany's National Socialist period, the rise of Neo-nazism, especially in the former GDR, made it seem even more pressing to keep the memory of Germany's crimes alive, as well as to continue to accept responsibility for them by acting accordingly in the present. In addition, since East Germany never really faced its Nazi past, but had largely projected responsibility onto the "fascist" West, there seemed to be an urgent need to address National Socialism more objectively and without distortions. The relationship to the Nazi past was thus still vital for finding a new self-definition for unified Germany. However, the conditions had become even more complex after 1989/90, since now two past systems – Nazi Germany and East Germany – had to be dealt with.

Not surprisingly, these conflicts concerning the German past were again (and still are) mirrored in activities of architectural destruction and reconstruction. While in West Germany reconstruction had been the major priority right after the war, East Germany, mainly because of financial reasons, had been much slower in rebuilding its cities. Even though initially many plans were made to rebuild destroyed historical sites, their instigation was frequently only fragmentary. Later, these plans were often abandoned completely and, under the influence of the Soviet Union, East Germany focused on building what are now seen as monuments to its Socialist regime, such as large parade avenues and governmental structures, as well as the aesthetically displeasing uniform apartment blocks ("Plattenbauten").

In the city centers, due to the constant lack of money and materials, many older buildings were simply left to crumble away. Consequently, while the postwar rebuilding of the cities in West Germany was mostly completed by the

1960s, it was still possible to encounter ruins from World War II when strolling through an East German city after reunification. By the time of the fall of the wall, the GDR was completely bankrupt and Germany again found itself in a fever to rebuild both its economy and its cities. Just as in West Germany in the 1950s, decisions had to be made about the manner in which urban transformation was to be achieved. The attitudes adopted reveal again the position of memory in German national identity. A good example of how the decisions about reconstruction mirror the approach taken to the memories of the most recent German past(s) is the rebuilding of the Frauenkirche in Dresden. The Dresden Frauenkirche (Church of Our Lady) had been constructed between 1726 and 1743 by the master builder George Bähr. The architecturally extraordinary church became an integral part of the Dresden silhouette, which earned the city the description of being the Florence on the Elbe, and was immortalized by the pictures of the Italian painter Canaletto (Bernardo Bellotto) in the mid-

The view of Dresden as painted by Bernardo Bellotto in 1748. Reproduced in black and white with permission by Staatliche Kunstsammlungen Dresden, Gemäldegalerie Alte Meister.

eighteenth century. When Dresden became the site of a devastating attack by Allied bombings on February 13 and 14, 1945, the Frauenkirche was one of the architectural casualties of the air raids. While at first apparently withstanding the bombs, it collapsed into a pile of rubble two days after the attacks. Overall, about fifteen square kilometers of the city were completely destroyed (Paul 314). After the war was over, Dresden, just like many other German cities, immediately started to make plans to rebuild their historic old town in order to restore it to its prewar condition. The city began collecting and cataloguing blocks of the Frauenkirche to use for the reconstruction, despite the fact that all of Dresden found itself in the most desolate situation. However, a change of direction in the

The Frauenkirche after the bombings in 1945. Reproduced with permission from Sächsische Landesbibliothek - Staats- und Universitätsbibliothek Dresden, Abt. Deutsche Fotothek/Photo: Edmund Kesting

East German government and the unavailability of proper funds prevented the rebuilding from ever starting. Instead, new plans arose which were less concerned with the city's historic character and more with the idea of radically separating it from its royal "Residenzstadt" flair, an appearance that was perceived as necessarily opposing Socialist ideals. In the spirit of this need for cleansing, much rubble was controversially removed from the city center. Yet some of the Dresden officials and conservationists never let go of their rebuilding plans for the Frauenkirche, and tried to save the building from being cleared away in its entirety. Consequently, the remains of the Frauenkirche were neither completely removed, nor was the church rebuilt.

Instead, the Socialist government finally decided to turn the destroyed building into a memorial " 'To the tens of thousands of dead, and an inspiration to the living in their struggle against imperialist barbarism and for the peace and happiness of man' " (quoted in Buruma 300), as the official East German plaque read. The destructive force of the air raids flown by Western Allies that the ruins represented were thus turned into an instrument in the East German struggle against the West as soon as the Cold War began. Always depending upon the particular relationship between the Soviet Union and the U.S. at the time, the anniversaries of the destruction of Dresden were either seen as reminders of the horrors of war or times for official demonstrations against the West, the destroyers of Dresden and the imperialist-fascist enemy of socialism (Steele T2). By portraying the Western powers as fascist systems, and the bombing of Dresden as a fascist act, East Germany ultimately equated the destruction of Dresden with the crimes committed under National Socialism, strengthening the idea of East Germans as victims and thus suppressing the causal relationships of the war. In East Germany it was, therefore, not the reconstructed cultural icon from a prewar past, as in the case of the Goethehaus, that became a site for identification of both individuals and the state, but the ruins of the Frauenkirche that became a visible symbol for East Germany's official self-definition as a cultural anti-thesis to the West. Starting in 1982, these ruins were also associated with another meaning, when Dresden inhabitants lit candles there for peace as a silent protest against their government – again using a site of cultural and historical importance as a place for redefining themselves and their place within society.

When reunification occurred, it was also "die Wende für die Dresdner Frauenkirche" as the official publication of the Society for the Promotion of the Rebuilding of the Frauenkirche Dresden happily proclaims, since plans for an exact rebuilding of the church were immediately enacted after the wall fell (Paul, Kantschew, and Kröger). Implicit in this statement is, of course, the perception that the time had finally come to rescue the Frauenkirche, which had been a victim of World War II as well as of the Socialist East German government that had refused to rebuild it after 1945. The Frauenkirche project is in many aspects very similar to the reconstruction of the Goethehaus immediately after the war. Both buildings were considered important cultural icons in Germany and in each case original plans and photographs of the buildings were available, which made a historical reconstruction possible. It is thus not surprising that the Frauenkirche project, like its Goethehaus counterpart, also stirred strong emotions among its supporters and critics. Similar to the postwar era, modern architects voiced, and still voice, their protest against the restoration of a historical silhouette which had not been present for nearly fifty years. They warn against the erection of what could, at best, be seen as a copy, and they emphasize the need for "vorbildliche Bauten der Gegenwart" (Delau).[28] Others, like Christof Ziemer, who had been one of the leaders of the rallies for democracy in 1989, argued for keeping the ruins in order to keep memory alive, to display the "offene Erinnerungswunde"

---

[28] "exemplary contemporary buildings"

(Kohlhaas 26),[29] a position that was even supported by the Protestant church (Steele T2). Yet despite this opposition, the so-called "archeological rebuilding" of the Frauenkirche did get underway, albeit under the condition that the 250 million Deutschmark project had to be financed with private donations.

Even though the supporters of rebuilding the Frauenkirche promise to return to the world one of its most striking monuments, this argument rings as hollow as it did in the case of the Goethehaus fifty years earlier. Since the Frauenkirche in Dresden was completely destroyed, rebuilding it cannot be justified as the preservation of a historical monument, as there will be only a very small number of original pieces of the church included in the building. Experts thus question the reality of the "archeological rebuilding" of the church: "[E]s muss hier vom denkmalpflegerischen Standpunkt aus ganz eindeutig und unzweifelhaft - trotz aller gegenläufigen Behauptungen - von einem Neubau gesprochen weren, der die Formen der Dresdner Frauenkirche wiederaufgreift" (Trimborn 141).[30] In addition, the rebuilding not only depends on the most advanced computer technologies, but also includes some essential design changes in order to make the Frauenkirche safer and more stable than it was originally. These are all reasons why Dresden has even been called the new "Las Vegas an der Elbe" (Ruby) or a " 'Barock Disneyland' " (quoted in Delau). Since the emphasis placed on the archeological and historical nature of the project can be easily discredited, the reasons for the strong wish for the reconstruction of the Frauenkirche must lie elsewhere. It has been noted that the importance ascribed to the Frauenkirche project strangely surpasses its actual meaning: "Die Idee des Wiederaufbaus [wurde] von Beginn an merkwürdig überhöht. Als hätte sich plötzlich eine Schleuse geöffnet und einem lange aufgestauten Bedürfnis freie Bahn verschafft, flossen dem Unternehmen von Beginn an Schecks und Sympathien in nie gekanntem Ausmaß zu" (Neffe 295-296).[31] A comparison to the debate surrounding the Goethehaus in Frankfurt helps clarify some of this Frauenkirche-mania. The Goethehaus controversy revealed a strong connection between the rebuilding efforts and the design of a new national identity. Rebuilding the Goethehaus helped fulfill the dreams of creating a world unscarred by war that connect one back to the greatest periods of German culture and tradition. While not displayed as openly in the case of the Frauenkirche, probably because these expressions of nostalgia and selective memory about history are now less commonly accepted and more criticized than after the war, these inten-

---

[29] "the open wound of memory"

[30] "Applying the criteria of the institute for the preservation of historical monuments, one has to speak undoubtedly, and despite all claims to the contrary, of a new building, which has the historical shape of the Dresden Frauenkirche."

[31] "The idea of the rebuilding was strangely exaggerated from the start. As if suddenly a flood gate had been opened, and this allowed a long suppressed need to escape. The rebuilding, from the beginning, received large amounts of checks, support, and good wishes to an extent never experienced before."

tions are nevertheless present throughout the whole controversy as well. With the Frauenkirche, the negating process even surpasses that of the Goethehaus, as it not only wipes out the visible marks of the consequences of the war, but also over forty years of Socialism. The project is the flagship of the trend in Dresden to reverse any changes the city has endured both during the war and its GDR times, a heritage both city officials and a large part of the population would like to erase as completely as possible (Düwel and Gutschow 270).

The rebuilt Frauenkirche thus provides a vehicle for an idealization of the pre-Nazi past and the suppression of the years 1933 to 1990. As many comments reveal, in a time of redefinition and change after reunification, cultural identity is connected retrospectively to the existence of the reconstructed Frauenkirche. The self becomes inseparable from what is perceived to be its physical manifestation. This connection also explains sentimentalizations, such as the claim that every Dresden resident knows "from memory the precise location that each piece of rubble belongs" (Asch 4). Erecting the Frauenkirche is understood as the possibility to rebuild one's true and lost identity. The words of a Dresden resident exemplify the projection of one's own destiny onto the physical entity of the Frauenkirche:

> "For two hundred years my family has been connected to the Frauenkirche. My grandmother was confirmed there, my greatgrandmother baptised, and I had books and pictures recalling those years [...]. I know the church from top to bottom. I was only a boy at the time but I loved the Frauenkirche. The day after the raid we stood on our balcony where we lived. The smoke lifted for a moment ... it was unbelievable. I shouted to my mother, 'look, the Frauenkirche is still standing.' We stared again, and saw through reddened eyes it was true. Yet shortly afterwards it collapsed, as if not wanting to survive the insanity. The disaster was now complete." (quoted in Asch 4)

This yearning for an identity defined through an idealized personal past is similar to the conservative view of the Adenauer era and also corresponds to the wish of Kohl and his supporters to recreate a German national identity. "Wunden heilen, nicht Wunden offen halten" (c.m. 4),[32] the credo of the Dresden struggle in rebuilding their baroque silhouette could also have been that of either politician. It is thus not surprising that this myth of the old Dresden and the emotional approach to the rebuilding of the city was used by Kohl for his message of the new nation. Several times the Frauenkirche served as a campaign stop for the politician and when in the early 1990s Kohl was asked what he would like for his birthday, "he conceded that a reconstructed Frauenkirche would be the fulfilment of his ideal" (Asch 3).

However, it is not only a sentimental yearning for the Germany of high culture that makes the Frauenkirche so attractive for the conservative movement in Germany. The destruction of the Frauenkirche of course stands for the wiping

---

[32] "to heal wounds, not to keep them open"

out of Dresden and its population in a massive air raid which did not destroy anything but civilian targets and was so close to the end of the war that many now contend that it was not necessary. It is true that Dresden can serve as yet another reminder that war is cruel and brings terrible sorrow and suffering. It is in this spirit that many Dresden residents and other Frauenkirche supporters justify the rebuilding of the church. They hope to create, as the web site of the Society for the Rebuilding of the Frauenkirche Dresden proclaims, a "Weltfriedenszentrum im neuen Europa." Yet is Dresden truly the right place for a center of world peace? In 1995, the writer Ralph Giordano warned in an open letter to President Roman Herzog about the dangers of his plans of giving a speech at the Frauenkirche in Dresden at the 50th anniversary of the bombing. Giordano does not try to minimize the horror of the events, since he himself knows the terrible effects of large area bombings from his own experience when he survived the destruction of Hamburg in 1943. However, he points out that Dresden will also always stand for attempts by revisionists to offset the wrongs committed by Germans. He expresses the fear that

> das Jahr 1995 auch die große Stunde der professionellen Aufrechner werden könnte, die Hoch-Zeit unentwegter deutscher Verdränger. Und deren Paradebeispiel, ihr Lieblingsmodell, war und ist die Zerstörung Dresdens in jener Februarnacht durch die Halifax- und Lancasterbomber der Royal Air Force! Wer immer bei uns das Thema behandelt, er wird mit dieser unheimlichen Nachbarschaft zu rechnen haben - und einer äusserst schwierigen Abgrenzung zu ihr. (Giordano 10)[33]

The supporters of the Frauenkirche project are, of course, well aware of these issues and try to avoid publicly any such associations. The President emphasized in his speech that " '[n]o one wants to offset the wrongs committed by Germans in the Nazi state against anything else' " (quoted in Cowell A6). The Society for the Rebuilding of the Frauenkirche also stresses in its pamphlet "The Rebuilding of the Frauenkirche Dresden," in which it calls for donations, how the newly constructed church will have symbolic value for the world: "The Frauenkirche, rebuilt from its ruins, will become a monument for the reconciliation of nations and a visible exhortation for peace in the world." Yet how believable – or how naive – are these good intentions? Interestingly enough, the English text of the donation pamphlet for the Frauenkirche is a direct translation of the German text printed on the opposite side, with one difference, namely about the symbolic character of the building quoted above: "Die aus den Trümmern wiedererstandene Frauenkirche wird *ein Symbol für die Heilung der durch den Krieg*

---

[33] "the year 1995 could be the time for those who try continuously to erase one event with another, the best opportunity for those Germans who hope constantly to exorcize the past. And their key example, their favorite model, was and is the destruction of Dresden on the night in February by means of the Halifax and Lancaster bombers of the Royal Air Force! Whoever deals with this topic in Germany has to expect the frightening closeness of these ideas - and also how difficult it is to distance oneself from them."

geschlagenen Wunden sein, ein Denkmal für die Versöhnung der Völker und eine sichtbare Mahnung zum Frieden" (emphasis added).[34] As becomes obvious when comparing the two texts, not only does the English version lose the emotionalizing and exaggerated religious symbolism suggesting both the resurrection of Christ and the rise of the Phoenix from the ashes, but it completely leaves out the words that directly state the healing function the society claims for the rebuilding of the Frauenkirche. Germans are here portrayed as innocent victims, in need of healing from the effects of the horrors of war, and the precursors of the events are suppressed. The organizers of the fund-drive for the rebuilding project are very conscious of these implications. By leaving out these particular passages in the English translation, they show that they understand that this idea of German victimhood could irritate some international donors, who will not see the rebuilding of the Frauenkirche as a 21st-century bandage for the sorrow suffered at the hands of the Germans.

Consequently, the Frauenkirche is more than a call for the future prevention of the destructive forces of war. Under the cover of historical preservation, the Frauenkirche becomes a site where opinions can safely be uttered which would otherwise be objectionable. Rebuilding the Frauenkirche is thus also an act of defiance against losing the war, against losing a world order that many could identify with and now sentimentalize about, as well as against over forty years of Socialism. More than ever before, the rebuilding offers the opportunity to modify publicly the parameters for forming an identity that have been developed since 1945, as it can be used to blur the distinction between perpetrators and victims.[35] It thus becomes another form of the zero-sum calculations which, as early as 1946, Karl Jaspers in *Die Schuldfrage* had condemned as unjustified, but which are repeatedly brought into play by revisionists: the suffering from the bombings supposedly making up for the crimes committed during National Socialism. Jaspers tells us that perpetrators can also experience pain, but that does not alleviate the guilt of their crimes. In the Dresden hype surrounding Germany's own hardship, the true horrors and the extent of crimes under National Socialism are often minimized while German suffering is emphasized. In 1995, the *taz* reported just such an incidence:

> Die Dresdner Musikfestspiele stehen in diesem Jahr unter dem Motto: "Apokalypse"; und Intendant Michael Hampe schreibt im Geleitwort des Programmhefts: "1995 jährt sich zum fünfzigsten Mal das Ende des Zweiten Weltkrieges und die Zerstörung

---

[34] "The Frauenkirche, resurrected from the rubble, *will be a symbol for the healing of the wounds inflicted by the war*, a monument for the reconciliation of the nations and a visible exhortation for peace in the world" (emphasis added).

[35] Interestingly enough though, while interpreted as a sign of overcoming Socialism, the rhetoric used is not only representative of revisionism, but also, even though unconsciously on part of the participants, in many ways a continuation of the East German standpoint that had fostered this view of the German victims of Western imperialism for propaganda purposes.

Dresdens, jenes apokalyptische Ereignis, das wie kein zweites zum Symbol des Un-
tergangs, des Grauens und des Leidens wurde, das jener Krieg über die Menschheit
brachte." (Krell 5)[36]

Here, the writer does not shy away from raising the destruction of Dresden to
the same level as the horrors of Auschwitz, and thus singles out an incident of
German suffering as the epiphany of the horrors of the war. This crass example
openly reveals the shift in perception of German history which forms the highly
questionable political foundation of the Dresden rebuilding project.

It is, of course, to be expected that a nation which has gone through a major period of transformation such as reunification searches for new ways to define itself. It is also normal that its population tries to create visible symbols
which can serve both as mirrors to reconfirm their national identity and as tools
for communicating this self-understanding to others. However, as the similarities between the Goethehaus debate and the Frauenkirche phenomenon show,
the current trend to define one's self-view through the rebuilding of historical
structures is by no means novel, but instead based on coping mechanisms established after World War II. In times of change, Germans are continuously drawn
to processes of avoidance and suppression, redirecting the perception of German
history away from Nazi Germany and its consequences to what is seen as a more
glorious prewar past. It is thus not surprising that many of the sentiments expressed about the Frauenkirche and the need to rebuild it resemble what was felt
and said about the Abbey St. Anton by characters in Böll's *Billiard um halbzehn*,
in which the author captures beautifully the mood of the 1950s in Germany. The
often predictive nature of Böll's novel shows how much of the 1950s thought-
patterns are still alive today. Just as the silhouette of the Frauenkirche is seen
as essential to Dresden and its identity, so the Abbey's rebuilding is hailed as
restoring the city to the look it is supposed to have, to its old self. Once again
conservative restoration sentiments and the attempts to reclaim one's own are
hidden from the victors behind a front of reconciliation – reconciliation as a
cover for selective forgetting. Even the haunting overpowering structure of the
novel's Abbey, that in the end returns in the form of a cake model is paralleled
by the Frauenkirche. The church once again features prominently in the Dresden silhouette. The church is seen as the major achievement not only of one
person, but of a whole city. While not yet available in cake, one can celebrate
the Frauenkirche's greatness by purchasing a model made out of porcelain, or
by strapping the church around one's wrist on a watch. Just as in the case of
Jaspers' sentiments, Böll's warnings are still meaningful, and both can serve as
important reference points for Germans today in how to deal with their past.

---

[36] "This year, the Dresden Music Festival has the theme 'apocalypse,' and music director Michael
Hampe writes in the introduction of the concert guide: 'in 1995, it is the 50th anniversary of
the end of the Second World War and the destruction of Dresden, the apocalyptic event which,
unparalleled by any other, has become the symbol of destruction, horror, and suffering which
this war has brought to mankind.' "

The situation after reunification, and in particular the Dresden example, also shows that almost sixty years after the war it is easier to embrace restoration than to emphasize the idea of the importance of memory of the Nazi past. Neonazi skinhead activity is still widely answered by counter demonstrations and verbal condemnations, but the proponents of a constant awareness of the German Nazi past are searching for more permanent representations of the importance of memory and responsibility, especially since most eye witnesses of the Nazi years are rapidly dying. While the conservative national movement can restore the Frauenkirche as a pillar of their identity, modern architecture as found, for example, in Berlin can convey a departure from the past independent from reshaping it, but cannot provide an emphasis on remembering that should also define Germany's landscape. The opening of Jewish museums and the restorations of synagogues are one way of trying to create lasting places for the awareness of and the responsibility for German crimes during National Socialism in postwar, postreunified Germany. Another is the building of the Holocaust memorial which is being constructed in Berlin after a decade of discussions. The idea behind the memorial is not only that it should be a symbol of past crimes, but that of continued German memory of its deeds, with design suggestions emphasizing the burden of history that still affects every German and should influence their behavior. In its conception, the memorial tries to be a reminder that it is important not to forget, but to give memory room in our lives, it is intended to evoke "ein kontinuierliches Weiterwirken der Schuld bis heute" (Mittig 281).[37] The design, which covers a large area with pillars of different heights, was formed in the hope that the dimensions of the memorial, which occupies a large space in the middle of the German capital, are translated into the consciousness of every viewer. The memorial aims at being a visible scar that does not heal (Kulick), a scar in the city, in German history, and also in everyone's life. It is thus the direct opposite of the Dresden project, where the wound is being erased from the city.

While it remains to be seen whether the memorial will be misused as a place where memory can be safely and ritualistically contained even though it is otherwise completely banned from consciousness, it seems to be an honest attempt to preserve the awareness of the Holocaust and the responsibility that comes with being German. As Andreas Huyssen points out, despite its drawbacks, monuments can fulfill an important function: "the Holocaust monument, memorial, and museum could be the tool Franz Kafka wanted literature to be when he said that the book must be the axe for the frozen sea within us. We need the monument and the book to keep the sea from freezing" (*Twilight Memories* 260). Indeed, the Dresden rebuilding project demonstrates how important it is to keep memory and a sense of responsibility, and maybe even feelings of guilt, alive in Germany. It is a key factor in counteracting new movements aimed at reshaping the past by trying to make German history seem more agreeable and less trou-

---

[37] "a lasting effect of guilt till today"

blesome. It is clear, however, that almost sixty years after the end of the war, Germany necessarily has to rethink its strategies in terms of how to deal with its National Socialist past and World War II. Most of the perpetrators are now dead, and even the ones who were children at the end of the war are slowly disappearing. New generations are searching for different ways of approaching their history in order to define their own position about events they were not directly part of, but which had, and continue to have, a deep impact on their lives.

Yet, as has been shown, the two trends surrounding the memory debate that emerged in the 1980s, one emphasizing responsibility, the other a conservative nationalism aiming at alteration and forgetting, can still be readily observed in German politics, culture, and society today. In its most pointed forms this conflict of memory has become a dispute on victimhood, an attempt to set Dresden against Auschwitz. Dresden, and with it the whole experience of the air raids on Germany during World War II, has thus in the past been monopolized by those who want to reshape history and lessen the guilt and responsibility Germany carries because of its National Socialist past. Early on, many intellectuals such as Jaspers rejected the idea that suffering from the bombings can offset the crimes committed against Jews and other persecuted groups, as well as the death of many soldiers. However, Jaspers does not suggest that the horrific experience of Germans during the bombings and after the war in the devastated cities be denied or suppressed. Jaspers hopes that the new approach after 1945 will be characterized by "truth" in every aspect which arises when one reflects, debates, and questions (8). It seems that the official silence surrounding these German experiences of suffering actually indirectly supported the inappropriate comparisons between Auschwitz and Dresden because it negated a more objective look at events and thus opened them up for exploitation.

In reunified Germany, which is now mostly shaped by postwar generations, the wish for a more complete picture of the past has been growing. The emerging interest in the bombings can be seen as one indication that the established reluctance to discuss and debate German guilt and memory might be softening. It has become noticeable that recollections of German suffering which were previously merely talked about privately, suddenly can be voiced publicly (Jarausch 22). The debates started by Sebald's *Luftkrieg und Literatur* and Friedrich's *Der Brand* are examples of this new openness about the air raids and their consequences. Yet it is naive to think that the passing of time and the generational changes have made it possible to talk about the bombings and the pain they caused among the population without consideration of its context. The vast support for the rebuilding of the Frauenkirche in Dresden and the exaggerated sentimentalization and mythical elevation of the process show that many Germans are still eager to define themselves, consciously or unconsciously, as the true victims of the war. For them, the rebuilding of the Frauenkirche serves as a symbol for the overcoming of their suffering and the resurrection of national pride. This way of dealing with the destruction and suffering caused by the air raids in Germany is an inappropriate path when one does not want to reinforce attempts to offset German crimes with the bombings. At the same time, it is precisely the Dresden situation that shows how important it is to reclaim from the revisionists the topic of the air raids and the suffering they entailed. Only when the topic is analyzed objectively and in the appropriate context will it be impossible to misuse it as a pseudo-justification to deny or forget German guilt and responsibility.

Clearly, Germany's dealings with its past have shown how writing about the bombings or discussing them was, and still is, extremely problematic. A work depicting the air raids will necessarily also be looked at as a political contribution. It is thus not surprising that writers used to be extremely hesitant to depict their bombing experiences. To avoid misreadings, German guilt must serve as an underlying current for literary production. In literary texts, this can be achieved by a sensitive and truthful treatment of the topic and by authorial decisions such as choosing an appropriate form, style, or perspective. The awareness of the guilt and memory debate takes on an even more important role in criticism. Literary criticism that aims at dealing with the literature of the bombings has the difficult task acknowledging the psychological suffering expressed in the texts as well as putting these realizations into the proper context. An objective approach using psychiatric theory, as outlined in the previous chapter, in conjunction with a study of German guilt and its role since 1945, provides the tools to reduce misunderstandings and to counteract the misuse of the air raids to try to mitigate German guilt.

Chapter 4
The View from Within: The Air War in German Writing

The discussion surrounding the air raids in Germany and their representation in literature, initiated by the late writer and literary scholar W. G. Sebald, is seen by many critics as one of the most exciting events in German literary study in the last few years. The discussion revolves around the German perception of history, German guilt and memory taboos, and also poses questions about the function of literature. Surprisingly, arguments rarely include full consideration of texts which are written directly about the bombings. Names and titles bounce back and forth in the culture sections of the newspapers, the number of books are added up and people ask themselves how many works would be enough to disqualify Sebald's assumption of a German taboo surrounding the events, while other critics question whether the debate is even appropriate. The existing literary accounts themselves, however, which describe the air raids and their consequences, are hardly explored. Yet it is precisely in these texts and their surrounding circumstances that answers are found to many important questions in the debate. More than anything else, they offer insight into the lasting pychological effects of the bombings and their manifestations. Since most of the writers lived through the bombardments, their texts also allow one to explore the relationship between a writer experiencing trauma and his or her literary production. Personal statements indicate that these events can indeed play an important role in future artistic development. To understand more clearly how the air war was perceived and what prompted authors to write or not to write about them, it helps to analyze individual portrayals of the air raids and the techniques which are employed to capture this exceptional experience. Close scrutiny of the relationship between trauma and guilt in their works reveals the difficult position of German authors when writing about the bombings, and also sheds light on the validity of some critics' assumption that a literary work about the air raids and their terrible consequences is necessarily revisionist in its tendency.

4.1   Early Reactions: Hans Erich Nossack, Wolfgang Borchert, and Gert Ledig

Hans Erich Nossack's *Der Untergang* (*Doom and Destruction*), which describes the destruction of Hamburg in 1943, is one of the earliest and probably one of the best known German literary publications about the bombings. Born into a rich Hamburg merchant's family in 1901, Nossack was subject to the stifling rules of the bourgeois life style which he started to despise early on. He finally broke with his family when he was twenty-two, even rejecting their financial help. Working during the day to support himself, Nossack followed his real passion at night when he wrote poetry and plays. It was the identity of the writer which he was striving for most, but political circumstances repeatedly hindered publication of his works. When the dangers of National Socialism became more imminent, both he and his wife joined the Communist Party, hoping that the Communists could stop the rise of the Nazis. This step led to serious consequences for Nossack in 1933, when he was immediately prohibited from writing and publishing and had to endure continuous searches by the SA. As Nossack relates: "nach der vierten oder fünften Haussuchung mußte ich mich entscheiden: emigrieren oder nicht. Und ich emigrierte in die Firma meines Vaters. Es war das, was ich am wenigsten wollte. [...] Aber nun mußte ich die Firma meines Vaters übernehmen. Dadurch geriet ich aus dem Blickfeld der Gestapo" (Rudolph and Nossack 183).[1] Under National Socialism, Nossack was thus condemned to live a double life. Officially, he had returned to his bourgeois roots and was a merchant in the family business. Only in his spare time could he write, but, as was most frustrating for him, secretly and for his desk drawer rather than for an audience.

When Hamburg experienced its most destructive air raids towards the end of July 1943, Nossack and his wife were spending a short vacation in a small hut fifteen kilometers outside of the city. It is from here that Nossack observed the bombardment:

> Man wagte nicht, Luft zu holen, um es nicht einzuatmen. Es war das Geräusch von achtzehnhundert Flugzeugen, die in unvorstellbaren Höhen von Süden her Hamburg anflogen. Wir hatten schon zweihundert oder auch mehr Angriffe erlebt, darunter sehr schwere, aber dies war etwas völlig Neues. Und doch wußte man gleich: es war das, worauf jeder gewartet hatte, das wie ein Schatten seit Monaten über all unserm Tun lag und uns müde machte, es war das Ende.[2]

---

[1] "after the fourth or fifth search of our home I had to make a decision: either to emigrate or not. And so I emigrated to my father's firm. It was the last thing I wanted to do. [...] But now I had to take over my father's company. This way I kept myself out of the light of the Gestapo."

[2] "One didn't dare to breathe in order not to breathe it in. It was the noise of eighteen hundred airplanes, which were flying at unbelievable heights and approaching Hamburg from the South. We had already gone through two hundred or more attacks, some of them very strong ones, but this was something completely new. And yet one knew right away: this was what we had all been waiting for, for months it had overshadowed everything we were doing and had tired us out, it

Only three months later, Nossack wrote *Der Untergang*, hoping to avoid, as he says, "daß es sich wie ein böser Traum allmählich verwischen wird" (8).[3] Nossack opts for the form of a report to describe the destruction of Hamburg. He portrays himself as being in the role of the objective observer, the "Zuschauer" (7) who does not get emotionally involved but only describes what he sees. It allows him to talk about the events despite the sensitivity of the topic while at the same time dissociating himself psychologically from the horror he encounters.

Throughout the text, it is obvious that Nossack is deeply affected by the events. One can detect both in himself and the people he depicts many examples of typical symptoms of acute and posttraumatic stress disorder. The account is marked by a sense of unreality concerning the destruction of Hamburg, presenting the events as located beyond understanding: "es [wird] der Vernunft niemals möglich sein [...], das, was damals geschah, als Wirklichkeit zu begreifen und dem Gedächtnis einzuordnen" (7-8).[4] In the Hamburg refugees, Nossack encounters deep traumatization:

> Warum klagten und weinten sie nicht? Und warum diese Gleichgültigkeit im Tonfall, wenn sie von dem, was hinter ihnen lag, sprachen, diese leidenschaftslose Art der Rede, als berichten sie von einem furchtbaren Begebnis der vorgeschichtlichen Zeit, das heute nicht mehr möglich ist und dessen Erschütterungen nur noch durch unsere Träume nachklingen? (28)[5]

The reaction to loss and devastation is one of inner destruction. The passage illustrates the numbness and emotional detachment of the victims who are also plagued by the horror of the events intruding into their lives through dreams. Interestingly enough, Nossack at first refers to only the refugees ("sie"), but then includes himself in the description of their situation ("unsere Träume"). He thus understands and shares their reaction. The excerpt also points to an aspect of depersonalization among the survivors. In fact, Nossack describes their state as almost 'dehumanized.' When talking about a group of refugees, he refers to their sitting together as "tierisches Zusammenhocken" (35), another time a woman screams like a "todwundes Tier" (34).[6] This descent from the human world becomes evident in other aspects as well. The report reveals a lack of interest in the bombing victims about the world around them. Previously normal

---

was the end."

Hans Erich Nossack, *Der Untergang* (1948; Frankfurt am Main: Suhrkamp, 1996) 13-14. All subsequent references are parenthetical in the text.

[3] "that the memory would slowly become blurred as in a bad dream"

[4] "it will never be possible for the mind to understand the reality of what happened back then and to include it in its memory structures."

[5] "Why were they not complaining and crying? Why this indifference in their tone of voice, when they spoke about those things that lay behind them, this passionless way of talking, as if they were reporting a terrible event from pre-historic times which would not be possible today and only whose tremors were still felt in our dreams?"

[6] ... as "animal-like huddling," another time a woman screams like a "fatally wounded animal"

activities, for example reading the newspaper, have now become unimportant: "Wenn wir in jenen Tagen zufällig eine Zeitung in die Hand bekamen, lasen wir die Heeresberichte gar nicht erst, wir verstanden nicht einmal, wozu sie noch herausgegeben wurden [...]. Was außerhalb von uns geschah, existierte einfach nicht" (39).[7] The report is marked by the persistent avoidance of stimuli that would remind one of the traumatic events. Nossack and his wife actively refuse to go to places or discuss matters that would arouse recollections of the air raids, they try to act "als wäre nichts geschehen" (32).[8] Yet, as often is the case in trauma survivors, the event cannot be suppressed completely and repeatedly returns, just as in recurring dreams, in intrusive memories: "wie schwer es war, diese Täuschung aufrechtzuerhalten. Alle fünf Minuten wurde sie durchbrochen, wenn es aus uns aufseufzte. Nichts konnte die Gedanken daran hindern, nach Hamburg zu gehen"(32).[9]

These are only a few examples that indicate the deep effect the bombings had on the Hamburg population and on Nossack. In fact, the existence of the work itself is an indication of its importance. Nossack is well aware of the dangers of writing about the events. He continuously reflects on why he is writing down his experiences:

> Wozu? Wozu dies alles niederschreiben? Wäre es nicht besser, es für alle Zeiten der Vergessenheit preiszugeben? Denn die dabeigewesen sind, brauchen es nicht zu lesen. Und die anderen und spätere? Wie, wenn sie es nur läsen, um sich am Unheimlichen zu ergötzen und ihr Lebensgefühl zu erhöhen? (44-45)[10]

The excerpt demonstrates Nossack's fears concerning writing about the experience of destruction. He knows that once committed to paper, the text is open to interpretation and could be misunderstood by the audience. He is aware of the difficulties such a work might encounter and the sensitivity of the issues he is touching upon. Coupled with his personal trauma it explains his hesitation of both speaking about the events and commenting on them. Still, Nossack feels strongly that he must record his experiences:

> Ich fühle mich beauftragt, darüber Rechenschaft abzulegen. Es soll mich niemand fragen, warum ich so vermessen von einem Auftrag rede: ich kann ihm nicht da-

---

[7] "When in those days we by chance got hold of a newspaper, we didn't even bother reading the reports from the front, we didn't even understand why they were still printed [...]. Whatever happened outside of us simply didn't exist."

[8] "as if nothing had happened"

[9] "how difficult it was to keep up this illusion. Every five minutes it was interrupted, when a sigh rose up in us. Nothing could hinder our thoughts from traveling to Hamburg."

[10] "For what? For what should I write all of this down? Wouldn't it be better to forget it forever? Because those who have been there do not need to read it. And others and those born later? What if they only read it in order to get excited by the horror and to heighten their sense of being alive?"

rauf antworten. Ich habe das Gefühl, daß mir der Mund für alle Zeiten verschlossen bleiben würde, wenn ich nicht dies zuvor erledigte. (7)[11]

Writing down the events is more than the creation of a witness report, but it becomes a necessity for Nossack, the artist. He needs to tell *Der Untergang* if he wants to continue to be a writer, or, maybe more accurately, if he wants to become one. The report is thus also a personal reflection about the meaning of the events for Nossak himself (Stephan 310). The destiny of the city becomes the destiny of Nossack the writer: "Ja, ich habe, wie ich es jetzt weiß, immer gewußt, daß es sich bei dem Schicksal der Stadt um mein Schicksal handeln würde" (18).[12]

The concentration on the self also explains the strange tension that underlies the work. On the one hand, Nossack continuously emphasizes its nature as an objective report, a document bare of any personal emotion. For example, after describing some of his feelings, he interrupts the flow of the text and asks: "Handelt es sich hier wirklich nur um ein ganz persönliches Gefühl? Denn dann würde es nicht in diesen Bericht gehören" (44).[13] On the other hand, Nossack's text reveals a symbolic structure that reaches far beyond a documentary. It is filled with metaphors and various other artistic devices and the concrete experiences that arise when the world around him is destroyed are widened to include a personal mythic dimension. It is the "Untergang" (7), a "Gericht" and a "Schicksal" (18, 32), determined by a "höhere Gewalt" (44), and part of the "Unterwelt" (17).[14] The entire incident is taken out of its concrete circumstances and perceived as a kind of play by powers beyond human understanding: "Eine viel tiefere Einsicht in die Dinge verbot uns, an einen Feind zu denken, der dies alles verursacht haben sollte; auch er war uns höchstens ein Werkzeug unkennbarer Mächte, die uns zu vernichten wünschten" (42).[15] The events become transformed into an artistic experience: "Jedesmal, wenn man sich aus dem Dunstkreis der Stadt wieder gelöst hatte, war es wie das Erwachen aus einer Ohnmacht. Oder man war verwüstet und vor Erschöpfung teilnahmslos wie ein Dichter, der mit Dämonen Zwiesprache hielt" (45).[16]

---

[11] "I feel that I have a calling to render an account of it. I do not want to be asked why I speak so presumptuously of a calling: I do not have an answer. I have the feeling that my mouth would be closed forever if I did not first take care of this."

[12] "Yes, I have always known, just as I know now, that the destiny of this city is also my own destiny."

[13] "Is this really only a personal feeling? Because then it would not belong in this report."

[14] It is the "end," a "judgment," and a "destiny," determined by a "higher power," and part of the "underworld."

[15] "A much deeper insight into things forbids us from thinking of an enemy, which was supposed to have caused all of this; it was also at most a tool of powers which we could not know and that were trying to destroy us."

[16] "Every time one had escaped from the atmosphere of the city, it seemed as if one were waking up from a fainting spell. Or one fell down and, because of exhaustion, was indifferent like a poet who had spoken with the demons."

While described as a general catastrophe and horrible in their consequences, the air raids thus play an important personal role in Nossack's life as an artist. To deal with the destruction and to get beyond the bombings' detrimental psychological effect, he reinterprets them as a meaningful personal event. The change of perspective also makes it possible for Nossack to avoid any questions of guilt and causality with regards to the air raids. By transforming them into timeless mythical occurrences, the difficult political background can be ignored and an understanding of the situation can be achieved. The destruction of Hamburg comes to be seen mainly as an artistic turning point, a point of departure. As he writes to his friend Hermann Kasack:

> Was mich angeht, so drängt es mich, nach Fertigstellung meines Bekenntnisses zu dem Erlebnis des Untergangs Hamburgs, auch über die sonstige geistige Vergangenheit mit nüchternen Augen Inventur zu machen, um danach entscheiden zu können, was davon wirklich mit untergegangen ist und was sich trotz Brandwunden etwa noch verwerten läßt. Das Gefühl, an einem Wendepunkt zu stehen oder vielleicht sogar schon ein paar Schritt darüber hinaus zu sein, ist nach wie vor in mir vorherrschend, und ich bin wachsam, mich nicht selbst zu versäumen. ("Brief" 13-14)[17]

This celebration of the opportunity to build something new in the midst of destruction is fostered by a new perception of time that goes along with the experience. Repeatedly, Nossack emphasizes the loss of linear time, and with it the loss of a sense of a past or a future: "Wir sind gegenwärtig geworden. Wir haben uns aus der Zeit gelöst" (71).[18] The idea of timelessness facilitates his reinterpretation of the present situation:

> Das, was ich als junger Mensch nicht ganz fertiggebracht hatte, sondern nur halb – die Ablösung von Familie und Konventionen –, das ergab sich nun durch die völlige "Zerstörung der Vergangenheit", wie ich es nenne.
> [...] Ich mußte mich nicht mehr mit irgendwelchen Konventionen belasten. Ich konnte mich ganz nach mir selber richten. (Rudolph and Nossack 185)[19]

In this sense, Nossack can make the catastrophe productive, he turns it into something positive which finally seals his destiny as an artist, and in this way the tragedy has a liberating effect (see also Maue 184). The reinterpretation of

---

[17] "Concerning myself, after I have finished my confessions about the events of the destruction of Hamburg, I also want to compile an honest inventory of my intellectual past, in order to decide afterwards what of it has truly vanished in the destruction and what, despite being damaged by the flames, could still be used. The feeling of being at a turning point, or maybe even a few steps beyond it, occupies me most, and I am careful not to miss myself."

[18] "We have become part of the present. We have been taken out of time."

[19] "What I did not manage to do completely, but only partially as a young man – to leave behind my family and societal conventions – was now accomplished by the complete 'destruction of the past,' as I call it. [...] I didn't have to burden myself with any societal rules. I could act solely according to my own wishes."

the destruction of Hamburg as a necessary artistic turning point becomes the foundation for all of Nossack's future work. Already before the heavy bombings, Nossack was exploring questions about the position of the individual in the world and repeatedly wished for a big event that would make it possible for him to break completely with the everyday life of reality and to enter the unpredictable chaos beyond this well-organized surface. Now, after the bombings, the horror of the experience and the force of destruction he observed become a constant echo in his work. As he states in an interview:

> Nossack: [...] Wenn eine Stadt in so kurzer Zeit kaputtgehen kann, dann bedeutet das doch etwas. Es bedeutet, daß man sich abfinden muß mit der Möglichkeit, daß so etwas zu jeder Zeit passieren kann. Das nenne ich das Unversicherbare. Und das ist für mich etwas Positives [...]
> Rudolph: Dann kann man doch sagen, daß Sie von der Erfahrung des Untergangs und des Todes ausgingen, als sie 1945 wieder anfingen zu schreiben?
> Nossack: Das möchte ich bejahen; denn ich bin einfach nicht zu denken ohne dieses Erlebnis. (Rudolph and Nossack 185-187)[20]

The experience of the bombardment of Hamburg truly makes Nossack the writer that we know. Nossack's literature after the war is one of existential questions, of a world in which one has to live with the awareness that nothingness is all around one and where there are no certainties one can rely on. This world is not ruled by the passage of time and by the way we organize and schedule our lives, but by the constant possible presence of death. It is a continuation of the state of timelessness that Nossack describes in *Der Untergang*. In the final pages of the text, Nossack thus sets up time as a rival to death, but shows death as the clear winner:

> Ihr sollt nicht immer mit dem Fremden zusammensein, sagt die Zeit, ich werde euch einsperren. - Ach, Mutter, warum denn nicht? - Er verdirbt euch, und es wird nichts Rechtes aus euch werden. - Mutter, du kennst ihn nicht. Er weiß so schöne Spiele. Er wohnt dort drüben, wo keine Häuser mehr sind. [...] Er ist unser Freund. Wir bitten ihn immer, uns dorthin mitzunehmen, wo er wohnt. Aber er will es noch nicht. [...] ihr bleibt jetzt hier. Es ist kein Umgang für euch. [...] Wir sind wieder auf die Straße gelaufen und spielen mit dem Tod. Da setzt sich die Zeit traurig in einen Winkel und kommt sich nutzlos vor. (71-72)[21]

---

20 "Nossack: When a city can be destroyed in such a short time, then this clearly means something. It means that we have to accept the possibility that this can happen at any moment. This is what I call the uninsurable. And that for me is something positive [...]/Rudolph: Then one can say that you based your writing after 1945 on the experience of the destruction and of death?/Nossack: I agree with this, because I am unthinkable without this experience."

21 "You shouldn't always be with the stranger, says Time, I will lock you in. - Oh, mother, why not? - He spoils you, nothing good will become of you. - Mother, you don't know him. He knows such nice games. He lives over there where there are no houses any more. [...] He is our friend. We always ask him to take us with him to the place where he lives. But he doesn't want to do it yet.

The excerpt demonstrates why Nossack views the insecurity of this universe ruled by death as something positive. Time, here significantly represented by the mother, stands for the life style of his bourgeois parents, in which one's future is decided from the start. It is a world full of certainty and one that stifles, according to Nossack, any true artistic impulse. A catastrophe such as the Hamburg bombing, however, which suddenly makes everyone aware that death can destroy at any point any such plans in an instant, opens up perspectives and insight into the world essential to creativity. Nossack, despite the horror and trauma he feels and observes in others following the July events, succeeds in overcoming their effects through personal artistic production and by channeling his feelings into creation. The destruction of Hamburg is interpreted as a rebirth and new beginning by Nossack, and this is the image with which he leaves the readers in *Der Untergang* as well:

> Dann kam einer zu uns in den Keller und sprach: Ihr müßt jetzt herauskommen, das ganze Haus brennt und wird gleich einstürzen. [...] Einige von uns hörten auf ihn. Doch es gehörte viel dazu. Wir mußten durch ein Loch hinaus, und vor dem Loch schlugen die Flammen hin und her. Es ist gar nicht so schlimm, sagte er, ich bin doch auch zu euch hereingekommen. Da wickelte ich mir eine nasse Decke um den Kopf und kroch hinaus. Dann waren wir hindurch. Einige sind dann auf der Straße noch umgefallen. Wir konnten uns nicht um sie kümmern. (72-73)[22]

When Nossack finally embarked on his writing career after the war, he was already over forty years old. He wrote until his death in 1977, but was increasingly seen as a representative of an older generation whose idea of literature and the arts was becoming outdated. In contrast, Wolfgang Borchert is often described, and has represented himself, as the spokesperson of a whole generation of young adults after the war, a "Generation ohne Abschied" ("Generation without Farewell"), as Borchert called it. When he died in 1947 of severe liver disease after long illness, he was only twenty-six years old and his writing career had only lasted a few years. The news of his death reached the Hamburger Kammerspiele theater at the final rehearsal for the premiere of Borchert's anti-war play *Draußen vor der Tür* (*The Man Outside*) that impressively captures the destructive forces of the catastrophe of World War II and calls for a new beginning outside of the old orders. The premiere of the play then became a memorial for Borchert:

[...] you stay here now. He is no company for you. [...] We run back out into the streets and are playing with Death. Then Time is sad, sits down in a corner and feels useless."

[22] "Then a man came down to us in the cellar and said: You have to leave now, the whole house is burning and will fall down at any minute. [...] Some of us listened to him. But it took a lot. We had to crawl through a hole and in front of the hole were flames going back and forth. It is not so bad, he said, after all I also made it through to you in the cellar. So I wrapped a wet blanket around my head and crawled out. Then we were through. Some broke down afterwards on the street. We couldn't take care of them."

Nachdem sich der Vorhang geschlossen hatte, blieb es still im Theater. Eine lange Minute des schweigenden Gedenkens und der Ergriffenheit folgte, dann brach Beifall los. Er galt gleichermaßen der herausragenden schauspielerischen Leistung Hans Quests wie der des Autors. Selten wohl war ein Premierenpublikum stärker ergriffen und aufgewühlt worden. Der da zu ihnen gesprochen hatte, war nicht mehr, war einer heimtückischen Krankheit erlegen, wohl mehr noch: er war an der Unbegreiflichkeit des Krieges und an der Wirklichkeit der Nachkriegszeit zugrunde gegangen. (Kraske 38)[23]

From then on, a mythlike aura has surrounded Borchert and his work. Today he is still widely regarded as the representative of a better Germany and is often referred to as the "Inbegriff des Leidenden am deutschen Elend" (Clausen 225).[24]

While Borchert had started writing before the end of the war, it was immediately after the war that he made his major literary contributions on which his reputation is now based. He wrote about his experiences in the destroyed postwar world surrounding him, the ruins, the rubble, the hunger, the hopelessness, and the loss of ideals. This environment and situation inspired Borchert to search for new ways of writing and living, as he defined them in his manifesto "Das ist unser Manifest": "Wir brauchen keine Dichter mit guter Grammatik. Zu guter Grammatik fehlt uns Geduld. Wir brauchen die mit dem heißen heiser geschluchzten Gefühl. Die zu Baum Baum und zu Weib Weib sagen und ja sagen und nein sagen: laut und deutlich und dreifach ohne Konjunktiv" (113).[25] This new type of literature that Borchert was now aiming for seems radically different from his earlier writing. As will be shown, this assessment can be easily confirmed when one looks at his literary reactions to the experience of the bombings and their consequences during and after the war. Yet since Borchert has been seen by many to be not only a writer, but a representative of a whole generation and the new Germany after 1945, it is necessary to combine this literary investigation with a look at Borchert's general ideas and attitudes towards Germany and towards questions of guilt and responsibility as they reveal themselves in his works and manifestoes. This might not only help to dispel the Borchert myth, but also to give insight into the general German reaction to the war and the postwar era.

---

[23] "After the curtain came down, the theater remained silent. A long minute filled with quiet remembrance and emotion followed, then the applause started. It was for both the outstanding acting performance of Hans Quest and for the author. Rarely had an audience at a premiere been touched or affected more strongly. He who had spoken to them was no longer present, he had become the victim of a malicious illness: even more he had been destroyed by the incomprehensibility of the war and by the reality of the postwar situation."

[24] "perfect representative of one suffering from the German misery"

[25] "We don't need a poet with good grammar. We don't have patience for good grammar. We need those with the hot, sobbing emotion. Those who call a tree a tree and a woman a woman and who say yes and no: loud and clear and three times without subjunctive."

When his home town Hamburg was severely bombed and largely destroyed, Borchert was recovering in a military hospital in Germany from the first symptoms of his liver disease. He was quite shocked and almost speechless about the events. As he writes to some friends in Hamburg: " 'Ich hätte Euch längst schreiben müssen, [...] aber was – angesichts dieses Ungeheuren, was Euch überfallen hat? Ist nicht alles andere klein und unwichtig dagegen?' " (quoted in Schröder 201).[26] At the end of August, Borchert succeeded in obtaining a vacation, and he proceeded to visit his parents in Hamburg. While his home had been spared by the bombs, the city he knew had been completely destroyed. Together with his mother he took the train through Hamburg all the way to Hammerbrook, observing the rubble and fields of ruins around him. However, while the experience was horrid, Borchert did not yet react artistically to the destruction. As a biographer points out, his poems about the experience "klingen nicht nach Zäsur. Auch die schlimmsten Tatsachen hindern ihn nicht, Herz auf Schmerz zu reimen" (Schröder 203).[27] What the critic expresses through this poetic no-no is confirmed by Borchert's poems of the time. After the war, Borchert switches to prose and uses a style aimed at clearly naming everything in short direct sentences, of straight-forward language, and plain descriptions of the broken world around him. This way of writing that we today identify with Borchert and that inspired Böll to call his work both historical "Dokument und Literatur" ("Nachwort" 19),[28] is nowhere to be found in these immediate literary reflections on the bombings:

Hamburg 1943

Der Mond hängt als kalte giftgrüne Sichel
über den hohläugig glotzenden Fenstern –
es knistert und wispert rings um den Michel
wie von tausend verirrten Gespenstern.
Da ragt eine Wand wie ein Schrei
in das Grauen der einsamen Nacht.
Gestern hat hier noch ein Mädchen gelacht –
und der Wind weht träumend vom Kai.
Und der Wind weht vom Meer -
und er weht über Freuden und Schmerzen,
er riecht nach Tauen, Möwen und Teer –
und er singt von Hamburgs unsterblichen Herzen!
(*Schatten und Mond* 252)[29]

---

[26] "I should have written to you long ago, [...] but what – in view of this dreadful event, that has come upon you? Does not everything else seem small and unimportant in comparsion to it?"

[27] ...his poems about the experience "do not sound as if after a caesura. Even the worst happenings did not prevent him from rhyming 'Herz' (heart) with 'Schmerz' (sorrow)."

[28] "document and literature"

[29] "Hamburg 1943/The moon hangs as a cold bright-green crescent/above the hollow-eyed staring windows –/it rustles and whispers around the Hamburg Michel/as if of a thousand lost

Borchert's style is wordy and the metaphors and similes are overdone, but the most striking element of the poem is its idealization of Hamburg. Even before his visit to the destroyed city, he expressed in a letter to friends in Hamburg: " 'Aber ich war doch immer bei Euch und in Hamburg - und jetzt, wo wir es verloren haben, fühle ich erst, wie sehr ich doch dahin gehöre' " (quoted in Schröder 201).[30] Hamburg, now that it is destroyed, becomes a paradise of wind, sun and fishing boats, it is his idyllic home, his "Heimat, Himmel, Heimkehr" (Borchert "Hamburg" 72).[31] Consequently, at this point Borchert reinterprets the destruction as a confirmation of his place in the world, an affirmation of where he belongs. Destruction is faced through the comfort of the belief in a better future because Hamburg's soul and, as seems to be implied, the spirit of the Hamburg inhabitants, cannot be destroyed. Instead, as he writes in another Hamburg poem, "Die Stadt" ("The City"):" 'aus dem Rhythmus neuer Tage steigt sie [Hamburg] verjüngt empor' " (quoted in Schröder 204).[32] While Borchert was clearly no Nazi, and repeatedly got into serious trouble for his opposition, it is not surprising that he managed to have these two poems published in the *Hamburger Anzeiger* shortly after the bombings took place. Borchert's sentimental outlook and passive reaction played too perfectly into the hands of Nazi ideology and the propaganda machine.

In his short stories on the bombardments and their effects after the war, best represented by "Die Küchenuhr" ("The Kitchen Clock") and "Billbrook," Borchert discarded his euphoric tone and most of his sentimental language as well as the idealization of the city. Instead, the destruction of the buildings and of the people who live there becomes the central theme of the texts. Their desolate state is not relieved by the hope for a better and brighter future, but now, after the war, these ideals have been replaced by both outer and inner devastation. In "Die Küchenuhr," the protagonist can only save a cheap white kitchen clock from his house which, in his absence, had been destroyed by an air raid and where his parents lie buried under the debris. The protagonist reports about the clock: "Die Zeiger sind natürlich aus Blech. Und nun gehen sie auch nicht mehr. Nein. Innerlich ist sie kaputt, das steht fest. Aber sie sieht noch aus wie immer."[33] This image of the clock is representative of the inner state of the pro-

---

ghosts./There a wall stands high like a scream/into the horror of the lonely night./Yesterday, a girl was laughing here –/and the wind blows dreamily from the harbor./ And the wind blows from the sea –/ and it blows over happiness and sorrow,/it smells of fishing ropes, sea gulls, and tar –/and it sings of Hamburg's undying heart!"

[30] "But I was always with you and in Hamburg - and only now that we have lost it, do I feel how strongly I belong there."

[31] "home, heaven, homecoming"

[32] "out of the rhythm of new days, Hamburg will rise rejuvenated"

[33] Wolfgang Borchert, "Die Küchenuhr," *Draußen vor der Tür* (Hamburg: Rowohlt, 1956) 103. All subsequent references are parenthetical in the text.
"Of course, the hands are only made out of tin. And now they don't work any longer. No. It's broken inside, that's for sure. But it still looks like it used to."

tagonist. In fact, it has been noted that the kitchen clock can serve as a symbol for all of Borchert's characters who survived the hardships of the war (Stark 122). Borchert shows that even what is physically spared cannot survive unscarred. While the protagonist of the story seems at first completely normal, his inner turmoil also comes through: "Er hatte ein ganz altes Gesicht, aber wie er ging, daran sah man, daß er erst zwanzig war" (103).[34] Similar to Nossack, the bombings are understood as a rupture, it constitutes an event that throws one outside of ordinary time and thus of linear, normal development. Through the events, the young man's natural development has been distorted, making it possible to be young and old, broken and working at the same time. Objective, linear time, as measured by clocks, does not exist any longer. In the words of a bystander: "Wenn die Bombe runtergeht, bleiben die Uhren stehen" (104).[35]

"Die Küchenuhr" also gives other indications of the traumatizing effects of experiencing or witnessing the bombings and their consequences. None of the characters have names, but are instead referred to as "der Mann" or "die Frau." The protagonist is even further reduced to simply "er." This reduction to generic terms fittingly captures the situation during and after the attacks. It illustrates the depersonalization which is often found among people who have experienced trauma. This state is coupled with a sense of numbness and emotional detachment in the protagonist. When talking about the destruction of his house, he acts as if he is happy: "Sie haben wohl alles verloren? Ja, ja, *sagte er freudig*, denken sie, aber auch alles!"(103, emphasis added).[36] He avoids articulating his loss, but instead solely focuses on the kitchen clock, the only thing that survived except for him. The death of his parents is only mentioned after he is specifically asked about them: "Dann fragte die Frau: Und ihre Familie? Er lächelte sie verlegen an: Ach, sie meinen meine Eltern? Ja, die sind auch mit weg. Alles ist weg" (104).[37] The memory of the dead parents finally leads to the end of the story, with his distress on being reminded of their death exploding into a mad laugh that can only be controlled by the protagonist ending the conversation, trying to avoid his recollection.

Borchert captures how war, and in this case specifically the bombings, affect people in their core. The young man is suddenly stripped of his role in the world. He has lost his place in the social structure as the son who was cared for by his mother (as he relates, every night she would get up when he came home late from work to give him something to eat). In addition, he has fallen out of the linear development of time, and has even lost his home, his space. Borchert makes clear that such confrontations with traumatic events shatter personalities

---

[34] "He had a really old face, but from the way he walked, one could tell that he was only twenty."

[35] "When the bomb comes down, the clocks stop."

[36] "You lost everything, haven't you? Yes, yes, *he said merrily*, can you believe it, everything!"

[37] "Then the woman asked: And your family? He smiled, embarrassed: Oh, you mean my parents? Yes, they are also gone. Everything is gone."

and world views and leave people wandering lost through the world. The naive childlike outlook with which many of Borchert's characters view their environment, is gone forever, but no new perspective has emerged. The confrontation with the bombings thus becomes an existential one, a defining moment, but not necessarily one that gets resolved. It is this lost state, this idea of belonging nowhere and the lack of guidance that Borchert presents as the condition of his generation. They are a generation without farewell because they never had the chance to develop gradually into adulthood. Instead, the war has cheated them out of chronology and has forced them to be on their own before their time.

A similar development can be observed in the story "Billbrook." Dealing with the effects of the Hamburg bombings, the protagonist of the text is actually a young Canadian pilot with the name Bill Brook who, when he visits the city after the war, is shocked by the complete destruction caused by the attacks in which he took part. In an interesting twist, Bill Brook feels especially connected to Hamburg because he notices that a part of the city bears his name: "Billbrook." Setting out on foot to find this area, Bill Brook moves deeper and deeper into the heart of the destroyed city which appears almost surreal. Even though he never reaches Billbrook, which is too far away, he succeeds in finding, according to Kurt Fickert, "in himself a heightened awareness of reality" (10). Yet he also experiences a complete loss of his earlier naive childlike perspective with which he had approached the war and Hamburg, leading to an identity crisis. In this sense, the story talks about the same existential problems as the previous text, even though the protagonist is actually a person "from above," a pilot involved in dropping the bombs whose effects he now experiences. While Borchert thus avoids giving a voice to a German victim of the air raids when describing the devastation, he still projects his own perspective onto the character, implying that the destruction affects everyone in the same manner, no matter on which side they stand or where they come from.

When Bill Brook starts out on his journey to find "his" part of the town, and thus himself, he is full of joy about the name coincidence:

> Doch einen ganz kleinen Stolz darüber gönnte er sich und eine großzügige gute Stimmung. [...] Er sah sich in Hopedale in der Küche stehen und seiner Mutter das Haar zerzausen vor Übermut und Gelächter. Er hörte das Gelächter im ganzen Haus in Hopedale und bis in den Hafen von Hopedale, wenn er das hier, das von dem Stadtteil, der Billbrook hieß, erzählen würde. (78)[38]

The childlike outlook with which Bill Brook starts on his journey is part of what has been described as an "absichtsvolles Renaivisierungsverfahren" (Elm

---

[38] Wolfgang Borchert, "Billbrook," *Das Gesamtwerk* (Hamburg: Rohwolt, 1949): 78. All subsequent references are parenthetical in the text.
"He allowed himself to feel a tiny bit proud of the fact and in a generous good mood. [...] he saw himself standing in Hopedale in the kitchen, ruffling up his mother's hair for sheer fun and joy. He heard the laughter throughout the whole house in Hopedale and all the way to the harbor of Hopedale, when he would tell the story about this city quarter that was called Billbrook."

273).[39] This perspective allows him to give a more immediate impression of the destructive consequences of the air war and the situation of the cities in 1945. When Bill Brook finally is forced to see the devastation that the bombs have caused, he is shocked and observes all the details around him in absolute disbelief:

> Welche der vier Richtungen er entlang sah, und er hatte das Gefühl, er könne in jede Richtung der Straßenkreuzung kilometerweit sehen: Kein Lebendiges. Nichts. Nichts Lebendiges. Milliarden Steinbrocken, Milliarden Steinstücke, Milliarden Steinkrümel. Gedankenlos vom gnadenlosen Krieg zerkrümelte Stadt. [...] Kein Haus, keine Frau, kein Baum. Totes nur. [...] Er stand in einer toten Stadt und er schmeckte es fade und übel auf der Zunge. Er war nicht mehr stolz. (81) [40]

Realizing that this was the result of only two days of heavy bombing, he, just like the young protagonist in "Die Küchenuhr," gets so overwhelmed by the horror around him and the recognition of the cruelty of war that he cannot react other than by breaking into a crazy, unstoppable laugh.

Back in his hotel, Brook tries to deal with his experiences by verbalizing them, by writing about them in a letter to his family. However, he is unable to put what he has seen and gone through into words and finally avoids mentioning them at all:

> Er nahm einen Briefbogen. Und dann saß er vor dem leeren Papier und sah in die Lampe. Er wollte von Billbrook schreiben, von dem Stadtteil Billbrook [...]. Von den Leichenfingern wollte er schreiben, von der toten Stadt und ihren zehntausend flachgedrückten Einwohnern. Von der toten Stadt wollte er schreiben und von dem Mädchen mit dem Ball. Davon wollte er schreiben. Das wollte er denen zu Hause schreiben, denen in Kanada, denen in Labrador. Aber dann schrieb er kein Wort davon. Dann schrieb er kein Wort von der toten Stadt. Dann schrieb er nur von Hopedale, vom Wind in Hopedale, vom Hafen in Hopedale und vom Wasser in Hopedale. Er sah in die Lampe. (101-102)[41]

Brook is unable to talk about his experiences directly and so ends up writing about his hometown, Hopedale, instead. Yet these remarks on Hopedale are in-

---

[39] "purposeful maneuver to re-introduce a naive perspective"

[40] "In whichever of the four directions he looked, and he had the feeling he could see for kilometers in each direction of the crossroads: No life. Nothing. No life. Billions of blocks and stones, billions of stone pieces, billions of stone crumbs. A city thoughtlessly crumbled to pieces by the merciless war. [...] No house, no woman, no tree. Only deadness. [...] He stood in a dead city and it tasted stale and sickly on his tongue. His sense of pride was gone."

[41] "He took some stationery. And then he sat in front of the empty sheet and looked into the lamp. He wanted to write about Billbrook, about the city district Billbrook [...]. He wanted to write about the corpses' fingers, about the dead city, and the ten thousand inhabitants that had been flattened by the rubble, and he wanted to write about the girl with the ball. This is what he wanted to write about. This is what he wanted to write home about to his family in Canada, in Labrador. But then he wrote not a single word about it. Instead he only wrote about Hodedale, about the wind in Hopedale, the harbor in Hopedale, and the water in Hopedale. He looked into the lamp."

terspersed with intrusions from his experiences. His musings on Hopedale are indirectly reflections on Hamburg. "Wind," "Hafen," and "Wasser" are not only part of Brook's hometown, but are closely connected with Hamburg and are images Borchert repeatedly invokes when writing about the city. Instead of these pleasant sights, Brook is confronted with a picture of destruction and death. His inability to write about his experiences mirrors the author's own problems in describing what he saw and felt. Just as Brook has to talk about Hamburg by writing about Hopedale, it is now easier for Borchert to reflect on the destruction and his personal development towards a more complex world view through the outsider Bill Brook.

Hamburg, 1945. Reproduced with permission from Keystone Pressedienst, Germany.

The stark contrast between these stories and the earlier poems about the destruction of Hamburg exemplify the large changes Borchert went through both in outlook and, in order to express this new perspective, artistically. It is this new way of seeing the world, together with his radical request to "Say NO!" to the war and its consequences, that forms the basis of Borchert's reputation today as the first voice of the new Germany after Nazism.[42] However, was Borchert truly as radical in his break from both his earlier writing and attitudes as is generally assumed? When one looks at the stories set amid the rubble of the destroyed

---

[42] "Sag NEIN" is the much repeated key phrase of his anti-war pamphlet "Dann gibt es nur eins!" that calls for everyone to take active steps to avoid war instead of passively going along with things (Borchert 110-120).

city, Borchert manages to capture the physical and psychological situation of Germans in the immediate postwar years. Yet there is very little, if any, true confrontation with the past and any guilt that could arise from it. While guilt seems to flow like an undercurrent through his stories, it never really rises to the surface. Borchert's heroes often have a guilty conscience, but it stays diffuse and elusive even if they try to pin it down to one event in their past (Mirtschev 176). Borchert thus calls out vehemently against war in all of his writings, but he does not give room for a true discussion about the Nazi past or the crimes that were committed in the twelve years of their leadership.

Borchert's non-fiction writings demonstrate this avoidance of the realities of German crimes even more strongly. It has been noted that in his manifestoes and pamphlets, Borchert displays a "Schwamm drüber" mentality (Reemtsma 240), instead of truly dealing with the past.[43] In "Generation ohne Abschied," for example, he describes himself and his peers as a generation without farewell, but one that has now arrived: "Wir sind eine Generation ohne Abschied, aber wir wissen, daß alle Ankunft uns gehört" (110), thus focusing almost exclusively on the future.[44] In "Das ist unser Manifest" ("This Is Our Manifesto") , he states more clearly what he hopes for in this future. Borchert wants to turn the categorical "no" with which he confronts the war into a positive change. While this seems necessary in a situation when one needs to build a new country from the ground up, his path is disconcerting. Borchert here conjures up the image of Germany, the beloved country for whose sake everything and everyone has to be embraced:

> Denn wir lieben diese gigantische Wüste, die Deutschland heißt. Dies Deutschland lieben wir nun. Und jetzt am meisten. Und um Deutschland wollen wir nicht sterben. Um Deutschland wollen wir leben [...]. Dieses bissige, bittere, brutale Leben. Wir nehmen es auf uns für diese Wüste. Für Deutschland. Wir wollen dieses Deutschland lieben wie die Christen ihren Christus: Um sein Leid.
> Wir wollen diese Mütter lieben, die Bomben füllen mußten – für ihre Söhne. Wir müssen sie lieben um dieses Leid.
> Und die Bräute, die nun ihren Helden im Rollstuhl spazierenfahren, ohne blinkernde Uniform – um ihr Leid [...]
> Und den Landser, der nun nie mehr lachen lernt –
> und den, der seinen Enkeln noch erzählt von einunddreißig Toten nachts vor seinem, vor Opas M.G. –
> sie alle, die Angst haben und Not und Demut: Die wollen wir lieben in all ihrer Erbärmlichkeit. (116)[45]

---

[43] a "Let's forget it" mentality

[44] "We are a generation without farewell, but we know that all arrival belongs to us."

[45] "Because we love this gigantic desert which is called Germany. This Germany we now love. And now most of all. And for Germany we do not want to die. For Germany we want to live [...]. This biting, bitter, brutal life. We take it upon ourselves for this desert. For Germany. We want to love this Germany like the Christians love their Christ: for its sorrow. We want to love the mothers, who had to fill the bombs – for their sons. We must love them for their sorrow. And the

The text couples an all-embracing love for everyone in Germany, no matter what they have done in the past, with manifestations of their suffering and the complete separation of the country from the crimes committed by its inhabitants. These aspects of the Manifesto create an atmosphere very much comparable to the idyllic ideals of Borchert's earlier poetry. Questions of guilt and responsibility are entirely suppressed and the experience of destruction is instead seen as a time to reaffirm one's love for one's country and one's place in the world. So despite the radical break Borchert proposes in much of his writing, he seems to be yearning for some of the cozy communal feeling and mood, the "Volksgemeinschaft," which the Nazis had skillfully created among Germans. The reaction of Martin Cordes, one of Borchert's contemporaries, to his "Generation ohne Abschied" summarizes this problematic attitude :

"Jeder suchte das Seine, nicht den oder die Anderen oder gar das Glück der Anderen. Ihr erlebtet Euer Ich 'unter der Kathedrale von Smolensk [...], in der Normandie [...], am finnischen See, auf einem Gut in Westfalen.' Und nun? Was bleibt als Erkenntnis? Schuld? Nein. Selbstgefühl! 'Wir sind eine Generation der Ankunft [...] auf einem neuen Stern, in einem neuen Leben.' Ja wird man denn dort wenigstens bleiben, beglückt und beglückend? Wohl kaum. 'Wir wissen, daß alle Ankunft uns gehört.' Das geht also ewig so weiter: 'Denn heute gehört uns Deutschland und morgen die ganze Welt.' " (quoted in Reemtsma 242)[46]

Similar to Nossack, who deals with the destruction of Hamburg by personalizing his experience and views it as a key turning point in his career as an artist and writer, Borchert gives the devastation a positive meaning by using it to reaffirm his belief in a better future for Germany. Both writers thus avoid the important question of guilt, which is necessarily related to the ruins they see around them. Nossack attributes the experience as having been caused by an undefinable higher power, Borchert ignores causalities completely through his all inclusive 'no' to the past and 'yes' to the present and the future. Even though in both cases the topic of guilt cannot be suppressed completely and lurks just under the surface of their artistic production, it remains diffuse and is not confronted or thematized. In this respect, the authors thus echo the attitude of denial about

---

brides, who now have to walk their heroes about in their wheelchairs, without sparkling uniforms – for their sorrow [...]. And the Private, who will now never learn how to laugh again – and the one who will still tell his grandchildren about thirty-one dead at night in front of his, in front of grandpa's, machine gun – all those who are frightened and in need and humble: We will love them in all their misery."

[46] "Everyone was only looking out for himself, not for others or even for the happiness of others. You experienced yourself under the Cathedral of Smolensk [...], in Normandy [...], by a Finnish lake, on a large farm in Westphalia.' And now? What do you take back as insight? Guilt? No. A proud ego! 'We are a generation of arrival [...] at a new star, in a new life.' Well will you at least stay there, so happy and so ready to share your happiness? Probably not. 'We know that all arrival belongs to us.' This means it will always continue: 'Because today Germany belongs to us and tomorrow the whole world.' "

German responsibility of much of the German population at the time. The accessibility of Borchert's texts and his lack of discussion about the painful questions of German guilt, together with his early death, have helped to surround the writer with a mythical aura and have produced, in part, the important position that he has assured in postwar literary culture. It seems that it is time, however, to ensure that his stories, while impressive, are read in a broader historical context and are more critically assessed by their readers.

Wolfgang Borchert requested a new grammar of German writing, a more direct language which would name things as they were and radically break with the past. Yet his writing still contained a fair amount of what a critic called "schluchzende[s] Pathos" which diminished the effect of the horror he described (Schoeller 4).[47] Other calls for a different way of writing, such as Wolfgang Weyrauch's idea of the "Kahlschlag," a complete break with the past and the precision in material without clouding the view through ideological ties, were also more often embraced in theory than in practice. Gert Ledig's novel *Vergeltung* (*Payback*) from 1956, however, truly fits the postwar ideas for a new form of literature. In *Vergeltung*, Ledig offers a collage of different stories that depict sixty-nine minutes of a heavy air raid attack on an unnamed large German city in 1944. The novel displays the complete horror of what Germans so fanatically called for when they wanted a "total war;" the title *Vergeltung* (payback, retaliation, revenge) suggests that the air raids are the answer to their desires. Like a geologist, Ledig explores layer after layer of a cross-section of the events from the bombers above to the people in the shelters below ground, using precise language without any artistic frills. Yet the destructive force of the bombs does not allow his investigation to be neatly organized. Instead, the novel becomes as fragmented as the events themselves. Ledig mounts its individual parts together into a collage in a way that provides an almost movie-like effect.

Ledig had already experimented with the direct, almost brutal language of *Vergeltung* in his previous and very first novel, *Die Stalinorgel* (named after a type of rocket launcher), which had been published in 1955. This war novel focuses on the experience of the soldiers at the front, specifically a three day fight between desperate German soldiers and advancing Russian troops around a swampy hill near Leningrad. Ledig illustrates the horror of the war: he presents it as nothing but a falling back into a world without civilization in which only one's own survival is at stake. The book became an immediate success and was highly praised by critics, particularly for its direct, unsentimental, and new language which stood in stark contrast to other bestsellers about the war, such as Hans Hellmut Kirst's popular *08/15* or Ernst Jünger's earlier aestheticisation of war in *In Stahlgewittern* (*The Storm of Steel*) (Kilb 21).

For *Die Stalinorgel*, Ledig tapped into his personal experiences as a soldier. When he turned eighteen in 1939, he voluntarily joined the German army and

---

[47] "sobbing pathos"

was also involved in the terrible fights around Leningrad in 1942 which left a lasting impression on him. He was seriously wounded twice, the second time in 1942 when his lower jaw was crushed, and he was allowed to go home. There, he became the witness to heavy air raids, particularly in Munich, which then served as a model for his second novel, *Vergeltung*. He is thus one of the few authors who experienced both the fighting at the Eastern front and the large area bombings of German cities. Ledig's two novels about the soldiers' and the civilians' war experiences, together with his third one, *Faustrecht* (*Law of Fists*) which describes the after-effects of the war in the "rubble society" of the postwar era, form a unique and impressive trilogy about World War II and its consequences.

It thus seems surprising that Gert Ledig had become virtually unknown by the 1990s until he was rediscovered in the course of the Sebald debate about the bombings and German literature. The reaction to his second novel, *Vergeltung*, was largely responsible for this development. While the audience of the 1950s was apparently ready for the literary depiction of the cruelty of war at the front, it could not deal with revisiting the realities of the "home front." Critics were appalled by the book, the audience largely ignored it:

> In den Gründerjahren der Bundesrepublik wollte man solche 'Perversitäten' und 'gewollt makabre Schreckensmalerei,' die jeden 'positiv gerichteten Ausblick vermissen' lassen, nicht mehr lesen. Der Soldatentod an der Ostfront in der *Stalinorgel* war noch zu tolerieren, nicht mehr die Tötung von Frauen und Kindern im Bombenkrieg. (Rode 66)[48]

The soldiers' experiences had been written about previously. Not only were they part of a literary tradition, but it was also perceived as acceptable at this point to reflect on the most recent cruelty of the soldier's lot. War was war and one could identify with the soldier's suffering. Dying, in some sense, was the soldier's job. Experiences at the front now seemed far away, not only in time but even in space, since they were mainly located in places that were now meaningless to the new Germany. The bombings, however, had been largely avoided in literature just as people tried to avoid the topic in their lives. These experiences had been too close to home and had suddenly brought war to civilians. When they were successfully covering up the results of the bombardments by clearing the rubble, erecting new buildings, and restoring others as if they had never been destroyed, it did seem "perverse" to many to be expected to read about the destruction of their cities in their spare time. As one critic suspects: "Das Buch löste 1956, als es erstmals erschien, einen Schock aus und der wurde seinem Urheber mit Verdrängung vergolten, als hätte er den Krieg eigens angerichtet" (Schoeller 4).[49]

---

[48] "In the founding years of the Federal Republic, one did not want to read such 'perversities' and 'purposefully macabre depictions of horror,' which were 'lacking any positive outlook for the future.' The death of soldiers at the Eastern front in *Stalinorgel* was bearable, but not the killing of women and children by the bombs."

When looking at the novel, the reaction of the audience of the 1950s, caught up in avoidance and the conservatism of the Adenauer era, becomes plausible. Ledig's text depicts sixty-nine minutes of sheer horror which was new both in its gory detail and in its style. The world Ledig describes is one that is largely stripped to its core. It is without the civilized behavior patterns a society might adhere to, and without typical points of orientation such as space and time. All figures are either constantly moving in search of someone they will never find, or confined to unnatural places such as cellars and bunkers, or buried in the rubble. Instead of sitting in school, young students are literally tied to anti-aircraft stations on top of a roof, or hide in the trenches. Perception of time, as has already been seen in Nossack and Borchert, has also clearly changed. Again, time has lost its linear function and its capacity to give orientation in this chaotic situation, or to order events. For example, when a house collapses and the people in its cellar cannot get out, the urge to know the time becomes the fundamental desire of everyone, as if knowing the time would somehow rescue them from their unclear destiny:

> "Also bitte?" fragte der Mann. "Wollen wir uns jetzt ausgraben?"
> "Natürlich," klang eine Stimme aus der Finsternis. "Wir haben vier Stunden gewartet."
> [...] "Woher wissen sie das?"
> "Ich habe einen Wecker!"
> "Sie hat einen Wecker," sagte die Witwe, "Wir fragen hundertmal nach der Zeit, und sie hat einen Wecker."
> Der Mann befahl: "Zeigen sie ihn!"
> "Sie können ihn nicht sehen! [...]"
> "Hören," antwortete die Witwe. "Lassen sie ihn hören."
> "Tick, tack," sagte die Stimme. "Tick, tack!"[50]

The scene exemplifies the hope invested in established structures such as time to provide guidance in times of turmoil, but also reveals the absurdity of this idea in a situation like the bombardments where time is seemingly suspended. In another scene about a rescue team on its almost inevitably pointless mission, the participants are already aware of the suspension of time and the lack of importance of these types of measurements when facing death. Looking at a watch is simply a habit, but it does not offer any information and the action is void of meaning: "Einer der Männer suchte seine Uhr. Als er sie hervorzog, blickten alle

---

[49] "In 1956, when the book appeared for the first time, it caused a shock that was avenged by suppressing the one who had caused it, as if he alone had started the war."

[50] Gert Ledig, *Vergeltung* (Frankfurt a. M.: Suhrkamp, 1999): 83. All subsequent references are parenthetically in the text.
" 'So what now?' the man asked. 'Will we now dig ourselves out?' 'Of course,' a voice sounded from the dark. 'We have been waiting here for four hours.' [...] 'How do you know that?' 'I have an alarm clock!' 'She has an alarm clock,' said the widow, 'we ask a hundred times what time it is and she has an alarm clock.' The man ordered: 'Show it to us!' 'You won't be able to see it! [...]' 'Listen,' said the widow. 'Let us hear it.' 'Tick, tock,' the voice said. 'Tick, tock!' "

auf die Zeiger. Erst nacheinander, dann gemeinsam [...]. Die Uhr blitzte silbern. Der große Zeiger und der kleine Zeiger richteten sich auf Ziffern. Niemand von ihnen sah sie. Weder die Ziffern noch die Zeiger" (52).[51] Only the readers are made aware of the short duration of the depicted events since Ledig gives precise information about the time at both the beginning and the end of the novel. However, when the reader is immersed into the text, the suspension of time affects him as well. Since simultaneous events are mixed together and one jumps from fragment to fragment, no continuity of plot arises and the reader experiences the temporal disorientation of the novel's characters.

In addition to the loss of orientational categories such as time and space, the situation is so beyond any human experience that none of the learned values and ideas seem to make sense any longer. Instead, everyone and everything is consumed by the firestorm that rages through the city, no matter how they behave or what they do. The short biographies interspersed in the voices of the thirteen people around which the various story lines evolve, drive home how much the bombings, and thus the constant confrontation with destruction and death, have changed their lives and their personalities. Each is only a fragment of his or her earlier self, mirroring how the world around them has gone to pieces. There are no strict categories, but everything, such as force and love, guilt and innocence, life and death, becomes fluid.

Within this flux, questions of morality or ethics become meaningless. Values are either ignored or, when still adhered to, have no positive consequences. All of the story-fragments reveal this inner and outer destruction. This is the reason why, in one story, what starts out as a shocking rape of a young woman who is buried alive under the rubble of a house together with a man she does not know, suddenly can end in a love act. Yet Ledig does not soften the brutality of their situation by letting true closeness arise between them. Love is only an illusion, in the end everyone is again on their own. Each is left "apathisch" after the event and they finally die separately (175-176). In addition, the young woman, who in this scene is portrayed a victim, had shortly before been anything but that. Overburdened by her responsibility to carry a sick old woman down to the cellar at every air raid alarm, she had pushed her down the stairs and killed her. In another narrative, it is again the supposedly innocent, a young boy, who oversteps the moral boundaries. Left behind from a rescue team he was assigned to by its leader in order to spare his young life, he actually provides in fanatic delight the murder weapon for the lynching death of an American bomber pilot whose plane had crashed and who was wandering, half crazed by the experience, through the firestorm he had helped to create. In other stories, Ledig presents

---

[51] "One of the men was looking for his watch. When he pulled it out, all of them looked at the hands. First one after the other, then together [...]. The watch had a silver shine. The large hand and the small hand were pointing at numbers. None of them saw them. Neither the numbers nor the hands."

people who are driven by fear and love for their children to run through the hell of the flames in their search for them. These insane and deadly trips are more than attempts to save their children, but they are intended to guarantee one's own survival, since it is precisely this love for their children that keeps them feeling alive and human. Yet Ledig again does not offer any happy endings. In one case, a mother is sent on a hunt for her supposedly injured son unaware of what everyone else knows, namely that he is dead (this search only ends ten years later with her death, as the reader finds out in the epilogue). In the other case, a father dies on his way to try to find his small son at the train station even though, or maybe because, he is aware that his son is most likely dead.

In this atmosphere of despair, Ledig dissects the horror of the bombing war. There is hardly a page without death, or, as a critic points out, "[d]ie Zahl der Zerrissenen und Krepierten übersteigt schnell die der Seiten. Es herrscht nicht der symbolische, sondern der serielle Tod" (Müller 57).[52] The true hero of the novel is consequently not one of the characters, but destruction itself. Ledig's *Vergeltung* is thus not a text that lets the reader in on clear descriptions of the psychological suffering of the individual characters. Instead, he only gives glimpses of the traumatizing effects of the horror. Readers can gain some access to the trauma by filling in the gaps with their imagination. Similar to the experience of suspended time, the confrontation with horror causes a haunting reaction in the readers which follows them even after finishing the book. The graphic pictures Ledig provides leave their imprint: people being grilled in the asphalt, human torches, children crawling through their own blood, child soldiers of the anti-aircraft stations who get their noses torn off and whose intestines hang out of their dead bodies, together with the short deeper glimpses at some of the characters leave their mark. Just as there is no God any longer in this hell on earth (in one scene a Christ figure is ripped from the cross by the bombs (198)), the text stands without any mediation or comments by an authoritative narrator that could give any meaning to the events. The novel thus leaves the reader "allein, verstört, verzweifelt, abgeschlagen, wütend. Siebzig Minuten Qual und Pein, 199 unerträgliche Seiten; das Ich zittert, aber Weiterlesen muß sein" (Roos 44).[53]

Ledig sets out to convey, and succeeds in recreating, the all-consuming fear that characterizes the experience of the bombings. In an interview with Volker Hage, Ledig, shortly before his death in 1999, defines this personal experience as vital for writing about this horror which is beyond normal human experience:

Er kennt Freunde in Kroatien, die er gelegentlich besucht – und etwas über den Bosnienkrieg zu schreiben, das hätte ihn gereizt. "Aber ich habe nur ein paar Seiten

---

[52] "the number of bodies which are ripped apart and have died horribly soon rises above the number of pages. This is not symbolic, but serial death."

[53] "alone, confused, desperate, depressed, angry. Seventy minutes of torture, 199 unbearable pages; the self starts shaking, but one must go on reading."

geschafft," sagt Ledig [...]. "Es ging nicht. Zuviel Distanz. Die Angst muß dir selbst im Genick sitzen, du mußt das genau kennen." (Hage "Ledig" 164)[54]

For Ledig, writing about trauma is thus inherently linked to own experiences. As discussed in Chapter 2, fictionalizing an experience can be particularly helpful in a process of working through trauma, since it makes it possible to immerse oneself emotionally in the events, while still offering distance from them through one's fictional character. Fiction consequently allows one to get close to one's own trauma, a step necessary in healing, without causing the same level of distress as a non-imaginary recreation would. *Vergeltung* offers a general picture of the bombing war and also reflects Gert Ledig's own experiences during the air raids on Munich. In his conversation with Volker Hage, it emerges that the bombings were a haunting memory for the author: "Ein Traum suchte ihn noch Jahre nach Kriegsende immer wieder heim: Er liegt auf einer Plattform, hoch oben, auf allen Seiten gähnt der Abgrund, keine Treppe, kein Schlupfloch – und dann kommen die Flugzeuge und beschießen ihn" ("Ledig" 162).[55] While *Vergeltung* focuses on the experiences of many different people during an attack, Ledig's own trauma is also included in the novel, but reinvented within a fictional context. One of the most haunting stories of the book concerning an anti-aircraft station, continuously under attack on the roof of a four story high surface bunker, is very much a reenactment and expansion of his nightmare scenario:

> Auf der Plattform lagen sie, und ihre Fingernägel krallten sich in den Beton. Die Stricke waren gespannt. Ihre Verbindung mit der Erde.
> "Abschuß," brüllte der Geschützführer. [...] In einer Wolke züngelte eine Flamme. Sie zersprühte als Komet. Blitze stürzten nach unten. Ein Schlag erschütterte gleichzeitig den ganzen Bunker [...]. Eine Sekunde später hob der Luftdruck ihn hoch und warf ihn auf den Rücken.
> Der Geschützführer schlitterte mit ausgebreiteten Armen [...]. Wenn die Stricke versagten, wehte es ihn in den Abgrund. Vier Stockwerke tief. (53-54)[56]

It might be this underlying authenticity that gives the novel such power in its effect on the reader. As Ledig himself emphasizes, without going through this ex-

---

[54] "He has friends in Croatia, whom he visits once in a while – and he was tempted to write something about the war in Bosnia. 'But I only managed to write a few pages,' Ledig said [...]. 'It didn't work. Too much distance. The fear has to grab you by the neck, you really have to know it.'"

[55] "A dream still haunted him years after the end of the war: he lies on a platform, high up, on all sides lurks the abyss, no stairs, no hiding place – and then the planes come and shoot at him."

[56] "They were lying on a platform, and their fingernails were clawed into the concrete. The ropes were tight. Their connection to the ground. 'Shoot,' yelled the leading gunman. [...] In a cloud, a flame was visible. It exploded into a comet. Lightning came down. The bunker started shaking from a hit at the same time [...]. A second later the air pressure lifted him up and threw him on his back. The leading gunman was sliding with open arms [...]. If the ropes broke, he would fall into the abyss. Down four stories."

perience, one cannot really create true literature: "Sonst bist du bloß ein Bericht-
erstatter, kein Schriftsteller" (Hage "Ledig" 164).[57]

It was the strong opposition of critics and audience to *Vergeltung* that finally
drove Ledig out of the business of writing literature after his third novel and
almost completely erased him from the memory of German literary history until
he was recently rediscovered. However, texts like Nossack's *Der Untergang* and
Borchert's short stories were known and read by the very same audience. Why
did Ledig's novel fail? This might be connected with the lack of any positive
outlook in the work. Both Nossack and Borchert succeed in turning the horror
of the bombings into something positive. Nossack does so by personalizing the
experience into the essential event that served as a point of departure for his
new life as a writer. Borchert depicts his generation as innocent victims who
had to suffer from the circumstances of the world they grew up in, and he takes
the destruction as the foundation to build a new Germany in which everyone is
embraced. Neither one of them deals directly with the truly burning issues of
the war events, namely the reasons for the bombings and the guilt Germany had
loaded onto itself during the Nazi era.

In *Vergeltung*, Ledig chooses a different path. He tries to get to the core
of the events, both in content and in language. While the audience was particularly appalled by the directness of the gruesome details and a language that
appeared as fragmented as the content, an additional underlying reason for their
strong rejection seems to lie in Ledig's attempt to address the guilt question as
well. Even though he does not talk directly about the German crimes against
Jews, he nevertheless deals with the topic to a greater extent than most writers
of the time. The concept of the title, namely that the bombings were a response
to Germany's deeds, is echoed in the novel itself. As one character says: "wir
bezahlen die Rechnung" (115).[58] In another scene, Ledig depicts the terrible
lot of some Russian forced laborers, who have been reduced to act almost like
animals, dreaming and thinking only about food, until even these thoughts have
been killed: "Nikolai Petrowitsch war lebendig gestorben. Er träumte nicht mehr
von Brot. Tote leiden keinen Hunger" (111-112).[59] It is also on the issue of guilt
that the constant stark, nonemotional tone of the novel is interrupted right before
the short epilogue which concludes the work, offering a glimpse of humanity
in the chaos. When the American bomber pilot, who is painted sympathetically
and in great detail in the novel, is brutally killed even though he is completely
defenseless, the witnesses to the murder in the bunker, who previously were full
of hatred for the pilots above, suddenly feel deep shame: " 'Ich schäme mich,'
sagte eine Stimme von der Mauer, 'für die, die das getan haben' " (194).[60] Yet

---

[57] "Otherwise you are merely a reporter, not a writer."

[58] "we're paying the price"

[59] "Nikolai Petrowitsch had died while still alive. He didn't dream of bread any longer. The dead
don't suffer from hunger."

Ledig shows that this sentiment has come too late and cannot stop what has been put into motion long before. As he states in the epilogue:

> Eine Stunde genügte, und das Grauen triumphierte. Später wollten einige das vergessen. Die anderen wollten es nicht mehr wissen. Angeblich hatten sie es nicht ändern können.
> Nach der siebzigsten Minute wurde weiter gebombt. Die Vergeltung verrichtete ihre Arbeit.
> Sie war unaufhaltsam.
> Nur das jüngste Gericht. Das war sie nicht. (199)[61]

In his text, Ledig does not allow religion or myth to distort the true facts of the causes of the war and its events, but poses the question of responsibility. Also, the last comments in his novel about the climate of denial that surrounds the bombings in the postwar world almost leads one to believe that he already foresaw the book's certain failure with its audience. Ledig was writing against suppression of the events, but obviously was well aware of the difficulty of this endeavor. Unfortunately, the novel could not break through the silence and was cleared away with the rest of the rubble that would remind one of the destructive consequences of the war.

4.2   Mosaics of Horror: Alexander Kluge and Walter Kempowski

Even though rarely compared in literary criticism, Alexander Kluge and Walter Kempowski have followed strikingly similar interests in their literary careers, in the form as well as the content of their writing. Both have been attracted to a documentary and montage style and have extensively focused on World War II. Here, they have both published on the battle of Stalingrad, but also about the air raids and their effects. One might even say that Kluge and Kempowski have made the war the central theme of their works and lives. This concentration on the war, particularly on the large area bombings that will be discussed here, might also be connected to their respective experiences as youths. When Alexander Kluge was thirteen years old, he witnessed the destruction of over eighty percent of his hometown of Halberstadt only a month before the end of the war. This event left a lasting impression on the author and has even been called "ein biographisches Urerlebnis" (Lau 15) for Kluge.[62] In the preface to his volume of stories that contains a text on the experience, "Der Luftangriff

---

[60] " 'I am ashamed,' said a voice close to the wall, 'for those who have done this.' "

[61] "One hour was enough, and the horror was triumphant. Later, some wanted to forget this. Others didn't want to know it anymore. They claim that they couldn't have changed it. After seventy minutes the bombing continued. Revenge was doing its job. It was unstoppable. But judgment day – that's not what it was."

[62] "a biographically highly formative event"

auf Halberstadt am 8. April 1945," or "The Air Raid on Halberstadt on April 8, 1945," the reader gets a glimpse at the power of the memory of the events. For Kluge, the bombings are not part of the past, but of the present, their effect has been so severe, that they are not perceived as history:

> Es hat den Anschein, daß einige Geschichten nicht die Jetztzeit, sondern die Vergangenheit betreffen. Sie handeln in der *Jetztzeit*. Einige Geschichten zeigen *Verkürzungen*. Genau dies ist dann die Geschichte. Die Form des Einschlags einer Sprengbombe ist einprägsam. Sie enthält eine Verkürzung. Ich war dabei, als am 8. April 1945 in 10 Meter Entfernung so etwas einschlug.[63]

Similarly, Kempowski also had traumatic experiences with the bombings. He was on the ground when air raids against his hometown of Rostock destroyed the entire old part of the town and overall one third of the city. Later, he barely survived the heavy air raids against Hamburg where he was staying with his grandfather in July 1943. Kempowski's comments in an interview show how also for him, just as for Kluge, these events were formative experiences. Today, he perceives them as an important caesura in his development: "von heute aus gesehen glaube ich, daß damit eigentlich meine Kindheit beendet war, es hat einen Schnitt gegeben" (Hage and Kempowski 265).[64] The events are lasting experiences that have been with Kempowski throughout his life; he reportedly remembers scenes of sitting in the cellars, frightened, during the attacks: "Ich sehe mich noch heute im Keller sitzen, und habe dieses widerwärtige Geräusch im Ohr, das Pfeifen der fallenden Bomben" (Hage and Kempowski 265), or running through the firestorm: "Ich spüre es fast heute noch an den Augenlidern, wie es mir da wehtat. Es war eine unglaubliche Hitze" (Hage and Kempowski 266).[65]

Interestingly enough, these experiences have also inspired each author to move in a similar direction in the way that they artistically work through these powerful events. Both embrace the technique of montage, particularly the collage of different quotations in order to translate the events into prose. For Kluge as well as Kempowski, the bombings (and the war in general) create a world completely different from that which traditional narrative techniques are able to convey. As Kluge states in his acceptance speech to the Fontane-Preis, he sees a radicalization of the conditions of our time in the twentieth century:

---

[63] Alexander Kluge, *Neue Geschichten. Hefte 1-18: 'Unheimlichkeit der Zeit'* (Frankfurt a. M.: Suhrkamp, 1977) 9. All subsequent references are parenthetical in the text.
"It appears that some of the stories do not concern the present but the past. They take place in the present. Some stories show reductions. Exactly this state is then the (hi)story. The form of the detonation of a high explosive bomb is easily remembered. It contains a reduction. I was there when ten meters from me, on April 8, 1945, one of them exploded."

[64] "from today's perspective, I believe that with this event my childhood was over, it was a caesura."

[65] "I still see myself sitting in the cellar and have the disgusting sound in my ear, the whistling of the falling bombs."
"I almost feel it still today on my eyelids, how it hurt me there. It was an unbelievable heat."

"Fontane hat z. B. Bombenangriffe, die manchen Berlinern ja noch wohl in den Knochen liegen, nicht gekannt. Es gibt da, wenn man es bildlich ausdrückt, immer zwei Strategien. Eine Strategie von oben und eine Strategie von unten. Über die Strategie von oben hat Clausewitz einiges geschrieben. Das ist die Strategie, die das Bomberkommando hat; und das hat ja auch die Mittel dazu. Was eine Frau mit zwei Kindern unten im Keller als Gegenwehr dagegenzusetzen vermag, das wäre Strategie von unten. [...] Das Problem dabei ist, daß die Frau mit zwei Kindern im Jahr 1944 im Bombenkeller im Moment überhaupt keine Mittel hat, sich zu wehren. Sie hätte vielleicht Mittel gehabt im Jahr 1928, wenn sie sich da noch, vor einer Entwicklung, die dann auf Papen, Schleicher und Hitler zuläuft, mit anderen organisiert hätte. Also die Organisationsfrage liegt 1928 und das dazu gehörende Bewußtsein liegt in 1944." (quoted in Vogt 19)[66]

According to Kluge, the vast abstraction added to the world by technological developments precludes recognizing connections or cause and effect relationships and runs contrary to concrete experience. In Kluge's opinion, the writing styles of the 19th century simply cannot express properly the interplay between the abstract and the concrete which has become such a fundamental part of modern life. Consequently, in the case of the bombings, the experience cannot be shared in established narrative traditions, as it can only be understood through abstraction (Bowie 184).

Over thirty years after the air raids, Kluge finally feels that he can set out to describe them, as it is only now that the full human experience of the events and its strange interaction with the world of technological warfare is accessible to him:

Wenn meinetwegen eine Bombe im Luftangriff auf Halberstadt in meiner Nähe niederfällt, bin ich in der Illusionsblase, in der so ein Kind sich befestigt hält, eigentlich der festen Meinung, daß ich nicht getroffen werde. Warum ich das glaube, weiß ich nicht. Ich fühlte mich eigentlich ausgenommen von dem Geschehen, das heißt: völlig inadequate Reaktion. Dreißig Jahre später kommen diese Gefühle eigenlich erst an die Oberfläche – jetzt plötzlich unter dem Gesichtspunkt: Wie ist es mit den Menschen in diesem Jahrhundert gemeint? Was für eine eigentümliche Brechung gibt es zwischen dem Urvertrauen, also der Idee, man sei als einzelner begünstigt worden und kriege vom Schicksal einen Rabatt, und diesen gewaltigen Maschinen, die getrennt marschieren und vereint schlagen und die die objektiven Verhältnisse darstellen. (Kluge "Eröffnungsbilanz" 82)[67]

---

[66] "Fontane, for example, did not know any air raids which many a Berlin resident today still feels in his or her bones. There are, if one wants to illustrate it, always two strategies. One strategy from above and one from below. Clausewitz has written extensively about the strategy from above. That's the strategy of the bombing command; and it has the resources for it. What a woman with two children would do against it below in the cellar, that would be the strategy from below. [...] The problem is that the woman with the two children in the year of 1944 in the air raid cellar in this moment does not have any resources in order to defend herself. She might have had some possibilities in the year 1928, if she then had organized herself with others before the development that was moving towards Papen, Schleicher, and Hitler. This means that the question of organization lies in 1928, but the consciousness that is needed for it lies in 1944."

Personal reactions to the bombings, such as strategies for distancing oneself, de-realization and avoidance stand in stark contrast to the objective reality of the experience. To capture both aspects, the personal reaction and the more abstract but objective reality of the situation have to be combined into one work of art. At the same time, the text needs to capture the fragmentation of the situation, which occurs due to the difficulty of determining the connection between personal perception and the objective reality of the technological world. This is why Kluge ventures out to explore new forms of representation through montages and the mixing of documentary and fiction. In the process, Kluge not only manages to capture recent historical events, but characterizes the general postwar human condition (Roberts 118-119).

"Der Luftangriff auf Halberstadt am 8. April 1945" exemplifies Kluge's technique. He indeed offers a unique way of approaching the bombing experience. While Kluge most likely did not know Gert Ledig's novel, in the general development of air raid literature Kluge's story can be seen as a radicalization of the literary documentary approach, which Ledig had already determined to be most appropriate for describing the bombardments. Even though Kluge at points offers much insight into the psychological reaction of the people he depicts, perhaps even more than Ledig, the fragmentation of the text is taken to a much higher level. In some sense, Kluge chooses a modern form of a "report" to talk about the bombings. He creates a montage of different individual perspectives and story lines, often filled with quotations, which he mixes with pictures, graphs, and interviews. He also uses humor and the grotesque to increase the fragmentation of the text and to defamiliarize the reader. The actual authenticity of the material is not important; instead, Kluge aims at the truthfulness of the text, at capturing the situation, which he thinks is best achieved by mixing the real with the fictional without making clear what is fact and what is not. In this manner, he gives a voice to both the people on the ground as well as the pilots above who were dropping the bombs. In addition, he explores through drawings and technical descriptions the media itself, the bombs, and the abstract organization needed to create an air raid. The text thus illustrates both the "strategy from above" and the "strategy from below," the abstract mechanisms involved in an air raid and the concrete, yet completely inadequate human reactions, of which the events are comprised. By fragmenting the experiences into many small units, of which each focuses on different aspects, and then combining them into

---

[67] "Let's say that a bomb in the air raid on Halberstadt comes down close to me, I am in a bubble of illusion, in which a child tries to keep sane, and I believe firmly that I won't be hit. Why I believe this, I don't know. I felt somehow that I was outside of the event, this means: completely inadequate reaction. It is really only thirty years later that these feelings come to the surface – now suddenly from the angle: How is it with human beings in this century? What is this strange break between the inborn trust, which means the idea that one alone has been singled out for preferential treatment and has credit from destiny, and these immense machines which march seperately and strike together and which represent the objective conditions."

one story, Kluge not only creates content, but also empty spaces, textless parts which lurk between the fragments. Kluge thus deemphasizes the role of the narrator and reemphasizes that of the active reader. Only by reading the text as well as its gaps, can a more complete experience and understanding be achieved of what an air raid is really like, both from below and from above.[68]

The inadequacy of different reactions, which Kluge also noticed in himself when he was faced with the bombing, is a recurring theme throughout his text. In the first section, for example, Frau Schrader, a theater manager, who survives the direct hit of a movie theater, desperately tries to fit the experience into her daily life and what she perceives as her reality. She thus searches continuously for causal connections between the events and her environment so that she can achieve some understanding of what is going on – a goal that necessarily is frustrated: "Die Verwüstung der rechten Seite des Theaters stand in keinem sinnvollen oder dramaturgischen Zusammenhang zu dem vorgeführten Film (35).[69] She also attempts to maintain her routine of "Ordnung schaffen" and "vier feste Vorstellungen," going through the motions of her daily life despite the building being largely destroyed (35-36):

> Dies war wohl die stärkste Erschütterung die das Kino unter der Führung von Frau Schrader je erlebt hatte, kaum vergleichbar mit der Erschütterung, die auch beste Filme auslösten. Für Frau Schrader, eine erfahrene Kino-Fachkraft, gab es jedoch keine denkbare Erschütterung, die die Einteilung des Nachmittags in vier feste Vorstellungen (mit Matinee und Spätvorstellung auch sechs) anrühren konnte. (35)[70]

In this spirit, she frantically cleans up for the next show even though this process includes collecting the body parts of dead movie goers who had been dismembered by the attack (36). Schrader's grotesquely inadequate behavior and absolute emotional detachment shows how the bombings have made her lose any sense of orientation within the world. All her attempts to reestablish herself through her work and actions fail since the reality around her has suddenly changed. In the end, after having given up trying to order her surroundings, she feels worthless and useless (37). The bombings have not only destroyed the building, but everything through which Frau Schrader had defined herself.

Similarly, in another story fragment, Frau Arnold and Frau Zacke, who radio information about enemy planes from the town's lookout tower to a central

---

[68] It is in this sense that Stephanie Carp is quite correct when she states that Kluge replicates "die Struktur eines Luftangriffes als Struktur des Texts" (Carp 141-142). ("the structure of an air raid as the structure of a text.")

[69] "The devastation of the right side of the theater stood in no causal or artistic relationship to the movie that had been shown."

[70] "This had probably been the strongest shock the movie theater had ever experienced under the guidance of Frau Schrader, hardly comparable to the strong emotional tremors that even the best films could cause. For Frau Schrader, an experienced movie theater specialist, there was, however, no shock strong enough to interrupt the division of the afternoon into four (with matinee and late night show, six) scheduled showings."

station, are completely unprepared for the events. For them, their work starts out more like a picnic with folding chairs, a thermos with beer, and sandwiches (44). When the large bomber units approach and start dropping bombs, the women keep reporting even though it is impossible to distinguish any longer where bombs are being dropped since they are everywhere. The church tower where they are located is on fire as well. Although they begin to understand the futility of their activity, they have no reaction to the inferno other than to keep acting as they have been instructed: "Die Frauen zwingen sich, in der Hocke, beide Hände am Gesims, weiterhin zu den Maschinen hinzusehen, die als zweiter Pulk anfliegen, etwa 2000 m Höhe. 'Kulk, Breiter Weg, Woort, Schuhstraße, Paulsplan.' Sie leiten sie aber nicht mehr weiter" (46).[71] Even after Frau Arnold lies buried under the church bell and Frau Zacke has to stand for hours with a broken leg on an area so small that she might fall any second, she does not really grasp the immensity of the situation and concentrates rather on the story-value of the events: "Sie kann natürlich was erzählen, falls sie noch gerettet wird" (47).[72] This is, of course, ironic, since we know that talking about these occurrences afterwards is extremely difficult as soon as the magnitude of the experience truly enters the consciousness.

The greatest insight into the impossibility of reacting adequately to the bombings is shown in a story about a school teacher, who had recently fled from the East and was now living with her three children in a little garden-shed in Halberstadt. She tries to respond to the bombings with logic, objectivity, and practicality, her "Strategie von unten" (55) as the section is entitled (and which Kluge repeatedly uses when he comments on the experience of the air raids).[73] Yet Kluge shows that these attempts are futile. Not only can she not communicate her strategies to her children, but they are also useless because she has no understanding of, or effect on, the strategy from above:

> Es war keine Zeit. Leitsätze einer "Strategie von unten," die Gerda in diesen Sekunden in ihrem Kopf zu versammeln suchte, konnten nicht übermittelt werden. Hier von ganz unten gesehen, zu den nicht sichtbaren Planern in 3000 m Höhe über der Stadt hinauf, oder auch ganz fern zu den Absprungbasen der Bomber hin, wo die höheren Planungsstäbe saßen. (56)[74]

---

[71] "The women force themselves, crouching on the floor, both hands on the railing, to continue looking at the planes which arrive as the second unit at an altitude of about 2000 meters. 'Kulk, Breiter Weg, Woort, Schuhstraße, Paulsplan.' But they have stopped communicating their observations."

[72] "She surely has a story to tell in the event that she is saved."

[73] "strategy from below"

[74] "There was no time. Key ideas for a 'strategy from below,' which Gerda in these seconds tried to put together in her head, could not be communicated. Neither from here, from all the way below, up to the invisible people who were planning the attack 3000 meter above the city, nor to the distant home airfields of the bombers where the higher-ups of the planning committees were located."

Gerda continues to try to use tactics and strategy (57) to escape from death, but this leads to almost grotesque forms of emotional detachment from the situation:

> Sie prüfte ernstlich, wen von den dreien [Kindern] sie mit Vordringlichkeit retten sollte, versuchte Vorteile daraus zu ziehen, daß sie sich selbst in die Aufzählung dieser Rangordnung einstufte: an verschiedenen Stellen, sie tastete ja erst. Vielleicht konnte sie etwas dazu tun, indem sie die nächste Staubdruckwelle vor den Lungen eines der Kinder, welches, wollte sie noch wählen, abfing. (57)[75]

Kluge makes clear through irony the illusion of her powers in the sight of these unknown "strategies from above:" "Ein zusammenstürzendes Kleinsthaus konnte sie freilich nicht auffangen" (57).[76]

The discrepancies between event and response are continuously shown to be related to the divergence of the absolute passing, and individual perception, of time. As in the other texts discussed so far, Kluge emphasizes this difference: "Die Katastrophe läuft jetzt seit anderthalb Stunden, aber die Uhrzeit, die gleichmäßig wie vor dem Angriff vorbeischnurrt, und die sinnliche Verarbeitung der Zeit laufen auseinander" (53).[77] Yet, as has been seen, Kluge views the problem not only as one of the individual who is unable to comprehend what is happening. Instead, the problem lies in the conflict between the individual who reacts to concrete experiences in the surroundings and an event that is based on abstract planning and organization, independent of individual concerns. The organizational patterns cannot be understood during the events, particularly since the effect of the complicated organization of the air raids is actually a very simple and primitive one: the city is burning down. What the proper reaction could have been can thus always become clear only after the fact, when the situation can be analyzed: "Mit den Hirnen von morgen könnten sie in diesen Viertelstunden praktikable Notmaßnahmen ersinnen" (53).[78]

When Kluge describes the strategy from above, he thus emphasizes the inherently abstract conception of the bombings by dissecting the attack in terms of its technical and organizational details. He compares the bomber units to factories that simply produce, without any concern of what the effect of their products are, or how the individual workers feel. In this atmosphere, what used to be part

---

[75] "She was seriously investigating which of the three [children] she should save first, tried to come up with advantages for why she considered herself in the ranking: at different positions, at this point, she was only exploring. Maybe she could help when, at the next shock wave, she would prevent the dust from getting into one of the children's lungs, which one she still wanted to decide."

[76] "Of course, she couldn't catch a small house collapsing."

[77] "The catastrophe has now been going on for one and a half hours, but clock time, which is still moving by as swiftly as before the attack, and the processing of the time by the senses, are diverging."

[78] "With the brains of tomorrow they would be able to come up with some practical emergency measures."

of warfare and what required a connection between problem or conflict and action, is now unimportant: "Gottvertrauen, militärische Formenwelt, Strategie, [...] Hinweise auf Eigentümlichkeiten des Ziels, Sinn des Angriffs usf. [wurden] als irrational ausgegliedert" (62).[79] The individual pilots only follow the strategy that has been decided by others, the goal of the mission does not matter and there does not have to be any sense behind the activity. What is of concern is only the perfect operation of the "factory." As Kluge has the British Brigadier Anderson tell a journalist: "Was das sollte, kann ich ihnen nicht sagen. Ich kann mich nur zur Angriffsmethode äußern." (76).[80] He then describes in detail the best way to bomb a city and kill as many people as possible. Once the machine is set in motion, it cannot really be stopped before it has completed its mission, no matter what happens on the ground and whether it produces unnecessary suffering, even among one's own people:

> REPORTER: Die Stadt war also ausradiert, sobald die Planung eingeleitet war?
> ANDERSON: Ich möchte mal so sagen: wenn ein paar besonders Eilige unter den Kommandeuren unserer eigenen Panzerspitze in einem ganz brillianten Vorstoß [...] die Stadt bis 11.30 Uhr erreicht hätten, so hätte das die Systematik unserer Pulks nicht geändert. (80)[81]

As mentioned before, Kluge further illustrates, and at the same time reproduces in his text, the abstraction that characterizes the air raids from above in maps, drawings, and descriptions. He displays and explains the different strategies that the bomber units employed in their flights and also offers technical drawings of the bombs. When reading these text and picture passages, the presentations of technical detail cause a very similar dissociation from the effects of the bombings that were seen just a few pages earlier. Kluge skillfully leads the reader down this road, creating more and more interest in questions of how best to carry out the attack instead of why it is being put into action or what its effect might be. When Kluge returns to the strategy from below, he encourages the continuation of this frame of mind in the reader while concentrating on activities on the ground, such as taking care of the wounded or putting out fires. The fire chief responsible for Halberstadt could just as well have been talking about creating fires as putting them out. There is little concern for the reasons why the bombs are being dropped or where they come from, any sacrifices being carried out, the safety of his men, or the suffering of the people, but what is

---

[79] "Trust in God, the military world of form and etiquette, strategy, [...] remarks about the characteristics of the target, reason and sense of the attack and so on [were] excluded as being irrational."

[80] "I cannot tell you why we did it. I can only tell you how we did it."

[81] "Reporter: This means that the town was eradicated as soon as the planning had started?/Anderson: Let me put it this way: If a few of our commanders had been in a particular hurry and our own artillery units had reached the city by 11:30 in a brilliant move forward, this wouldn't have changed the strategy of our unit."

important is only the functioning of his machine and the most effective way to stop the fires (in which he felt he was hindered by the emotional reactions of the city officials). Even his language expresses the war-like character of the affair:

> Richtig ist es, die Gesamtkräfte an den Stadtausgängen zunächst festzuhalten und bis zum Eingang einigermaßen zutreffender Informationen über das *Was*, *Wie*, *Wo* und *die Richtung* der Brandherde *nicht* einzusetzen.
> Aber versuchen Sie mal diese Vorgehensweise durchzuhalten gegenüber einem nervösen Oberbürgermeister, den Stadt-Juristen, den Vertretern der Partei usf. [...] Sehen Sie, wenn ich ganz unsentimental und fachlich von Anfang an auf Schwerpunkte hätte gehen können, wäre der Derenburger Angriff auf Schmiedestraße nach meiner Ansicht bis Martiniplatz oder Holzmarkt vorgetrieben worden. Eine wirklich interessante Sache, weil der Angriff in verzettelter Form ja rasch liegen blieb. (98)[82]

It thus shocks the reader when Kluge adds a two-page picture of the completely destroyed city of Halberstadt. The reader has to readjust his position and face the concrete consequences of what has been described before as nothing more than a production process. To this outer destruction, he adds a passage on the inner destruction of the people. It focuses on a psychologist who is collecting material for a study of the psychological effects of the bombings on the population. The people he finds are clearly marked by trauma. They are passive and can only talk about the events in stereotypical phrases, unable to express, or avoiding to express their true experiences: "Die Spekulation nach dem *Sinn*, die 'stereotypen Erlebnisberichte,' er hatte diese gewissermaßen fabrikmäßigen Phrasen, die sich aus den Mündern herausfütterten, schon gehört in Fürth, Darmstadt, Würzburg, Frankfurt, Wuppertal usf." (104).[83] They do not reflect on the events or their causalities, nor the German crimes that brought about the bombings. Instead, most of them would like to emigrate in order to avoid having to face the destruction around them, a wish typically seen in people affected by trauma. They distance themselves from the event and treat it, in the same way as Nossack's observations, as if it had never happened to them but lay in the past: "Die Situation lag 100 Jahre zurück" (105).[84] This forgetting, the suppression of the events and with it the causes that led to them, is even institutionally sanctioned. In the papers of the city archives, which report all the fires in the city

---

[82] "The correct way to do it is first to keep all the forces at the outskirts of the city and *not* to use them until there is somehwat reliable information available about the *what*, the *how*, the *where*, and the *direction* of the fires. But try to keep with this course of action with a nervous mayor, the city lawyers, the representatives of the party and so on. [...] You see, if I had from the start been able to set priorities, in my opinion the Derenburg attack on the Schmiedestraße could have advanced to Martiniplatz or Holzmarkt. A really interesting situation, since when they were conducted in this spread out format, the attacks soon became unsuccessful."

[83] "Speculations about the meaning, the 'stereotypical witness reports,' he had heard these factory-like phrases, which came out of their mouths, already in Fürth, Darmstadt, Würzburg, Frankfurt, Wuppertal and so on."

[84] "The situation lay a hundred years in the past."

since 1123, April 8, 1945, the day of a bombardment which created a firemstorm that destroyed over eighty percent of the city, does not appear (105).

Kluge thus leaves the reader with a strong image of physical and psychological destruction. The war and particularly the bombings created people which are "öd und leer wie die Stadtfläche" (106), they have become nothing but mirrors of the destruction around them.[85] At the same time, in this passage Kluge reaffirms his approach. While believing in the power of the documentary style, he here discredits actual witness reports since they are subject to the mechanisms of suppression and avoidance as well as being characterized by the inability of the witnesses to translate these exceptional experiences into anything but stereotypical phrases. This is why Kluge mixes fact with fiction, but still portrays the events as real, because it allows him to describe the experiences more accurately and to make them accessible to the reader without sacrificing authenticity. By adding the strategies from above, Kluge attests to the role and power of technology and the effect that this type of progress can have. He thus also uses the bombing of Halberstadt as an example of the tensions between the abstract, as created by technological advances, and the concrete experience in our modern world.

Kluge's story "Der Luftangriff auf Halberstadt am 8. April 1945" and the last chapter of Walter Kempowski's *Das Echolot: Fuga Furiosa* (*Sonar: Fuga Furiosa*), in which he deals with the bombing of Dresden, are separated by over twenty years, with Kluge's text appearing in 1977 and the second *Echolot* collection only recently in 1999. Yet they offer some striking similarities in the authors' intent, technique, and content that makes this difference in conception and publication almost invisible. Kluge recently even reissued the story as part of his new work, *Chronik der Gefühle*, confirming how he himself considers it to be important and current. In the same way as Kluge, Kempowski is concerned with the possibilities of representing important events that had, and have, a lasting effect on the individual, but lie outside traditional human experiences. He also embraces the technique of a montage of different perspectives as the only way a reader can grasp a situation in its full complexity, hence rejecting traditional forms of narration. In addition, however, Kempowski shows great concern about the danger of forgetting these historical events. More than Kluge, who has no problem inventing characters, perspectives, scenarios or quotations, and dressing them up as factual if necessary to achieve a desired effect, Kempowski is a collector of documents and facts. Kempowski's large archive has almost taken on mythic proportions in the culture sections of the newspapers, "es ist gigantisch, alle Medien sind vertreten, Bücher, Briefe, Fotoalben, Kassetten, Videokassetten. Drei, vier Räume voll" (Hennig 23).[86] As he has stated about his collector's obsession: "Um Gottes Willen, nichts wegwerfen!" (Hennig 23).[87]

---

[85] "... people who are bleak and empty like the city"

[86] "it is gigantic, all types of media are there, books, letters, photo albums, tapes, videotapes. Three or four rooms full."

Kempowski thus radicalizes Kluge's method of montage. In Kluge's work the narrator never disappears completely, not only because he selects and arranges the individual parts, but particularly because he still narrates, even if under the cover of giving authentic sources. This becomes especially obvious when he employs techniques such as irony or humor to make the conditions he is driving at more accessible. In contrast, Kempowski reduces the role of the author solely to that of a conductor (Guetg 67). He does not compose the individual parts, but only orchestrates the entire work by deciding about the selection and order of the material. The narrator and author disappear almost completely. His goal is the recreation of a collective experience:

> SPIEGEL: Lange nachdem Ihre erfolgreichen Romane erschienen waren, haben Sie damit begonnen, den Zweiten Weltkrieg in Form der Montage aus authentischen Stimmen darzustellen. Warum?
> KEMPOWSKI: Die Romane schrieb ich aus subjektiver Sicht. Später schien mir dieses Erlebnis vor allem ein kollektives zu sein. Dafür eine Form zu finden, war zunächst sehr schwierig. Ich habe sehr viele Tagebücher aus der Kriegszeit gesammelt, auch Briefe, Konvolute archiviert und immer wieder durchgelesen. So kam ich darauf, daß man doch eigentlich das Kollektive dieser Ereignisse zeigen müsse. [...] alles wird zu einem großen Chor komponiert, der der Wirklichkeit, der damals erlebten Wirklichkeit nahe kommt. (Hage and Kempowski 266)[88]

While Kluge and Kempowski both strive for truth and authenticity, and in doing so choose a montage to present the events, Kempowski does not think that it is enough to create the appearance of authenticity through the mixture of original material and fictional accounts, but instead only puts together original texts written by eye witnesses. While Kluge is a person of the present and concerned in his writing with describing general conditions that we find ourselves in today, Kempowski is caught up in his look back to the past, an attitude that has even been called "eine fast schon krankhafte Aversion gegen das Vergessen" (Reents 17).[89]

With his montages of authentic voices, Kempowski thus not only tries to create a picture of what he considers key events of the past, but also gives his personal literary answer to his fellow companion Kluge in the endeavor to produce documentary literature to present war events. Kluge, towards the end of his story, discredits the *sole* use of witness accounts to represent events. He em-

---

[87] "In God's name don't throw anything away!"

[88] "SPIEGEL: Long after your successful novels were published, you have started to portray the Second World War in the form of a montage of authentic voices. Why?/KEMPOWSKI: I wrote the novels from a subjective perspective. Later I started to think of the experience largely as a collective one. To find a form that would express this was at first very difficult. For a long time, I collected diaries from the war, also letters, I archived bundles of paper and read through them over and over again. This is how I came with the idea that one should show the collective effect of these events. [...] everything is composed into a large choir, which comes close to reality, to the reality as it was experienced then."

[89] "an almost obsessive aversion against forgetting"

phasizes their sterotypical expression and their evasive tendencies. In *Echolot*, Kempowski puts these assumptions to the test. With his *Echolot* project, Kempowski probes into the depth of history and historical experience; in analogy to sonar he tries to measure the presence of a certain event in the collective German mind. Instead of giving an overview of a long period of time, he concentrates his efforts on a very small time frame. The project started in 1993 with the publication of the first part of *Das Echolot*, that in over 3000 pages dealt with the time from January 1 to February 28, 1943 and was concerned mainly with the battle of Stalingrad. Kempowski then continued the project with *Das Echolot: Fuga Furiosa* in which he, again in four large volumes, covers the time from January 12 to February 14, 1945. Here, he focuses on the refugee treks from the East at the end of the war and the bombing of Dresden on February 13 and 14. As in the first *Echolot* edition, the work comprises as a collection of voices which form a large choir of historical experience, which the reader has to listen to and explore (*Das Echolot* 7)

Readers who embark on this project (which due to its length takes a lot of commitment) find excerpts from writings by varying sources, be they victims or perpetrators, young or old, English or German, known or unknown. The entries also stem from different times - some are immediate reactions, others have been written after the fact, sometimes many years after the events. All of the passages are given equal priority in the work, which means that an entry by Hitler can be closely followed by one from Victor Klemperer's diaries (see Chapter 5 for a detailed discussion of Klemperer's experience of the Dresden bombings). Kempowski absents himself completely from the final work. There is no commentary of any kind except birthdates and the names of the authors. In *Echolot: Fuga Furiosa*, Kempowski even does without a preface, unlike the first *Echolot* collection in 1993.

Nevertheless, the author can still be sensed through the choice of passages and in the way that he structured the work. In his volume on Dresden (Tuesday, February 13 and Wednesday, February 14, 1945), for example, Kempowski skillfully recreates the air raids, starting at a time before the bombardment, then describing the experience during the attack and finally the results afterwards. In the beginning, he fashions an atmosphere of calmness, with a surprisingly large amount of normalcy and relaxation. As Ernst Heinrich Prinz von Sachsen reports about his drive into Dresden:

> Der Verkehr wogte hin und her, ich genoß wie immer den wunderbaren Anblick der Silhouette der Altstadt mit dem Wahrzeichen Dresdens, der Kuppel der Frauenkirche, der Brühlschen Terrasse, dem Schloß, der italienischen Hofkirche, der Semper-Galerie und der Oper. Wohl kaum eine andere deutsche Stadt an einem großen Fluß wies ein solches Bild auf. Ich liebte meine Geburtsstadt und die Residenz meiner Väter mit allen Fasern meines Herzens, ich war geradezu verliebt in sie.[90]

---

[90] Walter Kempowski, *Das Echolot: Fuga Furiosa*, vol. IV (München: Knaus, 1999) 709. All subsequent references are parenthetical in the text.

Since it is the carneval period, children have dressed up in costumes despite the war and are having fun in the streets: "Am Fasnachtsdienstag kramten die Kinder allerlei Maskerade aus den Kästen des alten, bunten Bauernschrankes und zogen lärmend in den Straßen herum, was nun einmal das Privileg der Jugend ist, die sich dieses auch in der Kriegszeit nicht nehmen ließ" (710).[91] In the early evening, families sit around the dinner table and chat (722, 728), or listen to the radio ("Reichsprogramm: 20.15-21.00: Balladen und Lieder von Loewe, 21.00-22.00: Konzert, Werke von Mozart, Franck, Spohr" (727)), others take their dog for a last stroll (723).

Yet Kempowski interrupts this almost idyllic picture with many forewarnings of the impending disaster. Preparations for the attack are well underway from above, Bomber Command Headquarters in England have already ordered an air strike against Dresden:

> Früher bekannt für sein Porzellan, hat sich Dresden zu einer äußerst wichtigen Industriestadt entwickelt, und wie jede andere Großstadt verfügt es über vielfältige Telefon- und Eisenbahneinrichtungen. [...] Mit dem Angriff ist beabsichtigt, den Feind dort zu treffen, wo er es am meisten spüren wird, hinter einer teilweise schon zusammengebrochenen Front gilt es, die Stadt im Zuge weiterer Vormarsches unbenutzbar zu machen. (717)[92]

At the same time, excerpts from the diaries of Victor Klemperer reveal a different imminent threat. Although a Jew, he still remains in Dresden because his wife is not Jewish. On this day, he is ordered to deliver letters announcing deportation to most of the other few members of the Jewish community who, for one reason or another, had not already been sent to the ghettoes and concentration camps. Under these circumstances, of course, the threat of an air raid is relativized. The inclusion of these passages might remind some of the readers why these bombardments are happening in the first place. In order to encourage readers to ask further questions about responsibility and causes for the war, Kempowski also includes excerpts from Hitler's political testament in which Hitler reveals himself, even at this point in the war, still as obsessed with his ideas as before, reaffirming his hatred of Jews and trying to "prove" again their responsibility

---

"Traffic was going back and forth, as always I enjoyed the wonderful view of the silhouette of the old city with the emblem of the city, the dome of the Frauenkirche, the Brühl Terrasse, the castle, the Italian court chapel, the Semper gallery and the opera. Hardly any other German city on a large river offered such a picture. I loved my home town and the seat of my forefathers with my entire body, one could say I was in love with it."

[91] "On Fat Tuesday, the children pulled all sorts of costumes and masks out of the drawers of the old wardrobe and played merrily in the streets, which is after all the privilege of youth, and of which they did not let themselves be deprived, even in this time of war."

[92] "Dresden used to be known for its porcelain, but has now developed into an important industrial town and as is the case in every big city it has a diverse communication and transportation network. [...] The goal of the attack is to hit the enemy where it will feel it most; behind a partially crumbling front it is necessary to make the city unusable in the process of further advances."

for all the bad things that have befallen Germany, including losing this war –
passages which, Kempowski seems to hope, do the exact opposite and attest
to Hitler's and Germany's own responsibility. By including these diverse views
Kempowski, like Kluge, aims at presenting a multitude of perspectives of the air
raids and the war in general, both on the ground and from above.

Reactions to the bombings demonstrate again what detrimental psychological and physical effects this war strategy is capable of producing. Similar to
Kluge, Kempowski also chooses excerpts that exemplify not only the inadequacy of many people's responses to the air raids, but also the impossibility of
reacting in any other way to an event so beyond human experience. The scene
becomes almost unreal. When people who live in a small area ("eine kleine In-
sel" (741)) that was spared by the bombs for no apparent reason, step out of their
cellars after the attack and look at the burning Dresden, they are confronted with
a ghostly sight:

> Es war ein gespenstiger Anblick. Wir alle hatten Decken umgehängt. Bei einigen
> sahen Nachthemden oder Schlafanzüge hervor. [...] Um uns herum stand alles in
> lodernden Flammen. Ein heißer Wind trieb auf uns zu. Fassungslos und mit angstver-
> zerrten Gesichtern starrten wir uns an. Niemand sprach ein Wort. Langsam schlurfte
> einer nach dem anderen wie in Trance in die Häuser zurück. (741)[93]

The people are so horrified by the sight that they distance themselves emotionally from the events. They become passive, simply awaiting what will come as if
they were already dead. They avoid talking about the imminent danger they are
in and instead of devising survival strategies they retreat quietly to their houses.
How horrible the bombings must have felt on the ground is also captured in only
a few lines from a letter of a soldier who was on vacation in Dresden when he
was surprised by the attack: "Wir Frontsoldaten sind ja viel gewöhnt, aber das
war die Hölle auf Erden" (743).[94] As many others, he also does not know how
to react to events which do not even compare to his experiences at the front. He
thus falls back on ordinary behavioral patterns of daily life: "Ich dachte plötzlich
an mein Vesper im Brotbeutel. Sofort packte ich es aus und begann zu essen"
(743).[95]

The horror dehumanizes everyone by reducing them to their basic instincts.
In the cellars, people sit together like "todesbange Tiere" (765), often wishing
"daß ein Treffer der Qual ein Ende bereitet" (763), but when the question of
death or life arises, it is everyone for themselves: "Wer kann begreifen, daß man

---

[93] "It was a ghostly sight. All of us had blankets wrapped around us. With some of us one could
see nightgowns or pajamas underneath the blankets. [...] Around us everything was going up
in flames. A hot wind blew towards us. Unable to understand and with fearful faces we stared
at each other. Nobody spoke a word. Slowly, one after the other, and as if we were in a state of
trance, we shuffled back into our houses."

[94] "We soldiers from the front are really used to a lot, but this was hell on earth."

[95] "I suddenly remembered the food in my haversack. I immediately unpacked it and started to eat."

Dead civilians after the Dresden bombing. Reproduced with permission from Keystone
Pressedienst, Germany.

einen um Hilfe schreienden Menschen im Stich läßt? Es kann nichts Schlim-
meres geben! Zu helfen war nicht, und in den nächsten Minuten wären wir
estickt. So war die Lebensangst der Kreatur stärker und wir stürzten wie irrsinnig
dem Rettungsweg nach" (767).[96] After the attack, the survivors have only one
thought: "So schnell wie möglich diesen Hexenkessel zu verlassen" (784).[97]Like
Kluge, Kempowski leaves the readers with descriptions of devastation and inner
and outer destruction. Looking at the people still sitting in the ruins, it is not
clear whether they are alive or dead. Dresden, so praised for its beauty in earlier
excerpts, presents itself now as nothing but a desert of stones and rubble (822).

---

[96] "In the cellars, people sit together like 'animals who are scared to death,' often wishing 'that a
direct hit would end the torture,' but when the question of death or life arises, it is everyone for
themselves: 'Who can understand that one does not take care of a person crying for help? There
cannot be anything worse! There was no chance to help and in the next few minutes we would
have suffocated. So the creature fear of dying was stronger and we ran like crazy along the path
to safety.' "

[97] "As fast as possible away from this witches' cauldron."

Kempowski also includes the perspective from above amidst the devastation that he captures on the ground. However, whereas Kluge emphasizes the factory-like organization of the air raids, in which individuals play no role, Kempowski concentrates on personal utterances by the bomber pilots, specifically comments that express feelings of sadness about the attacks and concern for the people on the ground:

> Der phantastische Schein aus 320 Kilometer Entfernung wurde immer heller, als wir uns dem Ziel näherten. Selbst in einer Höhe von sechstausendsiebenhundert Metern konnten wir bei dem gespenstischen Schein der Flammen Einzelheiten erkennen, die wir nie zuvor gesehen hatten; zum erstenmal seit vielen Einsätzen fühlte ich Mitleid mit der Bevölkerung dort unten. (757) [98]

Kempowski thus exercises his positon of the "conductor" of voices to create a very different impression about the view from above during the bombardments. The air raids, which are completely void of human emotion in Kluge's story, now appear as individual acts that cause personal reactions of horror about the power of their destruction. The consequences are analyzed beyond the question of a successful mission and acknowledge the human cost caused by such technology.

The quotations and excerpts above illustrate that Kempowski is indeed correct when he considers the witness reports and letters to be powerful documents of the bombings. They reveal a lot of the horror and of the terrible effects the attacks had on the population. However, Kluge's assumptions are also valid. While Kempowski avoids repetiton of stereotypical depictions of the experiences by carefully choosing the texts and only giving excerpts instead of whole documents, the reader keeps wondering whether some of the events could not have been expressed better in fictional terms by an author, instead of by the diary passages. It is interesting to see how the language used in the excerpts often does not succeed in representing the horror. Stock phrases such as "nahm das denn gar kein Ende?" (816), "stürzten alle wie von Furien gejagt in den Keller" (807) or reflections such as "Da dachte ich all die Jahre zurück [...] über all die Zeit hinweg, die wir in diesem Hause in Kummer und in Sorgen, aber auch in Freuden verbracht hatten" (814), do not convey much to the audience.[99]

A further comparison of the two works, specifically the view of the air raid from above, reveals that Kempowski is indeed much more present in the text than he likes to admit. Striving for historical correctness, he nevertheless by his selection can easily distort the events. For example, by concentrating mainly on comments by bomber pilots who pity the population on the ground, Kempowski

---

[98] "The fantastic shine of the flames from a distance of 320 kilometers became brighter and brighter the closer we got to our target. Even at a height of six thousand seven hundred meters we could recognize details in the ghostly light of the flames; for the first time in many missions I felt pity for the population below."

[99] "would it never end?;" "all ran as if chased by furies into the cellar;" "Then I thought of all those years, [...] of all this time we had spent in this house in sorrow, but also in happiness."

implies a certain view that does not necessarily hold up under closer scrutiny. It has also been shown that witnesses are not always reliable. The authenticity and objectivity that Kempowski claims for his texts because of his exclusive use of actual documents is thus more than questionable since the witnesses themselves are not objective. Simply adding many voices does not change this fundamental issue, yet Kempowski leaves the passages without comment or interpretation that would clarify discrepancies.

The inclusion of excerpts by Hitler is problematic as well. While Kempowski attempts to work out some of the causalities of the bombings, the lack of any commentary can easily lead to misunderstandings about his intentions and might in fact have the opposite effect to that which he presumably intended. Furthermore, since all sources are put on an equal footing, but only one Jewish voice, that of Victor Klemperer is available, the collage is unbalanced. This is one of the reasons why sources typically do not stand alone in historical writing, but are complemented by interpretation. The dangers involved in this lack of evaluation of the sources reveal, as one critic describes it, the dark side of projects such as Kempowski's *Echolot* (Preisendoerfer 8). They claim to enlighten, but eye witness accounts or documents outlining Hitler's insane beliefs will never create actual historical truth.

Concerning such questions of guilt and responsibility, Kluge's technique is again more successful than Kempowski's. Kluge relies on his understanding of the text as literature, not history, but he is still concerned about the effect of the events he describes on the present. While Kluge excludes considerations of responsibility and the causalities of the war in his description of the bombing of Halberstadt, he does not completely omit these important issues. Only a few pages later he includes a story on the other, darker side of Halberstadt, the concentration camp "Außenlager Langenstein" located south of the city admidst the area's beautiful landscape. Since he is not bound to purely authentic sources, Kluge can create a collage that shows the horror of the concentration camp and also the later somewhat helpless dealings with the memory of it in East Germany. Introducing this part of Halberstadt's history necessarily connects Nazi crimes to the bombings. Consequently, while separating the two stories, yet focusing on the same location, Halberstadt, Kluge achieves a more complex view of the events even without interspersing actual commentary.

4.3   The Individual, Trauma and History: Dieter Forte

Walter Kempowski and particularly Alexander Kluge aim to present the bombings both as powerful collective and individual experiences. These experiences are simultaneously highly sophisticated and primitive, as well as abstract and concrete, and can only be captured by combining various angles and views. This technique conveys the difficulty in representing what is so clearly beyond normal human experience and cannot be grasped entirely by those who go through it. Yet their method of using a montage of either authentic, or seemingly authentic materials, also creates a distance between author and text, as well as reader and text, that is hard to overcome. For Kluge and Kempowski, this distance might be valuable as it allows them to control their own traumas. They can focus on their experiences that have stayed present in their mind without emotional involvement or directly revisiting their own past. They thus satisfy their need to talk about the events, while still managing to avoid their own trauma. However, this distance affects the reader's access to the experience. Their style offers more insight into the abstract nature of the bombings than the effects felt by individuals whose experiences are only briefly presented. The possibilities for emotional identification are limited. Yet these works do not only keep the reader at a distance, but there is an aura of non-literature surrounding both texts, particularly Kempowski's *Echolot* endeavor. In comparison, Gert Ledig in *Vergeltung* involves the reader more deeply than Kluge and Kempowski with their extreme fragmentation and estrangement techniques. Ledig recreates the horror of a singular attack within the reader. Still, Ledig's novel again conveys the serial rather than the personal event, the non-stop horror insead of the effect on each individual.

In contrast, Hans Erich Nossack and Wolfgang Borchert reduce the air raids to a purely personal experience. In order to deal with what has happened and the destruction around them, they turn them into positive events that allow personal growth and a fresh start, which minimizes and suppresses their detrimental traumatic effect. The question remains whether it is at all possible to create a work of literature that explores all sides of the experience equally, the personal toll they take as well as their collective meaning of horror, their abstractness and their inability to be understood and processed, and still provide access to the reader. A successful treatment of the events also needs to embed them into their proper historical context, so that the interdependence of the German crimes and the bombings is revealed and the causalities of the war are not distorted. Works such as Nossack's *Der Untergang* and Kempowski's *Echolot* exemplify the necessity of this second step for a successful mastery of the topic. In both texts, the question of German guilt is almost completely avoided. In one case, myth takes over where clearer statements are required, in the other the author hides behind the authenticity of his sources, trying to drown out these concerns by the chorus he creates. Nevertheless, questions of responsibility do arise in the reader and stay unsatisfactorily unanswered. The endeavor of writing about the bombings is thus obviously extremely difficult. The author not only has to overcome his or her own involvement and trauma, and feel the pressure to find the right balance between various aspects of the experience, but must also contend with the representation of suffering and the question of guilt.

In his partially autobiographical trilogy *Das Haus auf meinen Schultern* (*The House on My Shoulders*) from 1999, which contains the three previously individually published novels *Das Muster* (*The Pattern*), *Der Junge mit den blutigen Schuhen* (*The Boy with the Bloody Shoes*), and *In der Erinnerung* (*In Memory*), Dieter Forte strives for exactly this balance. The trilogy is a chronicle and depicts the development of two families, the Italian-French Hugenot Fontanes and the Polish, deeply Catholic, Lukacz'. The first novel, *Das Muster*, weaves together the two histories from the middle ages to the year 1933, where the two completely different families, by now both living in Germany, come together through the marriage of Friedrich Fontane and Maria Lukacz. The second and third novels revolve around the life in Düsseldorf of the unnamed "Junge," the son of Friedrich and Maria, in actuality a fictional reincarnation of the author himself. The pace slows down, now that the author's own experiences are incorporated in the text. The second novel, *Der Junge mit den blutigen Schuhen*, takes place in the Nazi and war years, the third, *In der Erinnerung*, in the immediate postwar era.

These latter texts, by focusing on the protagonist, his family and surroundings, describe time in Düsseldorf during the air raids and life in the ruins after the war. Düsseldorf, as an important industrial city, was the target of very heavy attacks throughout the time of the bombing campaigns, and trauma is an organizing thread throughout the two novels. When the first bombs fall it is expected, particularly by Gustav, the boy's grandfather, to be more or less an aesthetic and exciting event, a performance in the sky one cannot afford to miss:

> Als die ersten Bomben fielen, kletterte Gustav mit einem alten Feuerwehrhelm auf dem Kopf und einem Sofakissen zwischen den Zähnen auf das Dach, plazierte das Kissen auf den First, setzte sich rittlings darauf, zog seine Hosenträger über den Kamin, breitete seine Sternenkarte aus, schrie zur Dachluke, aus der Fins [his wife] Kopf heraussah, als geborener Agnostiker könne er sich unmöglich das göttliche Ereignis eines Weltuntergangs entgehen lassen, ein Ereignis, das alle Fragen mit einem Schlag in Antworten verwandle. Feuer und Schwefel falle vom Himmel, Blitz und Donner beherrsche die Welt, Rauch und Asche steige auf, alle in der Bibel angekündigten Plagen seien jetzt auf einmal zu besichtigen, das müsse man gesehen haben, da setze er sich nicht in den Keller. Ein Weltuntergang wiederhole sich nicht, das sei ein einmaliges Ereignis [...].[100]

---

[100] Dieter Forte, *Der Junge mit den blutigen Schuhen* (Frankfurt a. M: Fischer, 1995): 131. All subsequent references are parenthetical in the text.
"When the first bombs were falling, Gustav climbed up onto the roof with an old firefighter helmet on his head and a pillow between his teeth, put the pillow onto the ridge, sat down on it with his legs hanging down on each side, pulled his suspenders over the chimney, opened up his map of the stars, yelled over to the skylight, in which Fin's [his wife] head was appearing, as a born agnostic there was no way that he could pass on this divine event of the end of the world, an occurrence that would change all questions into answers in one blow. Fire and brimstone would rain from the skies, lightning and thunder would rule the world, smoke and ash would rise in the sky, all the plagues the Bible prophesized were now to be observed together, one must see this,

Yet Forte shows that the event has little to do with divine intervention, but is orchestrated solely by human organization and technological advances. When the planes arrive, the stars in the sky become invisible due to the large carpets of the bomber units, the spotlights of the flak, the munition, and the 'Christmas trees' planted in the sky as markers for targets (*Junge* 133). Gustav is brought completely back to reality when the house, hit by a bomb, goes up in flames, bursts under the pressure, and he, having been thrown down to the ground by the explosion, barely survives.

Soon, the air raids come so frequently that they replace the regular schedule both during day and night. Life is now structured by the warning sirens, full alarms, and the sirens signaling that the danger is over. Again, time has become distorted and even the sirens do not sound when they are supposed to: "Der Ablauf der Zeit wurde zuerst zerstört, weil Tag und Nacht nicht mehr existierten. [...] auch die Sirenen verloren den Zeitsinn und jammerten nur noch wahllos in die Bombenangriffe hinein" (136).[101] It is a world in which the powers of nature and its function in giving order to the world have been replaced completely by technological forces. These powers, although man-made, manifest themselves in a manner so beyond any regular human experience or comprehension that under their threat everything and everyone breaks down. One now learns that indeed the world can end over and over again. It leaves people in constant fear of death but, unable to react in a way that would allow them to avoid the danger, they simply remain passive and become deathlike during the events. By introducing into the text's syntax the destruction of any order an emotion except the most basic reactions and feelings, Forte achieves a powerful representation of the bombings that is unparalleled in other German texts:

> [...] jetzt donnerten da die fliegenden Festungen, die tiefer kamen, das Brummen ging in ein Dröhnen über, das die Trommelfelle betäubte und alle zum Schweigen brachte, denn die einzelnen Stimmen waren unter diesem Dröhnen nicht mehr zu verstehen, und wenn dann die schwere Flakbatterie aus dem Volksgarten loslegte, ihre Granaten heiser bellend in die Luft schickte, öffnete man schnell den Mund und hielt die Hände vors Trommelfell, sah sich mit aufgerissenem Mund, halb zugedrückten Augen und den Händen auf den Ohren gegenseitig an, zog sich in den Keller zurück, [...] und jeder wußte, in diesem Moment, daß er getötet werden sollte, daß man ihn, ja genau ihn, zerfetzen, verbrennen und ersticken wollte, und jeder ging auf seinen Platz in seinem Keller und ergab sich in sein Schicksal, der Boden schwankte und rüttelte, die Kellerwände bewegten sich, Mörtel und Steine wurden herausgedrückt, die Eisentüren bogen sich durch, das Licht erlosch, die Kellerluft verwandelte sich in Staub und Gase, in eine erstickende Hitze, das krachende, berstende Detonieren

---

in such a situation he would not sit in the cellar. The world would only be destroyed once, this is a once in a lifetime event [...]."

[101] "The natural course of time was the first thing that was destroyed, since day and night did not exist any longer. [...] even the sirens lost their sense of time and wailed only randomly during the air raids."

der Bomben kam immer näher in betäubenden Explosionen, lief auf das Haus zu, in dessen Keller in dem Moment die einzigen Menschen der Welt saßen, die wußten, daß sie jetzt sterben mußten, zerfetzt, verbrannt, erstickt, in diesem Weltuntergang, der über dem Haus zusammenschlug in einem einzigen, nie zuvor gehörten und niemals beschreibbaren Geräusch, das aus dem tiefsten Inneren der Erde kam – und sich entfernte, eine kurze, ohnmächtige Stille hinterließ, eine Totenstille, [...] in der man ohne nachzudenken spürt, was das ist, Leben, was das ist, Tod, und erfährt, wie man sich danach sehnt, weiterzuleben, und eine, die das nicht verkraften kann, wimmert vor sich hin, schreit los, schlägt um sich, will raus, will in den Tod, und einer wirft sich auf sie, und das Schreien geht wieder in ein Wimmern über, das aufhört, als die nächste Bombenwelle sich berstend nähert, die Explosionen, auf die man sich konzentrieren muß, die Luft zum Ersticken, der Boden bebt unaufhörlich, die Wände rütteln und brechen ein, und der Moment ist da, wo man sich lieber doch den Tod als so ein Leben wünscht, und wieder stürzt die Welt über einem zusammen, das ist jetzt wohl der Weltuntergang, da draußen lebt kein Mensch mehr, und das hier ist vielleicht der einzige Keller in der Stadt in dem noch Menschen apathisch hoffen, langsam ersticken, in der Glut vergehen, mit blutendem Körper und zerbrochenen Gliedern auf ihr erlösendes Ende warten, stundenlang, tagelang, nächtelang, bis einer das Kellerfenster oder die Außentür aufreißt und, umgeben von Rauch und Flammen, schreit "Rauskommen!" Die Auferstehung vom Tod zum Leben, für wenige Stunden und ohne Hoffnung, denn die hat man verloren, für immer verloren, von ferne hört man ein schweres Brummen, die Sirenen ertönen, der nächste Bombenangriff, ehe alle aus dem Keller sind, kriechen sie wieder hinein, der Tod ist ihnen gewiß. (137-139)[102]

---

[102] "[...] now the flying fortresses were thundering closer, they came lower, the rumbling sound became a roar which deafened the ear drums and silenced everyone because individual voices could not be understood any longer with this roar, and when the heavy anti-aircraft artillery from the park started, sending its whistling grenades into the sky, one quickly opened one's mouth and put hands on one's ears, looked at each other with wide-open mouths, half-shut eyes and hands on the ears, retreated into the cellar, [...] and everyone knew in this instant that he was supposed to be killed, yes, he himself was supposed to be ripped apart, burned, and suffocated, and everyone went to their place in their cellar and gave themselves over to their destiny, the floor was moving and shaking, the walls of the cellar were moving, mortar and stones were coming down from them, the iron doors were bending, the light went off, the air in the cellar became dust and gas, in a suffocating heat, the roaring and bursting detonations of the bombs came closer and closer in numbing explosions, came towards the house, in whose cellar were sitting at this moment the only people in the world, who knew that they had to die now, ripped apart, burned, suffocated, in this end of the world that was coming together right over their house in a single sound which they had never heard before and which can never be described, a sound that came from inside the deepest earth - and then wore off, leaving behind a short, helpless silence, the silence of death, [...] in which one feels without thinking what is life and what is death, and one realizes how one longs for life, and one who cannot bear this, is whimpering, starts screaming, lashes out, wants to leave, wants to die, and one throws himself on her, and the screaming becomes a wimpering again and then stops when the next wave of bombs comes closer, the explosions, one has to concentrate on, the air is suffocating, the floor shakes without stopping, the walls are rattling and start bursting in, and the moment has come, that one wishes for death instead of such a life, and again the world comes to an end above one, this is now the end of the world, there cannot be anyone still alive out there, and this might be the only cellar in the city in which there are still people who are hoping, listlessly, slowly suffocating, and melting in the heat, with bloody bodies and broken bones, waiting so that they will be relieved by death soon, waiting for hours,

In the horror of the experience, Forte's narration changes to a breathless, continuous tour de force. Through the breakdown of textual order, the lack of any periods that would divide the narration into sensible parts, it captures at least partially the destructive forces of the bombings both concerning the external world as well as the psychological condition of the people who have to live through them.

There is no question that the events leave the people on the ground deeply traumatized. The passage reveals individuals without hope, deathlike in their apathy, not sure whether they should wish for death or life, but expecting death at any time. People emerge from the cellars, marked forever by their experience, as if "aus einer Todesgruft zurückgekehrt in ein vorläufiges Leben, versehen mit dem Schrecken derer, die schon fast einmal tot waren, mit einem Kainsmal, das sie nie mehr verlieren sollten, das ihnen blieb ein Leben lang" (*Junge* 145-146).[103] This near-death experience will never lose its grip. Not surprisingly, the people the protagonist describes are without feelings. Their faces are motionless and numb like those of puppets (*Junge* 146), and they wander dreamlike through the ruins without seeing or reacting or caring about anything around them (*Junge* 147), clutching completely worthless objects as if they were of the utmost importance (*Junge* 148). Even though the boy is able to observe all these reactions around him, his life also becomes one of continuous and lasting trauma. Not being able to cope with the horror any longer, he flees into silence and for some time loses his ability to speak. During and after the constant attacks he also reveals an array of dissociative symptoms which are consistent with acute stress disorder. For example, when after an air raid his whole street is engulfed in fire with houses collapsing all around and people dying everywhere, the boy shuts off most of his senses, experiencing the situation "wie in Zeitlupe," "geräuschlos" and "fast bewegungslos" as if he were "allein auf der Welt und sähe alles aus einer einsamen Distanz, aus einer anderen Entfernung als bisher" (*Junge* 149).[104] His experience is reduced to still-life and the events are observed as if he were not part of them and as if they were not real – the only way the boy is able to process them at all.

These immediate reactions give way to signs of prolonged trauma. The horrific experience of fire, destruction, and death is a recurring and lasting image for the protagonist: "Das war das Todesbild, das der Junge nie mehr vergaß, das er

---

days, nights, until the window in the cellar or the door is ripped open and someone, surrounded by smoke and flames, screams 'get out!' The resurrection from death to life for a few hours and without hope, because it is lost, lost forever, from far one hears a heavy buzzing sound, before all have left the cellar one crawls back into it, death is certain."

[103] "... returning from the grave to a temporary life, marked by the horror of those who have been dead once before, with a mark of Cain, which they will never lose, which will stay with them for the rest of their lives."

[104] ... experiencing the situation "as if in slow motion," "without a sound," and "almost without movement" as if he were "alone in the world and saw everything from a lonely distance, from a different view point than before."

sein Leben lang mit sich trug. Solange er lebte, würde er das vor Augen haben"
(*Junge* 149-150).[105] Forte depicts how everyone who lives under the constant
rule of the sirens is marked by a combination of emotional detachment and increased arousal:

> [D]er Ton [...] setzte sich in den Menschen fest, machte alles grau und stumpf [...],
> [war] ständige Last auf den Schultern der Menschen, die mit schmalen Gesichtern
> gebückt durch die Hügellandschaft der Trümmer schlichen, halbverhungert in ver-
> lassenen Gebäuden herumsuchten, oft nicht mehr wußten, was sie suchten. (*Junge*
> 198)[106]

This deathlike numbness, because "wer in der Todeszone lebt, ist ein Toter, auch
wenn er sich noch aus alter Gewohnheit fortbewegt" (*Junge* 212), paired with
constant nervousness and movement, becomes a characteristic of the bombing
victims even when there is no danger of any air raids.[107] So when the boy, his
mother, and brother are evacuated to a village, they stand out because of their
"hastigen, schnellen, fahrigen Bewegungen" (*Junge* 229).[108] The protagonist is
haunted by his Düsseldorf experiences and, as is often found in PTSD victims,
the memories intrude into his life every night through dreams and flashbacks
which lead to the reenactment of earlier behavior: "Jede Nacht schreckte der
Junge hoch, hörte im Schlaf die Sirenen, sprang aus dem Bett, zog sich an, zerr-
te den Bruder aus dem Bett, zog ihn an, wollte mit ihm aus dem Zimmer rennen"
(*Junge* 229).[109] Even after the war is over, these flashbacks and intrusive memories do not stop and are now often triggered by certain images the boy associates
with the experience. For example, when he sees a broken mirror lying on the
street, he is reminded of a night under the bombs: "Die Sonne schien in den
Spiegel, blendete ihn mit ihrem Feuer, erinnerte ihn an die Brandnacht in der
Stadt, in der ein Mann das Feuer durch die Straßen trug, in einem Spiegel, den
er retten wollte."[110]

---

[105] "This was the picture of death the boy would never forget, that he would carry with him his
whole life. As long as he lived, he would have it in front of his eyes."

[106] "The sound became part of the people, made everything grey and dull [...], [was] a constant burden on the shoulders of the people, who with thin faces and bent over were creeping through the
hilly landscape of the rubble, half starved searching around empty buildings, often not knowing
what they were looking for."

[107] "whoever lives in the zone of death is dead, even if he still, according to his old habits, moves
about."

[108] "restless, fast, uncoordinated movements"

[109] "Every night the boy woke up in fear, heard in his sleep the sirens, jumped out of bed, got
dressed, pulled his brother out of bed, dressed him, wanted to run with him out of the room."

[110] Dieter Forte, *In der Erinnerung* (Frankfurt a.M.: Fischer, 1998) 21. All subsequent references
are parenthetical in the text.
"The sun reflected off the mirror, it blinded him with its fire and reminded him of the night of fire
in the city, in which he saw a man carry fire through the streets in a mirror he wanted to save."

At other times nightmares make him relive the horror of the bombings, leading him back to memories he would like to forget, but cannot: "die jaulenden, heulenden Sirenen, das Dröhnen der Bomber, das schrille Kreischen der herabstürzenden Bomben, [...] die zerberstenden Häuser, die zusammenbrechenden Straßen, deren Fassaden kopfüber in die hochschlagenden Flammen fielen, [...] die erstickende Hitze, die die Haut versengte (*Erinnerung* 150).[111] Again, linear time has lost its significance and, similarly to Nossack, Forte shows his characters captured in a moment without past or future, in the "Stunde Null," the "Niemandszeit im Niemandsland" (*Erinnerung* 75): "Stunden wie Tage und Tage wie Jahre, ohne daß man ihren Ablauf bemerkte, [...] als wäre da wirklich nur diese eine Stunde, die nicht zählte, die keine Zeit war, die die Welt anhielt, entstanden aus der Angst, die man nicht los wurde, entstanden aus den Totenbildern, die jeder in sich trug" (*Erinnerung* 75).[112] So while the war is officially over, it is still going on – both on the streets where people have to fight for their survival, and in their heads where war memories keep intruding and preventing any return to a truly normal life.

By dealing not only with the bombings, but also with the time before, during, and after the war, Forte manages to give a more complete picture of both the psychological and historical development than the writers discussed previously. Significantly, he also does not avoid questions of guilt in his text. He surrounds the central plot of the novels, which focuses on the 'boy,' with many individual episodes in which he explores the historical context of the events. Here Forte asserts the connection between the horror of the bombings and the horror caused by the Germans. Both become haunting images of the past that will carry forever into the future. In the novels, they are brought together in the same physical location, the quarter the boy lives in. Early on there are strong suspicions among the people in this part of Düsseldorf: "Ein dunkles Halbwissen verbreitete sich, Furcht und Angst vor den ungewissen Dingen, die da im verborgenen geschahen und die nach dem Krieg keinen wirklichen Frieden mehr zulassen würden" (*Junge* 174).[113] When the bombings start, Fin, Gustav's wife, clearly formulates the connection:

> So sagte Fin, als die ersten Bomben fielen und alle überrascht die Köpfe einzogen:
> "Angefangen hat es mit dem Lari. Das ist jetzt der Segen dafür."
> Der Lari war Bürger der Stadt, verheiratet, zwei Kinder, ein beliebter Steptänzer [...]

---

[111] "the wailing, roaring sirens, the roaring of the bomber planes, the shrill shreaks of the falling bombs, [...] the houses crashing down, the streets cracking with rows of houses falling forward into the rising flames, the suffocating heat which was burning the skin."

[112] "the zero hour, the no man's time in no man's land: Hours like days and days like years without one realizing the passage of time, [...] as if there were really only this one hour, which did not count, which was no time, which stopped the course of the world, created by the fear that one could not get rid off, and the images of death that all carried inside themselves."

[113] "A dark half-knowledge was spreading, fear of unknown things which were happening secretly and which, after the war, would never allow real peace."

ein junger, lustiger, immer lachender Kerl, der dunkelhäutig und mit einer Weißen
verheiratet war, der deswegen aus seiner Wohnung geholt und am Rheinufer erschla-
gen wurde, indem man sein Lachen im Rheinsand erstickte und ihm die Arme aufs
Kreuz drehte, ihn mit Messern erstach und mit Schüssen tötete. All das ging Fin bei
der Detonation der Bomben durch den Kopf, und deshalb sagte sie: "Angefangen hat
es mit dem Lari." (*Junge* 129)[114]

Later, the boy observes concentration camp prisoners who are being tortured by
their SS guard. This guard cruelly forces them to build senseless sandhills, just
to put the sand back into the wheelbarrows so that they can then make other
piles somewhere else (*Junge* 175). Forte thus illustrates the interconnection between German crimes and cruelty and the horror of the bombings to which the
population is subjected. Instead of avoiding the topic, as is the case for some
other authors, he strikes a narrative balance that allows him to voice his own
experiences within the historical context.

Forte's more poised literary account is partially a product of waiting many
years before writing about the bombardments. As Forte suggests, caught up in
avoidance, it takes a long time to be ready to face these traumas again and to
be able to capture these images of horror in language. In an interview, he describes suppressing the events as a necessary coping mechanism in order to be
able to continue to live: "die Bombennächte habe ich natürlich auch verdrängt,
um weiterleben zu können" (Hof and Forte 207).[115] Similar to the boy in his
work, Forte retreated into silence about his traumatic past, a reaction comparable to observations about PTSD victims. Before publishing his novels, he did
not speak about the war for fifty years: " 'Ich habe das lange verdrängt [...]. Ich
habe das nie jemandem erzählt, was ich selbst im Krieg und danach erlebt habe,
nicht einmal meiner Frau' " (quoted in Hage "Kälte und Hunger" 131).[116] He
thus belongs to a "Generation der Kinder in den Großstädten, die sich erinnern
können, wenn sie die Sprache dafür finden – und darauf muß man sein Leben
lang warten" (Forte *Spiegel* 222).[117]

By choosing the form of a novel and attempting to create a narrative about
the events that combines the abstract side of the air raids with a depiction of the

---

[114] "It all began with Lari. This is the response. Lari was a citizen of the town, married, two children, a beloved step dancer [...] a young, funny, always laughing guy who was dark and was
married to a white woman, who was pulled out of his apartment for this and killed at the banks
of the Rhine, when his laugh was suffocated in the sand of the Rhine, when his arms were turned
on his back, when he was stabbed with knives and when shot dead with bullets. All these things
Fin thought about when the bombs were detonating, and that's why she said: 'It all began with
Lari.' "

[115] "the nights of the bombs I, of course, also suppressed in order to be able to live on."

[116] "I suppressed it for a long time [...]. I have never talked about what I experienced during and
after the war, not even to my wife."

[117] "generation of children in the big cities who can remember, when they find the words to do so –
and for these words one has to wait a lifetime."

psychological damage they cause to the individual who happens to survive, Forte almost completely denies the distance between writer and subject matter. There is no room for dissociation from the events which techniques such as reports or collages of quotations allow. As he states in an interview:

> Der Junge bin natürlich ich, aber es lagen fünfzig Jahre dazwischen, und aus diesem Zeitunterschied heraus, der ein Geschehen auch objektiviert, habe ich versucht, die Erinnerung neu zu beleben, das, was der Junge erlebt hat, gesehen hat, die Ängste des Jungen, da habe ich mich nicht geschont, da habe ich mich schon reinversetzt, da bin ich auch durchgebrochen. (*Schweigen oder sprechen* 45)[118]

It is this inclusion of individual destiny, the boy, which allows the reader through identification to understand more fully the horror of the events. However, Forte does not and cannot focus on his character completely or foster absolute identification of himself or the audience with the boy. He needs what he calls a "distanzierte Nähe" (*Schweigen oder Sprechen* 46) both to perceive the events in a larger context and to get closer to his personal experiences without feeling overwhelmed.[119] The distance protects him from his own trauma:

> Ich wollte nicht zu autobiographisch schreiben. Es ist sehr schwer, so etwas noch einmal hervorzuholen. Ich wollte mich nicht selbst zerstören. Vor einem gewissen abgrundtiefen Schrecken versuchte ich haltzumachen, den Text wieder aufzufangen, ihn als Sprache zu halten, das Geschehen in der Sprache zu halten, die so etwas trägt. Deswegen habe ich so lange gewartet und habe mich bemüht, in der Distanz zu bleiben. (Hof and Forte 213)[120]

The novel is thus not a first person narrative, but remains in the third person. The boy has no name and in the last part of the trilogy is even reduced further to the third person, "he." There are also several instances in the work, when Forte appears almost to lose control over his material, leaving the boy behind and exploring independently the world of his novel. Even though some have criticized these digressions and the impersonal treatment of the boy, they are understandable and may be even necessary to convey the traumatic experience of the bombings. The air raids often caused a feeling of being distanced from one's environment, of being numb, almost deathlike and hardly human any longer. It is a world in which one's personality, the subjective "I" disappears and instincts

---

[118] "I am, of course, the boy, but fifty years have passed and it is from this time difference, which also objectifies events, that I tried to renew the memory. These events which the boy has gone through, has seen, his fears; I did not protect myself, but I put myself in his place and I broke through."

[119] "distanced closeness"

[120] "I did not want to write too autobiographically. It is difficult to revisit such an event. I did not want to destroy myself. I tried to stop in front of a certain deep horror, to get back to the text, to keep it in language, to keep the events in language, which can carry the burden of something like this. This is why I have waited so long and have tried to stay at a distance."

take over. Distance from the protagonist also facilitates inclusion of historical context in the novel, a context that a young child can hardly understand, but that Forte finds crucial for the portrayal of the times.

Due to the close connection between Forte's own trauma and his fictional story, writing is psychologically an extremely challenging task: "Es geht nur in einer Art Ohnmacht, in einer Art Absinken, das tief hinabführt in lang Vergessenes, das erst über die Sprache in die Erinnerung findet. Ein quälender Vorgang, man muß mit Zusammenbrüchen rechnen – ich weiß, wovon ich rede" (Forte *Spiegel* 222).[121] However, while the writing process caused Forte to feel even worse than when he had kept the events banned from consciousness, the decision to face the trauma, to put it into words, clearly also had a therapeutic effect. Not surprisingly, after finishing the trilogy, Forte felt a sense of freedom: It is "als ob ich zehn Jahre eine Zwangsjacke getragen hätte und sie jetzt ablegen kann" (Hof and Forte 200).[122] So even though the trauma never disappears, but stays with one for a lifetime and permanently damages one's existence (Forte *Spiegel* 223), writing down the story helps to deal better with the past: "man wird nicht befreit, man wird es nicht los, aber es wird einem bewußt" (*Schweigen oder sprechen* 52-53).[123]

Transforming the haunting images into language, creating a narration that is, while not necessarily correct in every detail, still true to the experienced trauma, can help one not only to create some order in memory, but also to make some degree of peace with the past. After it is allowed to surface, the trauma can be incorporated more naturally into one's life story, so that it loses some of its crippling power. At the same time, by ficitonalizing his past and sharing it with an audience, Forte gives readers the opportunity to gain insight into the experience of the destructive forces of modern technological advances as well as a glimpse at the detrimental effects trauma of such magnitude can have on the individual. However, Forte is under no illusion that one's own experience of the horror or the true depth of the trauma can ever be conveyed in its complete magnitude. Relying on the medium of language to convey his story, there are always memories that cannot be expressed, creating gaps in the narrative that the reader has to fill himself: "Es gibt ein Grauen jenseits der Sprache, ein unaussprechliches Entsetzen, es gibt Augen, Münder und Schreie, das ist nicht mehr zu artikulieren. Das wird untergehen mit denen, die es erlebt haben" (Forte *Spiegel* 222).[124]

---

[121] "It only works in a kind of unconsciousness, by lowering oneself into the depth of the long forgotten, which can only resurface in memory through language. A torturous process, one has to be prepared for breakdowns – I know what I am talking about."

[122] "as if I had worn for ten years a straight jacket which I can finally take off."

[123] "one is not freed, one cannot rid oneself of it, but it becomes conscious"

[124] "There is a horror beyond language, an unspeakable terror, there are eyes, mouths, and screams, that cannot be expressed in words. These impressions will die with those who have experienced them."

4.4   W. G. Sebald and the Air War-Taboo

When W. G. Sebald chose to address the question of German literature and the air war during World War II in his poetics lectures in Zürich in 1997, he did not venture far from the dominant concerns within his oeuvre. Sebald has continuously investigated the role of memory and the underlying hidden presence of past events in people's lives as well as the various ways writers communicate this condition. Experiences which lie outside of established human patterns of existence are of distinct interest to him in both his critical and literary works. In many ways, Sebald is thus a particularly apt person to evaluate the role of large area bombing experiences in postwar German society and launch a public discussion regarding the issues. Yet are his conclusions valid? Sebald, despite some opposition, insists in the publication of *Luftkrieg und Literatur* (literally *Air War and Literature*, but translated into English as *On the Natural History of Destruction*) two years after his lectures, that his original assessment remains true. He stands firm in his opinion that there is a deficit in adequate representation of the air raids in German postwar literature and explains it by the establishment of a taboo about the events right after the war, a silent *agreement* of the German population, including German authors, which was diligently adhered to by everyone (18). Yet one is left to wonder whether he reaches this conclusion on the basis of available material, or rather from the point of view of a preconceived hypothesis which he refuses to adjust. Not only does he underestimate the level of complexity of the postwar situation for authors in respect to both the issues of guilt and the consequences of the bombing trauma, but he also broadly omits or dismisses some of the most important literary attempts. In fact, underneath the surface of a critical analysis lurks a very personal quest by Sebald. Born in 1944, Sebald belonged to a generation of Germans that were never exposed directly to Nazism and the war but whose lives had, as a constant undercurrent, the memories and consequences of both. Searching for what he considers "adequate" literary representations of the bombings by other writers is thus also an attempt to find a way to live through experiences one never had, to drag these shadows into the open and make them controllable.

There is no doubt that Sebald asks valid questions in *Luftkrieg und Literatur* when he explores the (lack of) impact of the bombing experience on postwar German society. As has been seen, he is correct that, despite the necessarily long-lasting effects of the events, they neither became a dominant theme of postwar German literature nor indeed was there intense public discussion of the air raids in society as a whole. For Sebald, this limited reference to the topic, particularly among German writers, is a "skandalöses Defizit" (82)[125] and his judgment of German authors is harsh. Preoccupied with redefining themselves after the Nazi years, with concerns of how they would be perceived by others, they neglected to

---

[125] "scandalous deficit"

describe the realities of the war experience (7). They thus did not record history for posterity which, according to Sebald, is part of the author's responsibility.[126]

In the larger context, however, this assessment appears simplistic. Not only does it neglect the fact that most writers did not actually experience the bombings on German cities, be it because they were soldiers, exiles or because they were living in places that were not affected by the air raids, but it also does not consider the severity of the psychological and social pressures under which authors found and find themselves when trying to address the air war in their works and which have been described in the previous chapters. Clearly, the bombardments cannot be separated from the atrocities committed by Germany during the Nazi era and many writers felt deep shame about their country and themselves. These personal feelings of guilt are coupled with external definitions of collective guilt built around a strict division into victims and perpetrators, which leaves little room to explore events that cannot be assigned to one or the other. Instrumentalized from the start by various groups, writing about the bombings is not only an extremely demanding, but also a highly political, task as it is always under suspicion of trying to revise history in a way that could show Germans in a more favorable light or as victims themselves.

In fact, Sebald's own text exemplifies the problematic nature of the air raid theme. Sebald has never minimized Germany's role in the past, the Holocaust and the atrocities committed during the Nazi era have been central concerns in his work. When addressing the controversial issue of the air raids in *Luftkrieg und Literatur*, he also does not intend to suggest that the suffering incurred lessens the burden of the crimes that Germany committed, but rather wants to spur a discussion about this part of the war. However, even though Sebald shows sensitivity to these concerns in his other works and deals with them on a highly complex level, his lectures often appear surprisingly naive in regards to the questions that could be raised about the bombing theme. When lamenting the lack of representation of the bombardments and their effects in German literature, Sebald mentions many instances of German suffering under the air war, but only a few which deal with the pain inflicted by Germans. While one could assume the atrocities committed by Germany and their role in provoking the bombings to be permanently engrained in one's view of the war, as Sebald emphasizes in the third part of the essay, which he added to the book publication (119), his approach can at times be viewed as insensitive. The situation is amplified by a number of formulations, such as describing the bombings as "[d]ie in der Geschichte bis dahin einzigartige Vernichtungsaktion" (12).[127] Not only does

---

[126] Particularly in the context of postwar German literature, the connection between writing and political and historical responsibility has been strongly emphasized. However, it is, of course, debatable whether literature must play such a central role in the recording of events and their transmission, or in fact have any purpose at all.

[127] "the destruction, on a scale without historical precedent" (trans. 4)

this statement suggest that one can establish a "ranking" of destruction and suf-fering, but it supports the troublesome notion that the air raids can be singled out as the most horrible experiences of the war. The danger of these expressions did not only become apparent in some critics' unease with Sebald's standpoint but, as Sebald himself reports in the third part of his essay, were taken by a number of his readers as lending support to their ideas of German victimhood or even Jewish conspiracy theories (116-119).

The reactions that Sebald's own text provoked, which made it necessary for him to qualify his approach in publication of his book through additional commentary, highlights the complexity of the guilt issues when addressing the bombs even today. This additional chapter resembles a form of "damage control" as Sebald here clarifies the role of Germans in the war. Instead of concentrating almost exclusively on images of the destruction of German cities, he now repeat-edly reminds his readers about the proper order of responsibility for the air war and ends his essay with images of German bombings:

> Die rauschhafte Zerstörungsvision [von Hitler über London] geht in eins damit, daß auch die tatsächlichen Pionierleistungen im Bombenkrieg – Guernica, Warschau, Belgrad, Rotterdam – von den Deutschen vollbracht wurden. Und wenn wir an die Brandnächte von Köln und Hamburg und Dresden denken, dann sollten wir uns auch in Erinnerung rufen, daß bereits im August 1942, als die Spitzen der sechsten Armee die Wolga erreicht hatten [...], die Stadt Stalingrad, die zu jenem Zeitpunkt wie später Dresden von Flüchtlingsströmen angeschwollen war, bombardiert wurde von zwölfhundert Fliegern, und daß dort während dieses Angriffs, der Hochgefühle auslöste unter den am anderen Ufer stehenden deutschen Truppen, vierzigtausend Menschen ihr Leben ließen. (120)[128]

As the previous analysis has shown, the process of talking about the bomb-ings is further complicated by the deep personal traumatization many were left with and which made writing about it an extremely trying and psychologically challenging task. The literary accounts movingly show how the horror of going through the air raids day-after-day leaves people passive and deathlike, requiring them to distance themselves emotionally from the events to be able to cope with them. Overcoming these tendencies, and facing them by trying to convey them through literature, is a difficult and laborious step and these challenges color the texts that emerge. This study has revealed how the works are characterized by techniques which help protect the writers from getting too involved in their

---

[128] "The intoxicating vision of destruction [Hitler's about London] coincides with the fact that the real pioneering achievements in bomb warfare - Guernica, Warsaw, Belgrade, Rotterdam - were the work of the Germans. And when we think of the nights when the fires raged in Cologne and Hamburg and Dresden, we ought also to remember that as early as August 1942, when the vanguard of the Sixth Army had reached the Volga [...], the city of Stalingrad, then swollen (like Dresden later) by an influx of refugees, was under assault from twelve hundred bombers, and that during this raid alone, which caused elation among the German troops stationed on the opposite bank, forty thousand people lost their lives" (trans. 104).

German Stukas over the ruins of Stalingrad, Winter 1942/1943. Reproduced with permission from Keystone Pressedienst, Germany.

own memories – be it by interpreting the bombings as a positive experience, by hiding behind the perspectives or quotations of others, or by pulling back into a more abstract realm of narration when the focus on the individual becomes too painful. They are also marked by the difficulty of translating the usually sensory perceptions into language and into the coherence of a story. It is particularly surprising that Sebald does not acknowledge these aesthetic difficulties in regards to the bombings, since he himself faced them in his own literary output about traumatic past events. As an answer he developed a new style relying on an interplay of text and photography to address what often defies full expression through language. These photographs can both enhance or subvert, support or oppose the written text. In this manner, Sebald adds spaces in which meaning can arise that would otherwise fall into the gaps, and also illuminates the sensory and non-verbal quality of many traumatic memories.

Writing about bombings thus means overcoming several factors one would prefer to suppress, particularly the awareness of the atrocities committed by Germany that cause feelings of shame and guilt, the deep personal trauma and its effects, and the difficulty of creative aesthetic production about events beyond ordinary human experience. Under these circumstances and pressures, it is understandable that the bombings have not become a dominant postwar national theme in Germany and that many narrations took decades to appear. However, as the previous investigation has shown, contrary to what Sebald suggests the topic has not been completely draped in silence. In fact, even throughout his own essay, Sebald is required to reject more and more evidence to justify his original assessment. At first he still includes the private sphere, the "individual amnesia" of the German population (18), in his thesis, describing the exclusion of the destruction as an absence in any media, not just literature, "als ein Sich-Ausschweigen, als eine Absenz, die auch für andere Diskursbereiche vom Familiengespräch bis hin zur Geschichtsschreibung bezeichnend ist" (82).[129] Later, however, Sebald excludes the arena of private memory: "Wenn man Familienreminiszensen, episodische Literarisierungsversuche und [...] Erinnerungsbüche[r] [...] beiseite läßt, so kann man nur von einer durchgehenden Vermeidung oder Verhinderung sprechen" (108).[130]

Yet Sebald's extreme thesis not only fails to capture the situation in the private sphere, the literary accounts also disprove his idea of writers collectively adhering to a societal taboo against the air raids. Nevertheless Sebald holds on to his hypothesis even though it requires further exclusions. To mention just some examples, Gert Ledig and Dieter Forte, whose texts were available at the time of the publication of *Luftkrieg und Literatur* in 1999, do not receive the intense attention they deserve. Sebald treats Ledig's work briefly and superficially in his essay. While he acknowledges Ledig as an author whose "Romane [...] in nichts den Arbeiten anderer Autoren der fünfziger Jahre [...] nachstehen" (111-112), he at the same time dismisses the novel in a vague manner for its supposed aesthetic weaknesses which he leaves unexplained (110).[131] Forte is not acknowledged at all. Instead, the fragment *Die Kathedrale* by Peter de Mendelssohn, a document truly deserving of Sebald's criticism and thus proving his point of a failure in representation, is discussed in great detail.

For an objective literary and cultural analysis by a distanced critic, *Luftkrieg und Literatur* thus seems, while tackling important questions, at times strangely confused, unbalanced, and contradictory. The strictly critical approach is un-

---

[129] as "a self-imposed silence, an absence also typical of other areas of discourse, from family conversations to historical writings" (trans. 70)

[130] "Leaving aside family reminiscences, sporadic attempts to make literary use of the subject, and [...] books of reminiscences, one can speak only of a persistent avoidance of the subject, or an aversion to it" (trans. 93).

[131] "novels [are] in no way inferior to those of other authors of the 1950s" (trans. 96)

dermined consciously by Sebald when he uses the interplay of text and images he developed for his fictional works, and when he writes himself into the text, talking about his own relationship to the air raids. Yet he still at times underestimates how strong his personal involvement influences his conclusions. For Sebald, despite not having lived through the war, the bombing experiences are inseparably bound to his life, a life he represents as embedded between lasting childhood memories of cities in ruins (86) and the close proximity of his later home to the airfields from which the British bomber planes left for Germany. Sebald strongly defines himself through the events: "Dennoch ist es mir bis heute, wenn ich Photographien oder dokumentarische Filme aus dem Krieg sehe, als stammte ich, sozusagen, von ihm ab und als fiele von dorther, von diesen von mir gar nicht erlebten Schrecknissen, ein Schatten auf mich, unter dem ich nie ganz herauskommen werde" (83).[132] This identification with an experience one never had reaches a level that even Sebald views as somewhat perverse:

> [...] vor meinen Augen [verschwimmen] Bilder von Feldwegen, Flußauen und Bergwiesen mit den Bildern der Zerstörung, und es sind die letzteren, perverserweise, und nicht die ganz irreal gewordenen frühkindlichen Idyllen, die so etwas wie ein Heimatgefühl in mir heraufrufen. [...] Heute weiß ich, daß damals, als ich auf dem Altan des Seefelderhauses in dem sogenannten Stubenwagen lag und hinaufblinzelte in den weißblauen Himmel, überall in Europa Rauchschwaden in der Luft hingen, über den Rückzugsschlachten im Osten und im Westen, über den Ruinen der deutschen Städte und über den Lagern, in denen man die Ungezählten verbrannte [...]. (83-84)[133]

In his essay on Sebald's *Die Ausgewanderten* (*The Emigrants*), Jonathan Long has fittingly connected the type of memory that Sebald displays in his works with Marianne Hirsch's idea of postmemory (122). With postmemory, Hirsch refers to the situation of a generation which has not lived through traumatic events of the past directly, but nevertheless feels strongly connected to, and influenced by, them. These past experiences are so monumental that they can replace one's actual memories: "Postmemory characterizes the experience of those who grow up dominated by narratives that preceded their birth, whose own belated stories are displaced by the stories of the previous generation" ("Projected Memory" 8).[134] Hirsch's assessment of the second generation experience

---

[132] "Yet to this day, when I see photographs or documentary films dating from the war I feel as if I were its child, so to speak, as if those horrors I did not experience cast a shadow over me, and one from which I shall never entirely emerge" (trans. 71).

[133] "I see pictures merging before my mind's eyes – paths through the fields, river meadows, and mountain pastures mingling with images of destruction – and [perversely] enough, it is the latter, not the now entirely unreal idylls of my early childhood, that make me feel rather as if I were coming home [...]. I know now that at the time, when I was lying in my bassinet on the balcony of the Seefeld house and looking up at the pale blue sky, there was a pall of smoke in the air all over Europe, over the rearguard actions in east and west, over the ruins of the German cities, over the camps where untold numbers of people were burnt [...]" (trans. 71).

[134] While Hirsch developed her notion of postmemory in relation to children of Holocaust survivors, she expands its applicability beyond this particular group: "I believe it may usefully describe

accurately describes Sebald's situation. With his knowledge of the devastation associated with the war, the pictures of the rather idyllic reality of his childhood and youth in the Allgäu mountains in postwar Germany are banned from consciousness into the realm of the unreal and "Heimat" for Sebald is instead evoked by completely nonexistent memories of destruction (83). Hirsch does not understand postmemory as an "identity position, but a space of remembrance, more broadly available through cultural and public, and not merely individual and personal, acts of remembrance, identification, and projection" ("Projected Memory" 8-9). The problem Sebald faces is that the amount of cultural and public memory in Germany of the air raids after the war is not at all representative of the actual events and their effects. So even though the experience of the bombings is present as an undercurrent in society, the situation characterized by shame, guilt, and psychological trauma prevented the stories from becoming dominant narratives for post-generations. Postwar German society did not offer much space or points of departure for "imaginative investment and creation" (Hirsch *Family Frames* 22) with which some of the gaps between the actual experience and its available memories can be bridged for those who are only indirectly exposed to them.

It is thus not surprising that Sebald searches almost relentlessly for any possibilities of access to the experiences, for gaining at least glimpses of the events. Many forms of destruction feature prominently in Sebald's oeuvre and the bombings and their effects also frequently appear directly. These passages illustrate the continuous presence and importance of the (non)experience of the bombings for the author from early on and emphasize his limited access to them. In his first work of literature, for example, *Nach der Natur* (*After Nature*), Sebald tries to establish a foundation for the strong connection he feels to the air raid experiences, by insisting on an almost biological link between the events and his being. He describes how his mother in 1943 observes the burning city of Nürnberg after a bomber attack, the same day that she finds out she is pregnant with him:

> In der Nacht auf den 28. flogen
> 582 Maschinen einen Angriff
> auf Nürnberg. Die Mutter,
> die am anderen Morgen nachhause ins Allgäu
> zurückfahren wollte,
> ist mit der Bahn bloß
> bis nach Fürth gekommen.
> Von dort aus sah sie Nürnberg in Flammen stehen,

other second-generation memories of cultural or collective traumatic events and experiences" (*Family Frames* 22). Consequently, Hirsch's postmemory is a theory about indirect access to memory which is not attached to a specific event. Using her approach to assess a member of the German postwar generation should thus by no means be understood as an equation of the trauma of the Holocaust victims with German experiences of bombardments or other traumatizing events.

weiß aber heute nicht mehr,
wie die brennende Stadt aussah
und was für Gefühle sie
bei ihrem Anblick bewegten.
Sie sei, so erzählte sie neulich,
von Fürth aus am selben Tag noch
nach Windsheim zu einer Bekannten
gefahren, wo sie das Schlimmste
abgewartet und gemerkt habe,
daß sie schwanger geworden sei. (73-74)[135]

So while Sebald is inseparably linked to the air war, it also eludes him completely. Deprived of the actual experience, its lasting effects are perceived without any knowledge of the events. As Sebald describes in *Schwindel. Gefühle.* (*Vertigo*), they become part of one's world view, which is, however, distorted by this complete divorce from the original cause: "in fast jeder Wochenschau sah man auch die Ruinenhaufen von Städten wie Berlin oder Hamburg, die ich lange nicht mit der in den letzten Kriegsjahren erfolgten Zerstörung, von der ich nichts wußte, in Verbindung brachte, sondern für eine sozusagen natürliche Gegebenheit aller größeren Städte gehalten habe" (204).[136] Consequently, at this point, what is actually located in postmemory cannot even be realized as being belated.

Part of Sebald's and his generation's life, after they understand the belatedness of their position, is thus colored by the attempt to obtain an understanding of the origins of what they feel and perceive, of what they have seen in glimpses, but what has not become the topic of public discussion. In his works, Sebald describes several strategies with which he tries to access the actual experience of the bombings. One way is through personal eyewitness reports. However, the immediate family fails to provide the information he craves. The mother, who is effectively witnessing the bombings for the unborn child, does not (or does not want to) remember and share what she saw and felt. Sebald describes other accounts as being full of stereotypical phrases and so does not think that they can truly demonstrate the realities of the bombardments - an opinion which is partially justified as the limitations of works such as Kempowski's *Echolot* illustrate.

In *Die Ringe des Saturn* (*The Rings of Saturn*), Sebald attempts to gain insight into the events from another angle, namely by exploring the technical as-

---

[135] "During the night of the 28th/582 machines flew an attack/against Nürnberg. The mother,/who wanted the next day/to go back to the Allgäu/only managed to get to/Fürth by train./From there she saw Nürnberg in flames/but cannot remember today/how the burning city looked/and what feelings she experienced/at the sight./She then, as she told me recently,/went the same day from Fürth/to a friend in Windsheim/where she waited till the worst was over/and where she realized/that she had become pregnant."

[136] "in almost every newsreel one also saw heaps of rubble of such cities as Berlin or Hamburg, which for a long time I did not connect to the destruction that occurred in the last years of the war of which I was ignorant, but which I thought to be a natural part of any larger city."

pects of the bombings. At a visit to the Somerleyton house and gardens in the eastern part of England, the narrator strikes up a conversation with a gardener on the estate who tells him about his own obsession with the air raids. When he was young, he saw many bomber formations, which had taken off from the air fields nearby, fly over the area towards Germany. Yet even though he has insight into the technological requirements of the attacks, the events themselves remain abstract for him as well. He is able to recite statistical information about the bombings, the duration of the air war, the use of gasoline, the number of bombs, and the number of casualties among pilots (52), but he could and can only imagine the effects of the bombs and the destroyed cities were nothing more than dots on a map to him. So the technical and strategic aspects of the bombings also fail to provide an idea of the actual experience of the events. The situations of Sebald and the British gardener become mirror images. Both have access to the events only from a distance, from the perspective of the outside, even though each feels personally tied to the experience and haunted by it. In fact, it is here that Sebald, through the words of the gardener, already formulates in a fictional framework part of his thesis of *Luftkrieg und Literatur*. The British gardener relates that he even learned German to be able to read reports about the bombings and life in the ruins, but he does not succeed in finding out more about the reality of the experience: "Zu meinem Erstaunen freilich mußte ich bald feststellen, daß die Suche nach solchen Berichten stets ergebnislos verlief. Niemand scheint damals etwas aufgeschrieben oder erinnert zu haben. Und auch wenn man die Leute persönlich befragte, war es, als sei in ihren Köpfen alles ausradiert worden" (53-54).[137]

Sebald's deep disappointment with German postwar literature is closely related to this futile search for insight into the bombing experience. Similar to personal accounts or the technical and strategic aspects of the air war, literature was another path through which Sebald was hoping to gain access to the events or at least a point of departure for his own imaginative creations about them. In *Luftkrieg und Literatur* he mentions that, while he was growing up, he was constantly under the impression that important information about his background was being kept from him, the feeling, "es würde mir etwas vorenthalten, zu Hause, in der Schule und auch von den deutschen Schriftstellern, deren Bücher ich in der Hoffnung las, mehr über die Ungeheuerlichkeiten im Hintergrund meines eigenen Lebens erfahren zu können" (82-83).[138] Sebald seems to feel that he is being failed by society and cheated out of a knowledge he needs in order to understand himself and his place in the world. He is particularly angry

---

[137] "To my surprise I soon realized that the search for such reports always ended without success. No-one seems to have written down anything back then or remembered anything. And even when one talked to the people directly, it was as if everything had been erased from their minds."

[138] "that something was being kept from me: at home, at school, and by the German writers whose books I read hoping to glean some information about the monstrous events in the background of my own life" (trans. 70).

with German writers, leading to a tone in his essay which Andreas Huyssen has described as resembling a "discourse of 'Abwicklung' " ("On Rewritings" 81). Sebald implies that their failure to produce texts about the bombings not only constitutes a literary problem, but also has had a significant societal impact. According to Sebald, it is essential for German authors after 1945 to record history and to act as public witnesses, as it is the function of literature to keep historical events from being erased from memory (8). Yet he notes, "daß sich die Nachgeborenen, wenn sie sich einzig auf die Zeugenschaft der Schriftsteller verlassen wollten, kaum ein Bild machen könnten vom Verlauf, von den Ausmaßen, von der Natur und den Folgen der durch den Bombenkrieg über Deutschland gebrachten Katastrophe" (81).[139] He thus holds writers partially responsible for the lack of public discussion of one of the fundamental experiences of Germans during World War II, and particularly of leaving his generation robbed of an understanding about the underlying structures of their identity.

Could literature realistically ever have filled this void? As Dieter Forte suggests, when writing about an experience such as the bombings which has such a deep traumatising effect on the individual, the notions of responsibility for others are not necessarily foremost in the author's mind: "der Glaube an nachfolgende Generationen ist in solchen Situationen stark lädiert" (*Schweigen oder Sprechen* 36).[140] Despite these circumstances, study of some of the available accounts has shown that they are powerful and can provide, within their limitations, some degree of understanding of the experiences. Not surprisingly, Sebald needs to dismiss and exclude much existing material for his argument of *Luftkrieg und Literatur* to stand in its extreme form. However, it appears to be more than his desire to prove the soundness of his preconceived theory that leads him down this path. Sebald needed to insist on the validity of his thesis, as for him personally it remained true throughout his life. In literature, Sebald was not only looking for descriptions of the bombings, but for a possibility to live through and to experience first-hand the events whose full reality eluded him, but which cast such a strong shadow over his life. Hirsch convincingly argues that in postmemory one can try through imagination to get closer to the traumatic events, but the real experience can never be completely understood (*Family Frames* 22)). Even though the introduction of fiction and imagination opens up possibilities to get closer to these events, literature also cannot ever fulfill this role completely, even if the authors actually lived through the air war themselves. Events such as the bombings, which lie completely outside of normal human experience, can never be fully conveyed through writing. While the texts can offer interesting

---

[139] "that if those born after the war were to rely solely on the testimony of writers, they would scarcely be able to form any idea of the extent, nature, and consequences of the catastrophe inflicted on Germany by the air raids" (trans. 69-70).

[140] "in such situations, the belief in future generations is severely damaged."

and touching glimpses of the air raids and their effects, they can never repro-
duce them in their totality as there is always horror beyond language. Reading
about the bombings will thus never be the same as living through them, making
Sebald's quest necessarily a disappointed one.

Chapter 5
A Welcome Catastrophe: Jewish-German Voices

The German literary depictions of the bombings, discussed previously, have in common the representation of vast inner and outer devastation. The narratives are marked by the traumatic quality of the air raids and their consequences. The bombings brought war to the civilian world and with it the awareness that one could die at any moment. The powerful physical and psychological effects of the bombings described in these texts were enhanced by the insecurity and deep fear about the future in general – what will happen to Germany and the Germans when the war is finally lost? Yet not everyone who experienced the air war shared this outlook. Obviously, the victims of Nazism did not first learn about fear and about the constant threat to their lives through the air raids, but had been living in this condition since Hitler's rise to power. For the ones who had survived thus far, the bombings, while on the one hand still traumatic and frightening, were on the other more than welcome events.

5.1   Werner Schmidt

The memoir by the physician Werner Schmidt, *Leben an Grenzen* (*Life on the Edge*), which was published in 1989, speaks of the deep ambivalence and complexity of the situation. In 1933, Schmidt, whose mother is Jewish, is in the middle of medical school. Despite considerable opposition, he manages to finish his studies, but is unable to realize his wish to emigrate to Great Britain because of both the financial commitment involved as well as the restrictions instituted by the British government against physician immigrants from Germany. Desperate to continue his medical education and to work in the profession he loves, he finally manages to get a position as a doctoral student and pathologist in Hamburg in October 1940. Here, Schmidt also experiences the horror of the air raids, leaving him with the double threat of being killed by the bombs or losing his life directly at the hands of the Nazis. The only way he can overcome these fears is through professional distance. Even when Schmidt is sitting in the cellar during the attacks, unable to breathe and swallowing dust, with the floor shaking, he tries to channel all his energy into studying medical literature. He is also fully aware that, despite their horror and deadliness, which he experiences every day first hand, the increasing number of attacks and the deaths that come with them are a clear sign that the Nazi rule is coming to an end. He knows that those dropping the bombs will also be his liberators. However, this knowledge is accompanied by even more danger. He not only needs to be scared of deportation or death by the bombs, but also of becoming the victim of acts of revenge against Jews in the shelters (153). Schmidt thus concentrates fully on his daily service at the hospital, suppressing his fears with the duty he feels towards his profession and the people who gave him a chance despite his background: "Am nächsten Morgen geht es dann über Schutt, Asche, Glassplitter, Drähte der Straßenbahnoberleitung und zahlreiche im Pflaster steckende Brandbomben zum Dienst" (97).[1]

Schmidt lives through, and measures, the war developments in the cool and sterile dissection rooms. While fellow doctors are called up to serve, steadily reducing the size of the autopsy team, the work load continuously increases with the progression of the war. Schmidt here observes the deadliness of the regime in its many forms. In the cellar of the hospital, the foundation of Nazi rule on death and destruction is clearly exposed. After every air raid, corpses start piling up:

> Erneute Bombenangriffe. Wir sezieren die Opfer, aus deren zerfetzten Leibern Bettfedern, Bombensplitter verschiedenen Kalibers, Steine, Mörtel, Glas, Holz, Stoffstücke, ja sogar in einem Fall ein Flakblindgänger zu Tage gefördert werden, ferner Erstickte, Verbrannte, Phosphorverbrannte, Verbrühte, Tote, denen eine oder mehrere Extremitäten abgerissen sind, denen Teile des Schädels fehlen. Unter ihnen befinden sich Kinder, Greise, Menschen, die noch im Vollbesitz ihrer Kräfte waren, und solche – bereits schwer krank –, denen der Krieg ein schreckliches Ende bereitete. (96)[2]

The horror of the bombardments and the force of this technologically advanced weaponry is not lost on Schmidt, and he also laments their effects and blames Hitler for these deaths. Yet in this sterile and white-tiled room, Schmidt also has ample opportunity to observe the direct impact of Nazi rule, clearly reenforcing the dangerous position that he and his family are in. Time and again he has to examine the dead bodies of Russian POWs or laborers who have died under suspicious circumstances: "Die Zahl der Fälle von russischen Kriegsgefangenen, die verhungert sind, sowie von an Flecktyphus verstorbenen Russen

---

[1] "The next morning, I am off to work, climbing over rubble, ashes, glass fragments, streetcar cables and numerous firebombs buried in the pavement."

[2] "Air raids again. We dissect the victims, from whose ripped bodies we recover bedsprings, bomb fragments of various calibers, stones, mortar, glass, wood, pieces of cloth, in one case even a dud from the anti-aircraft units. In addition, we examine bodies who died of suffocation, burns, phosphor burns, scalding, corpses whose extremities are partially ripped off, who are missing part of their skull. Among them are children, old people, healthy and strong people, and some – already seriously ill – whose life came to a horrible end through the war."

und Russinnen, die wir obduzieren müssen, ist zeitweise sehr auffällig. Woher die Fälle kommen, weiß ich nicht" (96).[3] Later, in the anatomy department at the University of Gießen hospitals, he sees the dead bodies of concentration camp prisoners:

> Im Keller der Gießener Anatomie zeigte mir Prof. Wagenseil einen Haufen ausgemergelter Leichen, KZ-Häftlinge. Man hatte sie an einem Bahndamm in der Nähe gefunden und in sein Institut geschafft; waren gewiss bei Nacht und Nebel aus dem Waggon geworfen worden. Was sah ich in Hamburg. Man hatte hier Russen verhungern lassen. Heimatland. (160)[4]

With this exclamation, "Heimatland," at the sight of the dead tortured concentration camp prisoners, Schmidt's distanced look of the medical examiner and researcher breaks down and his desperation about the state of his home country emerges. It expresses the deep conflict he feels within himself: The same country he grew up in and which he is attached to, which he pities for being destroyed by the cruelty of the bombings, is the one that wants to exclude and kill him and his family, has killed innumerable people already, and where he is forced daily to fight for survival, always on the border of death.

This dichotomous state becomes even more pronounced at a later event. By chance, Schmidt observes the bombing of Dresden in February of 1945 when he stays in a town near the historical city: "Am 13. Februar, abends zwischen neun und zehn, ist plötzlich ein tiefes Brummen in der Luft, das immer mehr anschwillt und bald so laut ist, wie ich es bisher noch nie erlebt habe. [...] Dresden also ist angegriffen worden, Dresden, die letzte der großen und schönsten deutschen Städte, Dresden, der 'Balkon Europas' " (183).[5] Schmidt dearly regrets the loss of the historical and cultural monuments of the city as well as the many lives by the attacks. When he later travels through Dresden, the devastation leaves him with impressions he never manages to forget because of their cruelty: the sidewalks are full of burnt and dismembered corpses and the people who did survive walk through the burning city with such passive gazes as if they were dead as well. Yet at the same time, despite the horror of the scene, Schmidt views them as necessary. In his opinion, it is not the Allies who are responsible

---

[3] "The number of cases we are examining of Russian prisoners of war who starved, as well as Russian men and women who died of typhus fever, is at times very conspicuous. Where the cases come from, I don't know."

[4] "In the cellar of the Gießen anatomy department, Prof. Wagenseil showed me a pile of emaciated corpses, concentration camp prisoners. They had been found at a railway embankment nearby and then brought to the institute; they were surely thrown out of the train car in the middle of the night. What I had seen in Hamburg. There they let Russians starve. Home country."

[5] "On February 13, between nine and ten in the evening, there is suddenly a deep drone in the air, which steadily increases until it is soon louder than anything I had experienced before. [...] So it is Dresden that was attacked, Dresden, the last of the big and most beautiful German cities, Dresden, the 'Balcony of Europe.' "

for the loss of this cultural center, but Hitler and the rest of the National Socialist leadership. He hopes that these attacks will finally hasten the end of the war despite their potential to kill innocent people: "Gott sei Dank, daß den Eltern das erspart geblieben ist, daß sie nicht zufällig in Dresden leben. Den 'Herren' wird der Mut schon vergehen, wenn sie von Dresden hören. Es ist aus, ganz und gar aus, sie können nicht mehr zurückschlagen" (183).[6] Yet Schmidt soon learns how extremely dangerous the regime still is in its final months. The same day as the bombardment, February 13, when he was worrying about Dresden and mourning the loss of one of the last sites of intact German cultural icons as well as the lot of its inhabitants, his mother was picked up by the Gestapo and deported (185)![7]

From Schmidt's reflections emerges the double role of the air war in the lives of those who were under constant threat by National Socialism. Despite the havoc they wrought and the destructive consequences that necessarily accompanied them, the bombs were definitely also understood as signs of freedom and the beginning of the end of the war. Indeed, all Jewish narratives reflect to some degree this dualism of the experience. However, there are precious few Jewish accounts of the bombings. Sadly, this is the consequence of the gruesome fact that, by this time in the war when large area bombings became a key element of the Allied warfare, almost all German Jews had been killed or deported, if they had not managed to emigrate to safer lands. The few texts which are available are thus invaluable sources which give further insight into the perception of the air war from this unique perspective.

5.2   Victor Klemperer

Victor Klemperer's diaries *Ich will Zeugnis ablegen bis zum letzten* (*I Will Bear Witness*) were only published posthumously in 1995. They were rediscovered among his unpublished works and became an immediate success when they appeared. The texts chronicle in almost daily entries Klemperer's experiences as a Jew in Dresden under National Socialism. Writing them, he took great risks, both for his own life, and the lives of his wife and the people who were hiding the pages. Klemperer used passages of the diaries in his first work after the war, *LTI* (1947), or *Lingua Tertii Imperii*, in which he collected his observations about the language of National Socialism, but they only offer fleeting glimpses into Klemperer's personality and his difficult situation from 1933 to 1945. The

---

[6] "Thank God that my parents were spared this event, that by chance they don't live here in Dresden. The 'Masters' will now lose their courage, when they hear about Dresden. It is over, completely over, they cannot counter-attack any longer."

[7] After the war is over, Schmidt is told that his mother had been deported to Theresienstadt. He travels there and indeed finds her alive. He then manages to take her and a number of other Jews who had also been deported from Gießen back to the town.

diaries more vividly reveal the tension between the constant threat of death and the wish to live a normal life which characterizes Klemperer's situation in the Third Reich. They also illustrate Klemperer's difficult relationship to his Jewish background and to Germany – attitudes that color his outlook on Nazi Germany and its crimes, the war, and all the events he describes.

Klemperer grew up in an assimilated Jewish household. Even though his father was a Rabbi, he worked in a reformed community in Berlin that had adapted Jewish traditions to their Christian environment. Sabbath was held on a Sunday and the service was conducted almost completely in German, the members of the community did not cover their heads, and the traditional Bar Mitzvah was replaced by a ceremony for boys and girls when they were sixteen years of age (Jacobs 15). Three of Klemperer's brothers actually converted to Christianity early in their lives. Growing up in these circumstances, it is not surprising that he also followed this path of complete assimilation. He converted to Christianity not so much out of religious reasons, but because he viewed himself as part of a unified German community and thought that he would be more readily perceived in this manner if he became a Christian. He thus deliberately chose to sacrifice his heritage for a feeling of belonging more fully to German society. His specific goal was to be part of the academic world and participate in the German tradition of scholarship as a professor of French. Yet life as a Jew, even if converted, at the university was not easy as anti-Semitism was deeply engrained and it was not uncommon that Jewish scholars were ignored for leading positions.

However, Klemperer's wish for German integration went so far that it blinded him to these realities of the academic world he so idealized. He refused to accept that this anti-Semitism was also directed against him and instead doubted his abilities as a scholar. Even when, as Heide Gerstenberger relates, "ihm 1919 die Braut seines Kollegen Lerch ins Gesicht sagte, 'Ich verkehre nicht mit konvertierten Juden,' war er tagelang verstört und notierte: 'Was habe ich mit dem Ghetto zu schaffen?' " (12).[8] Instead of blaming the anti-Semitic structures and the people around him, Klemperer thus expresses a form of Jewish self-hatred, a sense of embarrassment at his own heritage. It is this loyalty to what he defines over and over as true Germanness, belonging to a country of knowledge and academic endeavor, as well as literature and culture, that then makes it even harder for Klemperer to accept the horrid realities of the Third Reich and leaves him blind to some of its consequences.

Even at a very late stage he underestimates the true danger of the regime. After Hitler comes to power, he and his wife still decide to go ahead and build a house, which takes up most of their savings and which they only a few years later have to leave. Although he has good opportunities to go to America where

---

[8] "when in 1919 the bride of his colleague Lerch told him to his face that she does not associate with converted Jews, for days he was deeply troubled and noted down: 'What do I have to do with the ghetto?' "

his brother Georg has already established himself, his emigration attempts are also half-hearted. He starts learning English a few times, but immediately stops and instead spends the time working on his writing projects, which allow him to ignore to some degree the developments around him. In this time, he lets many chances to leave the country slip by. As late as 1939 he still feels too connected to Germany to leave: "Georg [...] schrieb, er habe eine sehr aussichtsreiche Verbindung geknüpft, werde mir im Juni nach seiner Rückkehr nach USA Bestimmtes mitteilen können, hoffe mich noch Ende dieses Jahres drüben zu sehen. Ich weiß nicht, ob ich mir das wünschen soll. Wie gesagt: Ich vergrabe mich in Curriculum und Romains" (1937-1939 146).[9] Despite the ever worsening persecution of Jews, Klemperer keeps holding on to his ideals. So even though he suffers terribly because of German anti-Semitism, Klemperer rejects his Jewishness and describes himself only as German: "Die Jüdischen Gemeinden in Deutschland tendieren heute alle schroff zum Zionismus; den mache ich genausowenig mit wie den Nationalsozialismus oder den Bolschewismus. Liberal und deutsch forever" (1937-1939 175).[10] When he is finally forced to wear the stella on his coat, he does not want to leave the house any longer – not so much out of fear, but particularly because he feels terribly ashamed and embarrassed about being so clearly identified as Jewish (1940-1941 167).

Having kept a diary since his youth, writing in it takes on a special meaning during this time of persecution and personal confusion about his own ideals. For one, working on his personal notes as well as his private studies about LTI are a route for escape from the daily horror he faces. Similar to Schmidt, who tries to deal with the developments through the distanced look of an objective physician, Klemperer finds a helpful distance by putting his experiences into language and by studying the events with the philological tools of his profession. In this sense, writing allows him to retreat to a place of safety (Dirschauer 152), where he can still keep his dignity: "Es handelt sich nur darum, Haltung bis zuletzt zu bewahren. Bestes Mittel dafür ist Versenkung ins Studium, so tun, als hätte das Stoffspeichern wirklich Zweck" (Klemperer 1944 172).[11] That even this kind of safety is, of course, only an illusion is clear when one thinks of the danger Klemperer faces solely by the act of writing. He is well aware that the discovery of his diaries would equate with an immediate death sentence. Despite the precarious situation, however, Klemperer keeps going, because it is the only place where he can still be who he wants to be and thus rise from the "Nichtsein"

---

[9] "Georg [...] wrote that he has made some promising connections, and will be able to give me concrete information when he returns to the U.S. in June; he hopes to see me over there by the end of this year. I am not sure whether I should wish for this or not. I bury myself in work on the Curriculum and Romains."

[10] "The Jewish communities in Germany today all rigorously embrace Zionism; I won't go along with it, as I won't go along with National Socialism or Bolshevism. Liberal and German forever."

[11] "One can only keep one's dignity until the end. The best way to do so is to immerse oneself in one's studies, to act as if this type of recording of the events really has a purpose."

(1945 15) to which National Socialism has condemned him.[12] Not only are these texts places where he can reflect on his feelings and his difficult position, but they represent a sanctuary for the German ideals he believes in and which the Nazis try to corrupt. It is also the place where, through his LTI studies, Klemperer tries to preserve and save the German language, which the Hitler regime is robbing of its purity and integrity. In this sense, the diaries are more than personal or historical documents, they are a technique of survival. At the same time, they also become works of literature. A skilled writer with journalistic experience, Klemperer shows himself in his diaries to be a compelling storyteller and, as Hans Reiss suggests, evokes a reader response comparable to that produced by literary works:

> We as readers are the spectators of a terrible tale, but, unlike the hero of a tragedy or Klemperer, we know the outcome. We see how, like a tragic protagonist, he remains far too long blind to the full consequences of Nazi terror [...], how the noose tightens from 1933 onward and how death threatens him more and more. Even the end of his story has characteristics of tragedy, for, macabre as it may sound, he is saved by an intervention from above; like a *deus ex machina* the bombing of Dresden by Allied planes in February 1945 makes his rescue possible. (67)[13]

Reiss is correct that in Klemperer's case the bombs on Dresden, like a divine intervention from above, bring sudden and unexpected freedom, since the confusion following the heavy air raids gives Klemperer the opportunity to flee. As he reports in *LTI*:

> Am Abend dieses 13. Februar brach die Katastrophe über Dresden herein: die Bomben fielen, die Häuser stürzten, der Phosphor strömte, die brennenden Balken krachten auf arische und nichtarische Köpfe [...]; wen aber von den etwa 70 Sternträgern diese Nacht verschonte, dem bedeutete sie Errettung, denn im allgemeinen Chaos konnte er der Gestapo entkommen. (330)[14]

---

[12] "nothingness" or, literally, "non-being"

[13] Consequently, in the diaries, due to both style and content, reality appears almost fictional, and fictional devices can be used to access and understand reality. This interrelation, however, does not weaken the work's power as an authentic document depicting the daily horrors Klemperer had to go through. The text's apparent closeness to works of fiction, even if in large measure unintended, makes it easier for readers to identify with the "protagonist" and to become absorbed in the "story." This style might also inspire them to read the text more carefully and to look at additional, hidden layers of meaning. At the same time, the form of the diary and the awareness that this text, while individual chapters might display structural designs, was not conceived after the fact, but grew entry by entry without any knowledge of what will happen next, and depicts real occurrences, give it unparalleled authenticity.

[14] "In the evening of February 13, the catastrophe came upon Dresden: bombs were falling, houses collapsed, phosphorus was flowing, the burning beams fell both on Aryan and non-Aryan heads [...]; however, for the ones of the ca. 70 people who had to wear a star and survived the night, this catastrophe meant salvation, since the general chaos allowed them to escape from the Gestapo."

Despite his liberation, however, his more detailed account of the bombings in his diaries reveals that the destruction of Dresden which he witnessed also deeply affected Klemperer psychologically as well as in his view of the world. He is thus left in the strange position of both welcoming the destruction and at the same time regretting the consequences of what he calls a "Katastrophe" (1945 31).

For most of the war, Dresden had been almost completely spared from the air raids which destroyed many other cities in the country. However, the diaries reveal how the threat of an attack constantly hangs over the city. Hearing about the destruction of Königsberg, his wife's hometown, in 1944, Klemperer is deeply moved by the account:

> Das erschütterte mich, und wie ich morgens – purpurnstes, glühendunkles Morgenrot – beim Abwaschen auf die Carolabrücke und die Häuserreihe drüben hinaussah, stellte ich mir immerfort vor, diese Reihe bräche vor meinen Augen plötzlich in sich zusammen – wie das ja tatsächlich in jeder Stunde geschehen könnte und ähnlich alle Tage irgendwo in Deutschland wirklich geschieht. Aber wenn nicht gerade in den nächsten Stunden Alarm kommt, sinkt diese Vorstellung natürlich zrück, und ich hoffe weiter auf "Churchills Tante."(1944 122)[15]

With the unblemished city as a backdrop, the mandatory air raid drills take on the atmosphere of an amusing game and do not prepare the residents at all for what the city will have to endure half a year later (1944 132).

On the evening of the bombing of Dresden on February 13, 1945, Klemperer is pessimistic and depressed by a more direct threat, since on this day he had to bring notices announcing their deportation and thus their almost certain death to most of the few Jews who still remained in Dresden. The news that Klemperer is forced to deliver is also a sure indication of his own destiny. He knows that after years of oppression, he will now also face this death sentence in the near future:

> Abends hatte mir Waldmann aufs bestimmteste versichert (aus Erfahrung und neuerdings aufgeschnappten Äußerungen), daß die am Freitag zu Deportierenden in den Tod geschickt ("auf ein Nebengleis geschoben") würden, und daß wir Zurückbleibenden acht Tage später ebenso beseitigt werden würden – da kam Vollalarm. (1945 31)[16]

---

[15] "This shook me up, and when in the morning while doing the dishes – with the dark morning sky shining in deepest crimson – I looked out over the Carola bridge and the row of houses opposite, I was imagining that this row would suddenly collapse in front of my eyes – as it could actually happen at any time and indeed happens every day somewhere in Germany. But, except when there is an alarm in the following hours, this imaginary scene fades and I keep up hope because of 'Churchill's aunt.' "

[16] "In the evening Waldmann had assured me (based on his experience and recent remarks he had overheard) that the people who would be deported on Friday were to be sent to their death ("put on a side track") and that we who were staying behind would be disposed of the same way a week later – then the alarm sounded."

This marks the beginning of the heavy bombardments of Dresden. A little over a week after the bombardments, Klemperer talks about the air raids in his diaries. After the first wave of attacks, the most severe Dresden has experienced thus far, Klemperer, although he is shaken and complaining of a loss of feeling for time, is still able to continue to report, to describe details, to take stock of the damage, and thus to analyze in the spirit of the detached witness he adopts in his text:

> Der Boden war mit Scherben bedeckt. Ein furchtbarer Sturmwind blies. Natürlicher oder Flammensturm? Wohl beides. Im Treppenhaus der Zeughausstraße 1 waren die Fensterrahmen eingedrückt und lagen z. T. hindernd auf den Treppen. Bei uns oben Scherben. Fenster eingedrückt auf der Diele und nach der Elbe hin, im Schlafzimmer nur eines. [...] Man sah große Brände über der Elbe und an der Marschallstraße. Frau Cohn berichtete, in ihrem Zimmer seien Möbel vom Luftdruck verrückt. (1945 32)[17]

Yet when the second attack begins, Klemperer suddenly finds himself in the middle of the events. In the turmoil he gets separated from his wife, is injured in the face by a splinter and starts to think that death, which he had been so close to for many years, has now finally arrived through the bombs: "Ich dachte nichts, ich hatte nicht einmal Angst, es war bloß eine ungeheure Spannung in mir, ich glaube ich erwartete das Ende" (1945 33).[18] Now that the air raid has taken on such proportions, Klemperer's behavior patterns and attitudes resemble symptoms that have been previously described by acute stress disorder. The bombings leave him completely disoriented and he walks around almost randomly in the firestorm. This disorientation has not worn off one week after the events, when he is actually writing the account. Instead, Klemperer is still overwhelmed by the horror of the experience and unable to process the events or fulfill his self-described role of the observer and witness. He instead repeats in his diary entry only the confusion he felt during the raids, without analyzing them from his later perspective: "warum kann ich nichts im Einzelnen beobachten, sondern sehe nur immer das Bühnenfeuer zur Rechten und zur Linken, die brennenden Balken und Fetzen und Dachsparren in und über den steinernen Mauern?" (1945 35).[19] Similarly to what has been seen in other bombing accounts, he responds by shutting off emotionally, describing himself as standing "wie im Halbschlaf" and depicting the conditions as "betäubend" (1945 35).[20] In order not to be com-

---

[17] "The floor was covered with shards of glass. A terrible storm was blowing. Of natural origin or a firestorm? Probably both. In the staircase of the Zeughausstraße 1 the window frames had been blown out of the walls and were lying on the stairs, so that it was hard to get past them. Upstairs in our apartment pieces of glass. In the hallway and towards the Elbe river the windows had been broken by the pressure, only one in the bedroom. [...] One could see large fires across the Elbe and in the Marschallstraße. Frau Cohn told us that in her room furniture had been moved by the air pressure."

[18] I wasn't thinking of anything, I wasn't even afraid, there was just an incredible tension inside me, I think I expected the end."

[19] "Why can't I observe anything in detail, but always only see the burning roofs on the right and on the left the burning beams and pieces and rafters in and on top of the stonewalls?"

pletely overwhelmed by the events, they are kept at a distance and transformed into the unreal. He perceives the horror almost as an aesthetic construct:

> Bisweilen lagen, klein und im wesentlichen ein Kleiderbündel, Tote auf den Weg gestreut. Einem war der Schädel weggerissen, der Kopf war oben eine dunkelrote Schale. Einmal lag ein Arm da mit einer bleichen, nicht unschönen Hand, wie man so ein Stück in Friseurschaufenstern aus Wachs geformt sieht. (1945 37)[21]

During the bombing and, as his writing suggests, also after it was over, Klemperer avoids any reflection on what is happening around him: "ich war durchaus dumpf. Ich dachte gar nichts, es tauchten nur Fetzen auf. Eva – warum sorge ich mich nicht ständig um sie" (35).[22] In addition, again the objective and subjective perceptions of time do not match: "Ich war ohne Zeitgefühl, es dauerte endlos und dauerte auch wieder gar nicht so lange" (35).[23] Klemperer is a passive participant in the events, everything feels unreal to him and he can only either blindly follow people or act instinctively (1945 36). It is only through the encouragement of others and the initiative of his non-Jewish wife Eva that Klemperer succeeds in fleeing from Dresden and further persecution.

Klemperer's ambivalent attitude towards the bombings is thus an indication of the powerful psychological effects of the air raids, but it is also a reflection of his earlier conflicts. Klemperer repeatedly emphasizes how the bombings affect both Jews and non-Jews equally. A few days before the air raid on Dresden, he mentions, "[a]n ein rasches Ende glaubt keiner, und Jud und Christ fürchten auch gemeinsam die Bombenangriffe" (1945 24).[24] Talking about the destruction of

---

[20] "...describing himself 'as if he were half asleep' and depicting the conditions as 'paralyzing.' "

[21] "From time to time lay small and primarily bundles of clothes, dead bodies scattered on the pavement. From one of the bodies the skull had been ripped off, the head was a dark-red bowl. Once there lay an arm with a pale, not unsightly, hand similar to what you can see made out of wax in the windows of hairdresser shops."

[22] "I was emotionless. I didn't think of anything, only fragments came to my mind. Eva – why wasn't I worrying more about her."

[23] "I was without any feeling for the time, it lasted forever and at the same time didn't last that long."
In particular this loss of an ordinary perception of time has a lasting effect on Klemperer. It is repeatedly mentioned in one form or other throughout the rest of the diaries. The entries for June to December of 1945, published under the title *Und alles ist so schwankend* (*And Everything Is in Flux*) in 1996, reveal similar perceptions of having lost access to ordinary time: "Ich frage unterwegs immer wieder: wieviel Uhr? Antwort regelmäßig: ich habe auch keine mehr. [...] In der Begerburg haben sie mir eine hübsche Standuhr gegeben, die zuverlässig gehe – bloß die Zeiger sind abgebrochen (beim Plündern natürlich) und notersetzt: der Ersatz ist derart, daß sich die Zeit auf keine Weise ablesen läßt" (7) ("When we are out, I repeatedly ask others for the time. The usual answer: I don't have a watch either. [...] In Begerburg I was given a nice looking grandfather clock which was supposedly working reliably– the only problem was that the hands had been broken off (when the looting was going on, of course) and then were replaced: the replacement was such that there was no possible way to read the time").

[24] "no one believes in a swift end to the war, and Jews and Christians both fear the air raids."

Dresden in *LTI*, he emphasizes that "*derselbe* Feuersturm riß Jud und Christ in den Tod" (330, emphasis added).[25] When Klemperer flees, he can take advantage of this collapse of the differences between people amidst the confusion of the bombardments. In his diary he reports the advice of a Jewish acquaintance during the attacks: "Ich müßte den Stern entfernen, so wie er den seinen schon abgemacht hätte. Darauf riß Eva mit einem Taschenmesserchen die Stella von meinem Mantel" (1945 37).[26] No longer marked as a Jew, Klemperer and his wife blend in with all the other refugees, allowing them to leave Dresden and to survive the war.

The destroyed Dresden, 1945. Reproduced with permission from Keystone Pressedienst, Germany.

Even though they save his life, the bombings are a painful event for Klemperer and one that he can barely describe. Despite their significance, both in terms of their horror and in terms of his chance to flee, his entry about them is

---

[25] "the same firestorm brought death to both Jews and Christians."

[26] "I should take off the star, just like he had taken his off already. Eva then took a small pocket knife and used it to rip off the stella from my coat."

only eleven pages long. This lack of detail, so unlike Klemperer's usual style, indicates how deep the traumatization still was one week after the events, when he wrote the text. Horrific details are suppressed, and are only allowed to enter the text in some altered form, such as the aestheticized depictions of human body parts that litter the streets. Reflection or analysis are still not possible at this point and the events can only be described in their fragmented form. The coping mechanisms Klemperer developed in order to survive the horror of what he was experiencing are still in place and mirrored in the text itself.

While Klemperer is unable to discuss the sheer horror of the experience in any detail, leaving the reader to fill the gaps, he does view this utter destruction of Dresden also as a point of departure for his self-perception. Ironically, when ripping off the hated star from his coat, Klemperer finally reaches the point when he truly succeeds in being just like everyone around him, in some sense fulfilling his dream of complete assimilation. Yet he finally admits to himself that the Germany of the past, the Germany of the poets and thinkers, which he looked up to and strove for all his life, was truly gone and would never return. The ideals with which he almost blindly identified, and which, in his view, had been perverted by the "un-German" Nazis, are now completely and finally destroyed for him just as the famous architecture of Dresden, so representative of these German virtues and culture, has gone up in flames all around him. Even though starless, and almost embarrassed, he now more openly accepts his Jewish background and expresses some satisfaction with the effects of the air raids: "Sooft ich an den Schutthaufen Zeughausstraße 1 und 3 dachte und denke, hatte und habe doch auch ich das atavistische Gefühl: Jahwe! Dort hat man in Dresden die Synagoge niedergebrannt" (1945 45).[27] February 13, 1945, the day of the destruction of Dresden, will thus always be for him both the day of freedom and just revenge, as well as his "dies ater" (LTI 314), or day of tragedy. On this day, a beloved city crumbled, and with it came down the last bastions of a belief system that he had so long embraced, but which was based on ideas he now realizes were long gone.

5.3   Wolf Biermann

Klemperer's, and to some degree also Schmidt's, ambivalent attitude towards Germany even under Nazi rule, which influenced their self-view and the way they perceived the world around them, does not form a part of all Jewish narratives about the air raids. The songwriter and poet Wolf Biermann, for example, who was only a small child when he experienced the Hamburg bomb-

---

[27] "Every time I think of the pile of rubble which was Zeughausstraße 1 and 3, I thought and think, I had and have the atavistic feeling: Jehovah! This is where they burnt down the synagogue in Dresden."

ings and came from a background differing extensively from that of Klemperer and Schmidt, approaches the events quite differently in his writing. Biermann is mainly known for his critical songs about the East German government, a state he had voluntarily moved to as a committed communist when he was seventeen years old in 1953. He involuntarily left when the state, eager to get rid of the voice that was so strongly questioning its authority, withdrew his citizenship in 1976 and would not let him return to the country after a concert tour in West Germany. Almost his entire artistic career has been filled with reflections on Communism and critical evaluation of the East German system. However, starting in the 1980s and particularly after reunification, Biermann, now turning his back on Communism, has begun to explore other, more personal topics as well, such as his Jewish roots and personal memories of his youth.

He was the child of two committed and politically active Communists, Emma and Dagobert Biermann.[28] In addition to his political convictions, Dagobert Biermann was Jewish. Imprisoned since 1937 for his Communist activities, he was finally sent to Auschwitz in 1943 where he was killed in the same year. Overall, more than twenty members of Wolf Biermann's relatives on his father's side, among them his grand-parents, were victims of the Holocaust. Biermann's family thus suffered greatly under National Socialism, and he himself continuously lived under the double threat of his parents' known Communist convictions and his status as a 'half-Jew.' As Biermann describes it in his own words: "Als Mischling ersten Grades wäre ich nach dem Fahrplan der Rassengesetze etwa 1946 an der Reihe gewesen" (*Gedichte* 180).[29] It is no surprise that Biermann, when reflecting on the war, clearly sees its end and everything that contributed to it as victory and liberation, not as a German defeat (*Gedichte* 179, 186).

However, while the war was going on, Biermann was too young to understand the danger he was in because of his background and to reflect on his position. Instead, he was more influenced by his immediate experiences. One memory that Biermann will never forget was the bombing of Hamburg in 1943 which he witnessed when he was only six years old and which he wrote about in his poetry collection of 1995. While his mother is happy about the English bombers over Hamburg even though they also threaten their lives (a situation that Biermann calls a "Komplizierte private Interessenlage im historischen Kuddelmuddel" (*Gedichte* 180)),[30] Biermann emphasizes about himself the more direct and unreflected reaction of the child: "Ich verstand nichts im Luftschutzkeller, außer Luftholen und Mamas Hand" (*Gedichte* 180).[31] "Operation Gomorrah," as

---

[28] His political background is even reflected in his name. Biermann's first name is actually Karl-Wolf, after the Communist Karl Wolf who had been put to death in 1932 (Rosellini 11).

[29] "According to the (train)schedule of the Race Laws, as a mixed child of the first degree my turn would have come around 1946."

[30] (. . . a "complicated private conflict of interest in a historical hodgepodge")

the Royal Air Force called their devastating attack on Hamburg in July 1943, in which Biermann, after a horrifying flight, survived by holding on to his mother's back when she swam to safety through the canal, is thus indelibly burnt into Biermann's memory (*Gedichte* 180).

When the six year old finds himself in the middle of the bombs, they are not signs of the abstract concept of future freedom, but what he experiences, "[d]as ist der Tod."[32] It is the leimotif of his narrative and appears over and over again in the text. He describes how he increasingly moves into a deathlike state with the horror of the events killing any emotional reaction. It is a night in which no child cries or complains any longer (*Gedichte* 181), instead they are numbed by the inferno they see around them. He deals with the events through derealization: "Die blauen Flämmchen. Das geht uns nichts an" (*Gedichte* 183).[33] Biermann depicts himself as almost fatalistic in his outlook. When he loses his mother in the chaos, he only feels panic for a short moment:

Jetzt wieder durch eine Feuerwand! Und die Hand weggerissen. Mama, Mama. Die Leute schieben und stoßen und trampeln nieder, Mama. Ich bin allein auffer Welt. Die Menschen brüllen. Das ist der Tod. Ich stand ruhig am Rand des Getümmels mit meinem Eimerchen. Es war ja keine Gefahr mehr, es war das Ende. (*Gedichte* 182)[34]

Through the courageousness of his mother, Biermann survives, but the trauma he lived through became a lasting memory for him. Just as Borchert does, Biermann uses the image of the stopped clock to describe how the bombing of Hamburg had a strong psychological effect on him:

Es gibt ein tolles Foto vom ausgeglühten Gehäuse einer Taschenuhr in Hiroshima. Die Zeiger der Uhr sind im Zeitpunkt der Explosion auf dem Zifferblatt festgeschmolzen. Seit ich dieses Bild sah, wußte ich, daß die kleine Lebensuhr in meinem Rippenkäfig auch festgebrannt ist, sie ist stehengeblieben im Feuergebläse dieser einen Nacht. Sechseinhalb Jahre war ich damals, und so alt blieb ich mein Leben lang. Ich bin ein graugewordenes Kind [...]. (*Gedichte* 180-181)[35]

---

[31] "I didn't understand anything in the air raid cellar, except to keep breathing and Mama's hand."

[32] "[t]his is death"

[33] "The small blue flames. They don't concern us."

[34] "Now again through a firewall! And the hand is ripped away. Mama, Mama. The people push and shove and trample one down, Mama. I am alone in this world. The people are screaming. This is death. I stood there quietly at the side with my bucket, away from the crowd. After all, there was no danger any more, it was the end."

[35] "There is a great picture of a burnt out casing of a pocket watch in Hiroshima. The hands of the watch melted onto the dial at the time of the explosion. Ever since I have seen this picture, I have known that my small life clock in my ribcage has also melted down, it stopped in the firestorm of this one night. I was six and a half years old back then and that's how old I stayed for the rest of my life. I am a child turned gray."

Yet when one looks for literary depictions of the bombings in his poems and songs, one will be disappointed, for there are few. While his own experiences of the Hamburg air raids were clearly traumatizing, they are largely absent from the literary texts and only allowed to surface in more detail in the afterword to his *Gedichte* collection of 1995. Only here can the reader gain some understanding of the full extent of the powerful impression the air raids have left on Biermann. Yet Biermann never lets his audience get beyond a mere hunch: "Die Erinnerung an dieses Inferno ist mir eingebrannt wie nichts sonst. Alles vorher, alles nachher habe ich vergessen, aber über diesen Brand könnte ich einen Roman schreiben, wenn ich Romane schreiben könnte" (*Gedichte* 180).[36] Even though Biermann blames his inability to produce prose for his failure to write down his memories, the well-written, powerful account of his experiences suggests that it is not necessarily the author's limited skills, but rather the topic itself that makes writing the novel about the bombing of Hamburg impossible. Dieter Forte suspects that it is the psychological power of the events that keeps him from writing such a text: "Er könnte schon. Er muß wollen, er muß sich das antun, über einige Jahre. Er verfügt schon über die sprachlichen Mittel. Aber ich glaube, daß er Angst hat, sich dem auszusetzen, das noch einmal alles zu beschreiben. Das verstehe ich" (*Schweigen oder sprechen* 67).[37] While Forte is correct to point to the psychological toll it takes to immerse oneself again in one's memories of horror, the pain of which he is acutely aware from his own experience, Biermann's veiled refusal to write in depth about the bombings is also caused by additional pressures. The conflict between staying silent and telling, which characterizes many works about the bombings, is intensified in Biermann's case because of his unusual background. Biermann's choice not to speak appears deliberate and politically motivated.

Biermann's ideas about the function of art and writing, which also mark his choice of subject matter for his texts, confirm this assessment. "No, I don't write because I write" (Raddatz 51), Biermann states in an interview, embracing the concept that literature is not just produced for its own sake. Instead, it has to be written with an audience in mind, it should cause an effect and include a message. This is why for Biermann it is impossible to separate the political figure from the writer and at the same time to distinguish between the private and the public person. (*NZZ* 18). It is thus not surprising that Biermann hardly writes about the bombings even though they have been such an important event in his life. He clearly does not want to offer material that could give some the impression that one tragic event can relativize, or even erase, another. In a lecture, when

---

[36] "The memory of this inferno is burnt into me like nothing else. Everything before, everything after, I have forgotten, but about this fire I could write a novel, if I was capable of writing novels."

[37] "He could. He must want to do it, he has to do this to himself, for a few years. He already has the literary skills. However, I think that – and I forgive him for this – he is scared to expose himself to this, to describe all of this again. I understand that."

talking about Stalin and his crimes, particularly also about the Russian leader's recently discovered plans to eradicate the Jews in the Soviet Union, Biermann describes how problematic it is for him to discuss or write about terrible crimes other than those committed by the Nazis :

> Mich lähmt ein doppeltes Entsetzen. Diese Neuigkeit aus der Geschichte der Juden-verfolgung macht einen Riß durch mein Gewissen. Ich füttere mit solchen Fakten ja auch das gefräßige Monster der Selbstgerechtigkeit in manchem deutschen Rip-penkäfig. Na siehste, höre ich Hitlers Erbgemeinschaft tönen, unser Führer war gar nicht so einmalig schlimm. Mit der Zeit verschwimmen die historischen Konturen. In solch einem Geschichtsbild ebnen die Gipfel der Barbarei sich gegenseitig ein, Buchenwald und Dresden, Treblinka und My-Lai, Judenmord und Indianermassaker, Auschwitz und Archipel Gulag. Aber in Wahrheit ebnet sich gar nichts ein. Wer ein patriotischer Deutscher sein will und einen Rest nationaler Würde hat, der wird sich lieber an das Brechtwort halten: 'Mögen andere von ihrer Schande reden, ich rede von der meinen.' (*Verse und Lieder* 18-19)[38]

These feelings explain why, when Biermann does write about the bombings in 1988, he embeds his own memories in a depiction of the German air raid flown against Rotterdam in 1940:

> Jan Gat unterm Himmel in Rotterdam[39]
> 1
> Und als der Krieg noch jung und frech
> Und blitzkriegefröhlich war
> Da brach die Wehrmacht in Holland ein
> Das war im Vierziger Jahr
> Ein Bombengeschwader hat über Nacht
> halb Rotterdam ausradiert
> Das Feuer leckte die Holzhäuser weg
> – dem Hafen is nix passiert
> [...]

---

[38] "I am paralyzed by a double horror. This news about the history of Jewish persecution causes a rip right through my conscience. After all, with these facts I also feed the hungry monster of self-righteousness in some German ribcages. Well, there you have it, I hear Hitler's community of heirs boast, our Führer wasn't the only bad guy. With time, historical outlines become fuzzy. In this type of historical understanding, the peaks of barbarism are leveled to the same height by each other, Buchenwald and Dresden, Treblinka and My-Lai, murder of the Jews and massacre of the Native-Americans, Auschwitz and Gulag Archipelago. But in reality nothing is on the same level. Whoever wants to be a patriotic German and has left any sense of national dignity, will instead embrace Brecht's words: 'May others speak of their shame, I will speak of mine.' "

[39] Jan Gat refers to the memorial "The Destroyed City" which was created by the Russian-Jewish artist Ossip Zadkine and which was supposed to commemorate the air raid flown by Hitler's air force in 1940 against the city. The bronze figure stretches his hands out towards the sky and has, where his heart would be, a big hole. This is why the people in Rotterdam call the statue Jan Gat, or in English: John Hole (*Lieder* 397).

5
Jan Gat, ich kenne die alte Furcht
ich komm ja aus Hamburg her
Da bin ich gekrallt an meine Mama
Geflüchtet durchs Flammenmeer
In Hammerbrook durch den Kanal
So sind wir ins Freie geschwommen
Durchs Fegefeuer der Bombennacht
– so sind wir dem Tod entkommen
6
Und weil ich unter dem Gelben Stern
In Deutschland geboren bin
Drum nahmen wir die englischen Bomber
wie Himmelsgeschenke hin
[...] (*Lieder* 395-396)[40]

By making the Rotterdam raids the topic of the song, Biermann hopes to challenge the perspective that the bombings were only a war strategy solely of the Allies, used to target Germans. While all air raids are horrible and frightening when one is on the ground, no matter who sits in the cockpits of the planes, it was again Germany which had started using the tactic of large area bombings, delighting in their effects despite the civilian casualties involved. Biermann emphasizes that Germans are responsible for introducing this tactic into the war as well as for the war as a whole. The bombings of German cities were thus a direct consequence of the country's acts and crimes. He also ensures that his writings cannot be misused by Germans to understand them solely as confirmation of their own suffering during the bombings, but rather forces the reader to place the events in a historical context. Biermann, himself constantly threatened by death not only during the raid but during the whole Nazi era, consciously identifies with other victims of the war, the people of Rotterdam. Air raids on German cities are clearly marked as signs of freedom, and the end of the war as "presents from heaven." Interestingly, while in the afterword of the *Gedichte* collection a few years later he distinguishes between his mother's reaction to the bombings and his perspective of sheer fear as a child, here he includes himself in the happiness surrounding the attacks: "Drum nahmen *wir* die englischen Bomben/Wie Himmelsgeschenke hin" (emphasis added). This is not, like the narrative in the afterword, written from the perspective of a child, but it is Biermann the adult

---

[40] "(1) When the war was still young and fresh/And happy in its Blitz/The Wehrmacht broke into Holland/That happened in the year forty/A bombing squadron has overnight/Eradicated half of Rotterdam/The fire consumed the wooden houses/ – the port remained untouched/[...]
(5) Jan Gat, I know the old fear/I am from Hamburg, you know/There, holding on tight to my mom,/I escaped through the sea of flames/In Hammerbrook through the channel/That's how we swam away/Through the purgatory of the night of bombs/ – that's how we escaped death
(6) And because it was under the Yellow Star/That I was born in Germany/That's why we accepted the English bombs/Like presents from heaven/[...]"

reflecting about his past and making the decision to emphasize the horror caused by Germany, not only as being worse than that produced by the war tactics of the Allies, but as being the true reason for any suffering.

Five years later, in 1993, shortly before the publication of his *Gedichte* collection, the bombings are allowed to surface once again in Biermann's work in several stanzas of the poem "Die Elbe bei Hamburg" ("The Elbe in Hamburg"), placed as the last text in the anthology, directly before the afterword. In this poem, Biermann gives more insight into his personal experience and the meaning it has for him:

> In Hammerbrook erzähln die Trümmer unter dem Asphalt
> Vom Bombenteppich, Wasser brannte in dem Feuersturm
> Der Tod kam über uns mit menschgemachter Urgewalt
> Aus diesem Weltende kroch ich raus, ein Menschenwurm
>
> In jener Nacht fiel Schwefel aus den Himmeln in das Fleet
> Drei Männer brannten vor mir wie Heil-Hitler-Fackeln ab
> Das Dach von der Fabrik flog durch die Luft wie ein Komet
> Die Toten alle kleingebrannt fürs enge Massengrab
>
> So kam es, daß die helle Nacht auch noch den Tag verschlang
> Am Mittag konnte ich im Qualm gar keine Sonne sehn
> Ich hatte Glück und ward ein braves Kind mein Leben lang
> Genau auf sechseinhalb blieb meine Lebensuhr da stehn
>
> Seit jenem Tag hat mir der Glücksgott meinen Stern bewahrt
> Doch blieb ich immer, in der Liebe wie im Haß, verflucht
> Durch allen Wandel bin und bleib ich auch mit weißem Bart
> Gebranntes Kind, das neugierselig nach dem Feuer sucht
> (*Gedichte* 156-157)[41]

The poem indicates the horror of the events which, although they are created by humans, seem beyond human grasp. The air raid is an experience of primal apocalyptic force, under which the world is coming to an end through fire and brimstone. The natural order is severely disturbed and unpredictable: It rains sulphur from the skies, water catches on fire, the night is full of light from the

---

[41] "In Hammerbrook, the rubble underneath the asphalt/tells the story of the carpet bombing, the firestorm in which water was burning/Death came upon us with human-made elemental force/I crawled out from there, a little mite, when the world was coming to an end//During that night, brimstone fell from the sky into the loading channel/Three men were burnt down like Heil-Hitler torches in front of me/The roof of the factory flew through the air like a comet/The dead were all burned to tiny corpses for the tight mass graves//That's why this light night also swallowed up the day/At noon one could not see the sun because of all the smoke/I was lucky and was a good child all my life/At exactly six and a half my life-clock stopped//Since that day the God of Luck has kept my star/But I will always be cursed, in love as well as hatred/Through all change, and I stay so even with a white beard/a marked child, burnt, who, in curious bliss, searches for fire"

flames, while the day is dark with smoke. Biermann emphasizes twice that the only thing that prevented his death in this inferno was chance, but it did not save him from being permanently marked by the experience. Similar to Hans Erich Nossack, who talks about reaching an important turning point through the bombs, the survival is also a rebirth for Biermann, influencing him for the rest of his life. The price for survival is the burden of heightened responsibility, which continually forces him "to search for fire," to travel more difficult and controversial roads, even if they can lead to painful consequences.

However, when Biermann perceives himself as marked (by fire) it is not only because of his Hamburg experience. He recently elaborated more on his special position and this image, describing himself as "ein von Anfang an gebranntes Kind. In meiner Brust schlägt nun mal das verbrannte Herz meines Vaters. Außerdem war ich mit meinem eigenen kleinen Hintern durch das Höllenfeuer von Hammerbrook gerannt, 1943, als Hamburg im Feuersturm unter dem englischen Bomberteppich lag" (*Verse und Lieder* 29).[42] Both experiences, that of persecution and that of the bombings, are the most formative events for Biermann's view of the world. Yet while both affected him deeply, Biermann made a conscious choice of which one to emphasize. His loyalty lies with his father, and writing and living for Biermann is always also a fight against his father's death, the murder he cannot and will not accept for the rest of his life (Trende and Biermann 32-33). His poems and songs are consequently also works against forgetting of the German Nazi past and the terrible crimes committed under National Socialism. As he writes in the poem "Vom Lesen in den Innereien" ("Reading in Innards"):

verwelkt ist die blume vergissmeinnicht
fürs ganz große morden geht kein gericht
die Deutschen haben den Juden verziehn
– und bloß den Zigeunern noch nicht
wo alles grölt vor lachen, da kann
ich nichts als traurige lieder singen
[…]
i'm on my way
und komm schon von weiter her

in seinen verwehten fußstapfen nicht –
ich lauf ja mit meines vaters füßen
und weil er kein grab hat, treibts mich hier um
(*Gedichte* 122–123)[43]

---

[42] "a child marked from the start by fire. In my chest there beats the burnt heart of my father. In addition, I ran with my own small behind through the hellish fires of Hammerbrook, in 1943, when Hamburg lay in a firestorm from English carpet bombing."

[43] "the flower forget-me-not has wilted/for killing on a large scale there is no trial/the Germans have forgiven the Jews/ – just not yet the Gypsies/where everyone screams with laughter, i can

Biermann thus solves this private conflict of experiences by making a political choice; while the bombings have scarred him for life, the only way to deal with this trauma is to fight with the pen against all those who suppress and persecute and who bear ultimate responsibility for these events. The bombings thus cannot necessarily play a central role in his oeuvre. When they do come up, they have to be countered. In "Jan Gat unterm Himmel in Rotterdam" this is done by emphasizing the air raids flown by Germans, in "Die Elbe bei Hamburg" by alluding to the responsibility of the Nazi regime for the deadly events when comparing three men on fire to Heil-Hitler-torches and by mentioning Jewish persecution. Even in the afterword of the *Gedichte* collection, where Biermann so movingly narrates his experience among the bombs in Hamburg, he makes sure to point to the true causalities of the war. Consequently, he ends the story of the Hamburg attacks not with the horror of the bombings, but with the horror of the Nazi crimes: "Nun lagerten wir also mit den Überlebenden auf genau derselben Moorweide am Bahnhof Dammtor, wo sich zwei Jahre vorher die Hamburger Juden hatten sammeln müssen für den Abtransport nach Minsk. Das war der sichere Tod" (*Gedichte* 185).[44] While he experienced the bombing of Hamburg as "death," Biermann did survive his flight from the flames and did survive the war. Victims of Nazi persecution, however, he points out, were almost never so lucky. Their horror was "certain death" and the author wants to make sure that this fact is never forgotten.

5.4   Günter Kunert

Another witness to the bombings who shares a similar background and intention to Biermann is the poet Günter Kunert. Kunert was born in 1929 in Berlin. Since his mother was Jewish, Kunert's childhood was marked by anti-Semitism directed against his family, their relatives, and friends, and he remembers vividly how most of them were deported and killed. The experiences of alienation, loneliness, and death, which he was subjected to because of his Jewish background, feature as a definite undercurrent in his writing. The suffering of Jews under National Socialism is one of the central underlying concerns of his texts and repeatedly becomes the subject of an emphatic reconstruction in language, through which Kunert visits the places of torture and death he himself was spared (Heidelberger-Leonard 252). The feeling of homelessness, and exclusion, the estrangement from society, which Kunert experienced from early on, was further

do nothing but sing sad songs/[...]/i'm on my way/and i come from far away//not in his footsteps that have been blown away –/i walk with my father's feet/and since he does not have a grave, i am restless"

[44] "Where we were then lying with other survivors was exactly the same swampy pasture at the Dammtor train station, where two years earlier the Jews of Hamburg had to gather for their transport to Minsk. That was certain death."

fostered after the Third Reich by his position in East Germany, a country for which he at first had high hopes, but then grew increasingly disappointed. Criticized for his work, he had difficulty publishing in the GDR and finally had to leave the country in the aftermath of the Biermann expulsion when he joined other authors in signing a letter protesting the government's step.

Living in Berlin during the war, Kunert was also a witness to the repeated heavy bombings and destruction of the capital. One can assume that these experiences in the rubble-city both during and after the war were necessarily also formative for the poet and probably influence the repeated use of metaphors and symbols surrounding ruins, stones, and apocalyptic visions in his works. Yet Kunert talks very little directly about the bombings and it is clearly rather the deeply engrained trauma of Jewish persecution and its consequence of feeling pushed into an outsider position which informs Kunert's world view. It is thus not surprising that the ambivalence about the bombings, which was already visible in Schmidt, Klemperer, and Biermann, also shows itself in Kunert's texts.

Kunert, in contrast to Biermann, has expressed repeatedly that he does not see writing as a political act and that literature should be free of moral or didactic purposes (*Vor der Sintflut* 24). However, in one of his early and most famous poems "Über einige Davongekommene" ("About Some Who Got Away"), in which rubble features prominently, Kunert definitely displays a different kind of understanding of literature.[45] In this poem, the sobering effect of the vast destruction on the people who lived through the air war is challenged through irony. The title points to the survival of a disaster, but in a second meaning also to the possibility of having got away with something, of having escaped a punishment one deserved. In the main part of the poem, this double meaning is explored further:

Als der Mensch
unter den Trümmern
seines
bombardierten Hauses
hervorgezogen wurde,
schüttelte er sich
und sagte:
Nie wieder.

Jedenfalls nicht gleich.
(*Gedichte* 3)[46]

After the war, Germans face a world in ruins, everything around them and everything they believe in is shattered. As the use of the passive voice indicates, they

---

[45] One should mention that at this point in his career Kunert still believed in the possible success of the East German system.

[46] "When man/was pulled out/from underneath the rubble/of his/bombed house/he shook his body/and said:/Never again.//At least not right now."

can only survive and overcome this state with the help of others, incapable of escaping from their situation themselves. By shaking off the dust of the rubble, they also rid themselves of their false hopes and expectations, expressing their new insight gained from their experience with the typical "Never again" of the postwar years. However, the afterthought Kunert adds to the poem, the ironic "At least not right now," indicates Kunert's skepticism about this formulaic expression. He doubts the ability of the German population to learn from their misfortune and to understand truly the connection between German crimes and the destruction of their country. He thus questions and warns of such collective demonstrations of insight through catch phrases instead of actual change.

Still, although Kunert does not believe that they should be misused as signs for a German learning process, he is aware of the strong and lasting traumatizing effects the bombings have had on the population:[47]

> Die Sonne scheint. Aus den Fenstern
>
> Des neuen Hauses schauen die Frauen
> Auf spielende Kinder. Über den
> Himmel fliegt ein Flugzeug, über
> Die Gesichter zieht ein Schatten.
> Sie erinnern sich.
> (*Unter diesem Himmel* 36)[48]

New houses cover up the recent destruction and an idyllic scene of happy family life is portrayed. The sun is shining, and mothers observe their children playing. However, the memory of the war cannot be easily covered up completely, and a simple event such as a plane flying overhead can stir up the unpleasant past. So, like a shadow, the past lies over the population despite their efforts to banish it from their lives. The narrator of the poem, however, just as in "Über einige Davongekommene," takes a distant position. He is an outside observer and does not include himself in the scene.

Kunert talks in more detail about his own experiences during the air war much later, namely in his post-unification autobiography *Erwachsenenspiele* (*Adult Games*) from 1997. Of all authors, he most radically emphasizes the

---

[47] This poem is part of Kunert's second poetry volume from 1955, *Unter diesem Himmel* (*Underneath this Sky*). Jay Julian Rosellini has pointed out that this text is actually a rewriting of the 1953 Brecht poem "Der Himmel dieses Sommers" ("This Summer's Sky"). Even though it was only published in 1965, Kunert probably had access to the unpublished manuscript: "Hoch über dem See fliegt ein Bomber./Von den Ruderbooten auf/Schauen Kinder, Frauen, ein Greis. Von weitem/Gleichen sie jungen Staren, die Schnäbel aufreißend/Der Nahrung entgegen." ("High/above the lake flies a bomber./From the row boats/children, women, an old man look up. From far away/They resemble young starlings, opening their beaks/Towards their food.") (269-270).

[48] "The sun is shining. Out of the windows//Of the new house women gaze/Onto playing children./Across the/Sky flies an airplane, across/Their faces goes a shadow/They remember."

bombings as signs of freedom in his text, nearly dismissing their danger and traumatizing force. Kunert presents the air raids almost exclusively through the eyes of the teenage boy that he was during the war, who strongly identifies with the pilots as liberators:

> Welch ein Schauspiel! Und ich selber habe ja nichts zu befürchten, dessen bin ich mir ganz sicher. Auf mich haben die da oben es nicht abgesehen. Im Gegenteil. Was sie aus ihren Maschinen über den Dächern abladen, gilt nicht mir und kann mich somit auch nicht treffen. Ich unterliege ja nicht dem Strafgericht. Gemeint sind die anderen, denen damit die ausgleichende Gerechtigkeit widerfährt. (46)[49]

Bombs falling over Berlin, 1944. Reproduced with permission from Keystone Pressedienst, Germany.

Even though naive, during the war, under the constant double threat of persecution and bombing death, only such attitude can keep Kunert from complete despair. The idea of being "bombensicher" (46), of being completely safe from the bombs, gives Kunert the security he needs to survive, the hope of an end to

---

[49] "What a drama! And I do not have to fear anything, I am sure of it. The ones up there are not aiming at me. On the contrary. Whatever they unload from their machines over the roofs is not meant for me and thus cannot hurt me. I am not on trial after all. This is for the others; it is poetic justice."

a world where he or his mother could be picked up, deported, and killed at any moment. This way of distancing himself emotionally from the danger is made easier by the dulling effect which he describes setting in when the bombing experience becomes an almost daily routine, an effect, of course, that he shares with many who live through traumatic events. When he sees a dead air raid victim for the first time, he is overwhelmed and shocked by the sight, despite his repeatedly stated belief that the bombings are a just revenge (45). Yet when the air war continues, shock turns to habit (45) and it becomes easier for him to hold on to his view of the deaths as deserved punishment.

However, Kunert experiences almost every day how fragile a construct his position is and how easily it can be shattered by the bombs. Repeatedly, his family suffers from the attacks. In one of the first raids, a bomb falls onto and destroys the house in which his father usually works, while all the other houses in the same street remain unharmed (43-44). Similarly, during a later attack, the Kunert family is the only one whose apartment receives such extreme damage that they have to move out (61). There are only so many times Kunert can tell himself that this is the consequence of a navigational mistake and does not really pose a danger to him or his family. After a particularly severe daytime raid, his father does not return home on time and is feared dead. If his father as the only non-Jew of the family were killed, it would mean both his mother's and his own certain death. It is at these moments that the indiscriminatory danger of the bombs and the fear of them is finally allowed to rise to the surface for short moments. At one point Kunert refers to the bombing of their apartment as the point where his childhood came to an end:

> Nach Tagesangriffen [. . .] strolche ich umher. Oftmals enden meine Inspektionsgänge vor unserem Wohnhaus in der Köpernicker Straße, aus dem wir als einzige, als sei es beabsichtigt gewesen, verbannt worden sind. Ans Geländer gedrückt, schleiche ich die Treppen hinauf, löse den Drahtverschluß und betrete meine kürzlich abrupt abgebrochene Kindheit. Über die Verwüstung hat sich eine Staubschicht gelegt. Bücher, von Regenwasser verquollen, machen einen befremdlichen Eindruck – als hätten sie mir niemals gehört. (64)[50]

However, these moments are rare and Kunert keeps up an almost entirely light-hearted, satirical tone, particularly with respect to the bombings.

Today, Kunert is of course aware of the naivete of this approach and at one point qualifies his perspective:

---

[50] "After daylight attacks, [. . .] I stroll around. My inspection-tours often take me to our apartment house in the Köpernicker Street, from which we had been the only ones banished, as if it had been on purpose. Pressed to the railing, I slip upstairs, loosen the wire that holds the door closed and step into my childhood, which had shortly before been abruptly terminated. The devastation caused by the bombs is now covered with dust. Books, damaged by rain water, leave a strange impression – as if they had never belonged to me."

Ich bin ein Nachfahre des Simplicius Simplicissimus. Einer, der dank seiner überwäl-
tigenden Naivität fast unangefochten durch die Schrecken und Scheußlichkeiten prak-
tizierter Historie schlendert. Ein Seiltänzer auf brüchiger Trosse. Reichlich Gelegen-
heiten abzustürzen. (57)[51]

Kunert here not only describes his situation during the Nazi era, but also his
position today when he writes down his memories over fifty years after the war
is over. Going back to the past and exploring a time characterized by the threat
of death and the loss of many family members, is a painful act. He is depicting
a childhood and youth he actually never had. While he reveals in one passage
that the destruction of his house and his possessions was the end of his childhood, the title *Erwachsenenspiele* suggests that Kunert wants to emphasize that
it actually ended much earlier. When he visits the concentration camp Theresienstadt many years after the war, he finds the name Ilse Grünova among a list
of people who were executed there. Ilse Grün had been a cousin of his mother,
and seeing her name Kunert remembers: "Habe ich nicht sogar mit Ilse nach
den Klängen einer Schallplatte getanzt, weil in jüdischen Familien die Kinder in
die 'Erwachsenenspiele' miteinbezogen werden?" (50).[52] In fact, Kunert hardly
has any childhood, but very early on he is forced to become an adult because
of the constant threat of the Nazi era. Despite the title, the situation is clearly
not a game, but instead becomes a deadly reality, a daily dance with death. The
only way that Kunert can directly deal with the horror and pain of this past, and
maybe with his survival while so many others died, is by describing it in a play-
ful manner. Through the techniques of the picaresque novel, which also fits his
position as an outsider and observer, Kunert can reflect the horror of the times
through a satiric tone which creates the emotional distance from the events he
needs. By putting himself in the tradition of Grimmelshausen and his *Simplicissimus*, the quintessential German example for describing the horrors of war
through the picaresque lens, he hopes to avoid falling into the abyss of despair
that lurks to the left and right of his path.

Consequently, his youth during the Nazi era appears almost like a series of
adventures in the text. War, according to Kunert, is an exhausting affair (83),
characterized by the bombs, illegal underage visits to movie theaters, high cigarette consumption, first sexual encounters, and first drinking experiences. Even
when he speaks about the plight of the Jewish population and his relatives, he
tries to keep up the satirical element. In one instance, he describes the deportation of his grandfather as "abgereist worden" (48).[53] In another episode, he

---

[51] "I am a descendant of Simplicius Simplicissimus. One who, thanks to his extreme naivete, strolls
almost untouched through the horror and ugliness of practiced history. A tight-rope walker on a
brittle rope. Many opportunities to fall."

[52] "Did I not even dance with Ilse to the sounds of a record, since Jewish families include their
children in 'adult games'? "

[53] "being departed"

humorously illustrates the overnight stay of a Jewish family who has gone into hiding, which is complicated because of the enormous bodily proportions of a family member (50). However, concerning Jewish persecution, and particularly memories of relatives, Kunert's emotional defense through satire repeatedly breaks down. These are similar moments to those when the deadly nature of the bombings shows through, but their intensity and despair is much increased and the deep trauma of his experience is allowed to emerge. When he takes a last walk with his uncle, who has been ordered to report to the Gestapo, the haunting quality of this part of Kunert's past is revealed:

> Unabänderlich und so, als sei es gestern vormittag gewesen, spaziere ich an der Seite meines Onkels. [...] Das ist der letzte gemeinsame Gang mit meinem Onkel durch das zerfallende Berlin. Das letzte Mal, daß ich ihn sehe, innerhalb der sterblichen Wirklichkeit. Doch mein Gedächtnis wiederholt die Sequenz wie eine filmische Endlosschleife. [...] [Der Onkel und seine Ehefrau] verschwinden mit "Welle 47, 33. Osttransport v. 3.3.43" aus meinem und ihrem Leben. Sie lassen ein zartes Abbild im Kopf eines Knaben zurück, der drei Tage nach ihrem Abtransport seinen vierzehnten Geburtstag begehen soll. (47-48)[54]

Unlike the victims of the air war, who remain abstract and to whom Kunert lightly refers as "Ex-Erdenbürger" (47),[55] these dead have faces which live on in Kunert's memory all his life. The lasting image of despair about the Third Reich that burns itself into the reader is one of Kunert's mother after the war:

> Sobald sie daheim ist, bezieht sie Posten auf dem Balkon, um stundenlang die Straße hinauf- und hinunterzuschauen. Sie wartet auf Angehörige. Auf ihren Vater, ob er, den Rucksack auf dem Rücken, den Homburger auf dem weißen Haar, nicht von seinem Aufenthalt in Theresienstadt zurückkommt. Der Bruder, die Schwägerin, die Cousinen und Cousins, Verwandte und Bekannte, ach, irgendwer, so glaubt sie, muß doch auftauchen. Ein Glaube, trotz der Zeitungsfotos von den Leichenbergen, trotz der Berichte und Aussagen Überlebender im Funk, trotz der Dokumente, trotz des "Nürnberger Prozesses", trotz der Wochenschaubilder in den Kinos. Aber wir reden nie davon. (97)[56]

---

[54] "Ever unchanging, and so as if it had happened yesterday morning, I walk with my uncle. [...] This is the last walk with my uncle through Berlin in ruins. The last time that I see him within mortal reality. But my memory repeats the sequence like an infinite loop. [...] [The uncle and his wife] disappear from my life and their lives with 'Wave 47, 33rd Transport to the East at 3/3/43' They leave behind a frail picture in the head of a young boy, who three days after the deportation is supposed to celebrate his fourteenth birthday."

[55] "ex-mortals"

[56] "As soon as she gets home, she takes her position on the balcony to look up and down the street for hours. She is waiting for her relatives. For her father, to see if he, with his backpack over his shoulders and the Homburg on his white hair, won't return from his stay in Theresienstadt. The brother, the sister-in-law, the cousins, relatives and friends; someone, she believes, must come back. A belief despite the newspaper pictures of piles of corpses, despite the reports and accounts of survivors on the radio, depite the documents, despite the 'Nurenberg Trials,' despite the pictures shown in the newsreels in the movie theaters. But we never talk about it."

Haunted by these silent memories Kunert, like Biermann, thus makes a choice to minimize the danger of the bombings in his text in favor of emphasizing what he considers the true tragedy, the horror of the persecution under National Socialism. Consequently, after reunification, Kunert and Biermann, who earlier could not see eye to eye about literature, actually come closer together. Biermann, with the final disappearance of the GDR, gains some critical distance from his political convictions as well as from his didactic poetic goals. Instead, he starts to explore more personal issues, such as his Jewish background or his experience of the Hamburg firestorm. In *Erwachsenenspiele*, Kunert sets aside his idea of the freedom of literature from educational purposes and, even more than Biermann, stresses German guilt and the role of the bombers as signs of freedom. Even though packaged in irony and satire, *Erwachsenenspiele* surely has a didactic purpose as well. With this text, Kunert connects back to his earlier, more political poems about the bombings.

So despite the vast differences in age, outlook on the world, and political convictions of Schmidt, Klemperer, Kunert, and Biermann, their similar situations under National Socialism led to a comparable representational response to the bombings. Just as with other German authors, they show to various degrees that the air war was horrific and deeply traumatizing, suggesting that no one seems to be able to escape such destruction without being scarred. However, they also emphasize the positive role of the bombs and the destruction they caused as signs of a coming breakdown of the Nazi regime, of their possible survival despite Hitler. Among other German authors, much of the hesitation to write about the air raids comes from the psychological pressure to suppress the trauma, but is also influenced by a combination of being afraid of external accusations of revisionism as well as personal shame and feelings of guilt about what occurred in Nazi Germany. Many of the narratives that do exist about the bombings are thus often somewhat helpless in depicting the interdependence of German crimes and the bombings. In contrast, the Jewish accounts manage to convey the close connection between German guilt and the air war, since they are written from the perspective of the double victim, the victim of the air raids, ultimately also caused by National Socialism, and of German persecution. While accounts such as Biermann's and Klemperer's also illustrate the same difficulty in writing about the trauma because of the tendency to suppress it, it is this very awareness of German guilt that leads particularly Kunert and Biermann, and possibly also Klemperer, to deemphasize the experience in their writing and instead to point to Jewish suffering.

Kunert and Biermann make active decisions about structure and content in their texts to reflect their convictions; in Schmidt and Klemperer's cases, it is less obvious. Schmidt chooses to let the facts speak for themselves as much as he can, almost never leaving his observer role, but citing extensively from letters and documents. When personal feelings break through, they reveal despair with the situation, seeing the bombings as well as persecution as consequences of Nazism. Klemperer, by not publishing his diaries, decided not to share his whole personal experience of the Nazi era with an audience, even though he had been planning the publication of his notes while he was writing them. Instead, he put together *LTI*, his reflections on the corruption of the German language by the Nazis in which he included some short passages from the diaries. There are several possible explanations for this decision. First, it seems that Klemperer, in accordance with his goal of becoming a professor again, did not want to be recognized for such a personal work, but rather for a more philological endeavor. In addition, it might have been easier for Klemperer to work through his trauma from the past twelve years through this more distanced scholarly approach than by having to review the daily entries of his personal reflections. The diaries also show how blind Klemperer was for a long time and how strongly he still believed in the "true Germany" and its values, even though the Germany of the Third Reich was against everything he idealized. Only towards the end of the war, when everything around him was breaking down, did Klemperer finally let go of his ideals. It seems plausible that Klemperer no longer wanted to face how misguided he was, nor how hurtful it was for him to let go of the values he had so fervently embraced but which had proved to be only illusions. He also did not want to share these misperceptions with the public.

Klemperer thus might at this point be engaged in blaming the victim, himself, for his lot, in feeling some shame for his decisions, even though rationally he understands that it was not his fault. Some of this survival guilt also appears to influence Kunert in his authorial decisions, when he almost completely denies the horror of the air war experience and the great danger the bombs were posing to him and his family. In the face of the suffering of his relatives, the dangers of the air raids necessarily have to be eclipsed and their positive symbolic value centralized as signs of liberation and freedom.

Biermann, younger than the other authors during the war, is not subject to the same self-torment as Klemperer and, to some extent, Kunert. For him, guilt questions are much more straightforward and are closely related to politics. However, in contrast to Kunert, he readily admits the horror of the air raids and that Germans might have suffered in the bombings as well. In fact, he relates the bombing of Hamburg as his most vivid memory of the war. Yet these events are only rarely a topic for his literature and at the most one for an afterword. In his literary production, Biermann tends to strive for more clear-cut messages. He thus consciously decides not to write about the German bombing experience because he wants to emphasize the victims of German aggression, even if this excludes some events which he understands as extremely influential in his own life. Although reunification brought change to Biermann's topics and convictions, opening up space for reflections on his own past, the topic of the air war remains marginalized. His goal is still to educate his audience with his texts about the suffering Germans caused during the Nazi era and this sense of a mission takes precedence over any representation of other personal experiences.

Chapter 6
International Reactions to the Bombings

The air war has not only been taken up by German writers. In particular, Dresden, which is often understood as the central symbol of the destructive powers of large-area bombings, has inspired authors from outside Germany to address the topic as well. While Kurt Vonnegut's *Slaughterhouse-Five* is the first to come to mind when thinking about literary depictions of the Dresden raids, there are also two other novel-length examples: Dutch author Harry Mulisch's *Het stenen bruidsbed* (*The Stone Bridal Bed*) and French writer Henri Coulonges' *L'Adieu à la femme sauvage* (*Farewell, Dresden*). Interestingly, even though non-German authors do not experience directly the consequences of personal shame about the Nazi past, or external pressures about collective German guilt, the texts still display similar concerns and characteristics to the German accounts. As in their German counterparts, these novels not only deal with the strong psychological effects of the bombings and the search for proper modes of representation of the events, but also with the issue of guilt. Nevertheless, their relationship to the material also differs. The choice of the novel as the form used to address the air raids is interesting, as this requires a more lengthy treatment of the events, and many Germans have shied away from it. The publication dates (Mulisch's work, for example, was published as early as 1959), also suggest that non-German writers might have been less inhibited in dealing with the sensitive and traumatizing topic than German writers generally were. This observation is shared by Günter Grass when questioned about the scarcity of German writing about the bombings: "Vielleicht ist es für ausländische Autoren, die das erlebt haben, leichter gewesen, das zum Thema zu nehmen" ("Interview" 65).[1]

6.1   Kurt Vonnegut

Kurt Vonnegut's *Slaughterhouse-Five* from 1969 is the most famous novel about the (Dresden) air raids and their effects. Similar to many of the German narratives, the work, which has been widely discussed as an anti-war novel, is

---

[1] "Maybe foreign authors who went through this had an easier time in turning this into a literary topic."

based on the author's own experiences in World War II. As a German POW, Vonnegut witnessed the bombing and complete destruction of Dresden, and *Slaughterhouse-Five* is the author's manifestation of what he called "a process of twenty years [...] of living with Dresden and the aftermath" (Allen 163). Indeed, the words that describe the war, the Dresden events, and their effect on the people who experienced them did not come easily to Vonnegut. In an interview in 1974, he commented on the difficulties of articulating his experiences: "I came home in 1945, started writing about it, and wrote about it, and *wrote about it*, and WROTE ABOUT IT" (Allen 163). This agony is echoed in the first chapter of the novel itself:

> When I got home from the Second World War twenty-three years ago, I thought it would be easy for me to write about the destruction of Dresden, since all I would have to do would be to report what I had seen [...].
> But not many words about Dresden came from my mind then. [...] And not many words come now, either [...].[2]

Vonnegut's problems with articulation are evidence of the long term consequences that the author suffered after witnessing the destruction of Dresden as a POW. However, while critics generally recognize that the war and particularly the destruction of Dresden had a traumatizing effect on Vonnegut, the nature of this trauma and how it manifests itself in the novel has yet to be explored in a more systematic manner. A fresh look at *Slaughterhouse-Five* using the psychiatric theory outlined in Chapter 2 not only offers new insight into the work, but also opens a window into the author himself. Vonnegut's writing of *Slaughterhouse-Five* can be seen as a therapeutic process that allows him to uncover and deal with his own internal trauma. By using creative means to overcome his own distress, Vonnegut makes it possible for us to trace his own path to recovery. We slowly narrow in on his condition using the novel as a conduit first to the protagonist Billy Pilgrim, then to the narrator, and finally to the author himself.

Lawrence Broer has suggested that "[p]robably no characters in contemporary fiction are more traumatized and emotionally damaged than those of Kurt Vonnegut" (3). Billy Pilgrim in *Slaughterhouse-Five* certainly confirms Broer's assumption. Even his wife Valencia, who is unaware of Billy's psychological turmoil, gets "a funny feeling" that he is "just full of secrets" (121). Attempting to define Billy's psychological state more precisely, literary scholars have frequently associated *Slaughterhouse-Five* and its protagonist with schizophrenia, assessments most likely inspired by the author's own comments on the title page characterizing the novel as "somewhat in the telegraphic schizophrenic manner of tales of the planet Tralfamadore."[3] Yet it seems that even some of the crit-

---

[2] Kurt Vonnegut, *Slaughterhouse-Five* (New York, Laurel, 1969) 2. Subsequent references appear parenthetically in the text.

ics who describe Billy as schizophrenic are uneasy with this assessment. In the introduction to a recent collection of essays on Vonnegut, for example, Harold Bloom qualifies his description of Billy as suffering from schizophrenia with the parenthetical comment: "(to call it that)" (1). Symptoms of schizophrenia have to be present for at least six months before the disease can be diagnosed and it is not caused by an external event. Schizophrenics usually suffer from auditory or visual hallucinations,[4] and from social and/or occupational dysfunction (DSM-IV-TR 299). These criteria simply do not apply to Billy's situation. He does not suffer from hallucinations or delusions. Furthermore, he manages to lead, at least externally, a very functional life after he returns home from the war, exemplified by having a family, running a business, and being a respected member of society. This would be atypical for someone suffering from schizophrenia. Rather, Billy's problems are directly related to his war experiences. His fantasies seem to be the result of memories of particularly traumatic events, and a vivid imagination which he employs as a 'sense-making' tool to deal with his war trauma.[5] In contrast to the limited insight into Billy's psyche that schizophrenia provides, his symptoms and various facets of his state of mind in the novel can be more satisfactorily explained applying the criteria of posttraumatic stress disorder.

The symptoms of PTSD can be moderated or exacerbated by the response of the environment to the individual. It has been noted that the "psychosocial atmosphere in a society is clearly a factor that facilitates or hinders the process of coping with stressful life events" (Kleber, Figley, and Gersons 2). When Billy returns home, America does not provide him with the possibility of working through the traumatizing nature of his war experiences, particularly the bombing of Dresden. For a long time, the Dresden raids and their consequences were not a topic of interest in the United States. In fact when Billy, long after the events, does speak out once about Dresden, he is immediately silenced with the 'official' position towards the Dresden bombings. After his plane crash, Billy shares a room in the hospital with a retired brigadier general in the Air Force Reserve, official Air Force historian, and Harvard professor Bertram Copeland Rumfoord, who is writing a book about air battles and bombings during World

---

[3] A few of the many examples include Leonard Mustazza in "Vonnegut's Tralfamadore and Milton's Eden" who refers to Billy as "schizophrenic" (302). Similarly, in *Sanity Plea*, Lawrence R. Broer characterizes Billy's state as "schizophrenic deterioration" (91) and in "*Slaughterhouse-Five* or, How to Storify an Atrocity," Peter Freese describes Billy's story as sounding "suspiciously like the biography of a man who develops schizophrenia" (212).

[4] Hallucination is defined as "a *sensory* perception that has the compelling sense of reality of a true perception but that occurs without external stimulation of the relevant sensory organ" (DSM-IV-TR 823, emphasis added).

[5] Billy's more externally observable erratic behavior after the plane crash and his wife's death by carbon-monoxide poisoning also does not comply with the criteria for the diagnosis of schizophrenia. Rather, it seems consistent with the consequences of a head trauma he might have suffered in the crash, possibly adding to Billy's traumatized state by worsening his psychic condition even further.

War II. When Billy tells his story, Rumfoord refuses to accept Billy's suffering and negates it by refocusing on the bombers rather than the bombed:

> "It had to be done," Rumfoord told Billy, speaking of the destruction of Dresden.
> "I know," said Billy.
> "That's war."
> "I know. I'm not complaining."
> "It must have been hell on the ground."
> "It was," said Billy Pilgrim.
> "Pity the men who had to *do* it." (198)

The long-term denial of the events and the lack of understanding about or acknowledgment of the suffering Billy endured, do not allow Billy the possibility of working through his experiences. He is supposed to go straight back to his prewar life, as if nothing has happened, which ultimately leads to Billy's chronic suffering.

The most striking symptom of Billy's condition is his altered perception of time. He sees himself as having "come unstuck in time" (23):

> Billy has gone to sleep a senile widower and awakened on his wedding day. He has walked through a door in 1955 and come out another one in 1941. He has gone back through that door to find himself in 1963. He has seen his birth and death many times, he says, and pays random visits to all the events in between.
> He says.
> Billy is spastic in time, has no control over where he is going next, and the trips aren't necessarily fun. (23)

Being "spastic in time," thus, is a metaphor for Billy repeatedly reexperiencing the traumatic events he went through in the war, particularly as a POW during the Dresden bombings. Psychologically, Billy has never fully left World War II, but instead, in Jerome Klinkowitz' words, he lives in a "continual present" (55). In *Trauma and Recovery*, Judith Herman describes a similar situation with regard to former captives suffering from PTSD. While imprisoned, they "are eventually reduced to living in an endless present" (89). Yet after their release or liberation, they "may give the appearance of returning to ordinary time, while psychologically remaining bound in the timelessness of the prison" (89). It has also been observed that a former prisoner "even years after liberation, [...] continues to practice doublethink and to exist simultaneously in two realities, two points in time" (Herman 89-90).

Billy's situation is comparable to that of the soldiers Herman describes. While "outwardly normal" (175), the traumatic memories persistently intrude into his thoughts in ways typical of people suffering from PTSD. Billy also finds himself at times at two different points of his life at the same time, for example "simultaneously on foot in Germany in 1944 and riding in his Cadillac in

Collapsed clock tower of the Dresden Frauenkirche. Reproduced with permission from Sächsische Landesbibliothek - Staats- und Universitätsbibliothek Dresden, Abt. Deutsche Fotothek.

1967" (58). In many cases, Billy relives the past through his dreams. In addition, he reexperiences the trauma as distressing recollections or flashback episodes. Certain "internal or external cues that symbolize or resemble an aspect of the traumatic event" (DSM-IV-TR 468) trigger in Billy painful memories or cause him to relive the war episodes. Psychiatrists specifically point to "sensory phenomena, such as sights, sounds, and smells that are circumstantially related to the traumatic event" to "reactivate traumatic memories and flashbacks" in PTSD sufferers (Miller 18). This symptom is readily observed in the protagonist and explains the novel's abundance of both psychological and structural "linking devices" (Klinkowitz 78) between different scenes of Billy's life. For instance, the novel repeatedly mentions certain colors (for example "ivory and blue," "orange and black") or smells ("mustard gas and roses"), which carry significance in Billy's past.

The combination "ivory and blue" appears throughout the novel, usually as a reference to bare feet and implying cold and/or death. The image originates in the war when Billy sees "corpses with bare feet that were blue and ivory" (65). The significance of the colors "orange and black," which reappear in the striped pattern of a tent put up for his daughter's wedding (72), is connected to the POW train Billy rides during the war and which was "marked with a striped banner of orange and black" (69). The recurring smell of "mustard gas and roses" is also connected to death, and its significance arises from Billy's experience of having to dig victims out from under the Dresden ruins after the raids: "They didn't smell bad at first, were wax museums. But then the bodies rotted and liquefied, and the stench was like roses and mustard gas" (214). Other examples of triggers for flashbacks and memories include certain sounds such as a siren (57, 164), which Billy associates with the Dresden air raid alarms, so that it "scared the hell out of him" (57) and "he was expecting World War Three at any time" (57). Not surprisingly, seconds later he is "back in World War Two again" (58).

In another episode, it is the sight of men physically crippled by war going from door-to-door selling magazines that immediately causes Billy, himself mentally crippled by the war, great distress:

> Billy went on weeping as he contemplated the cripples and their boss. His doorchimes clanged hellishly.
> He closed his eyes, and opened them again. He was still weeping, but he was back in Luxembourg again. He was marching with a lot of other prisoners. It was a winter wind that was bringing tears to his eyes. (63)

Similarly, the optometrist barbershop quartet performing at his anniversary party causes a strong response in Billy, since they remind him of the four German guards in Dresden who, when they see the destruction of their hometown, "in their astonishment and grief, resembled a barbershop quartet" (179). This memory of the German guards lies at the center of Billy's trauma, the destruction of Dresden. In this case Billy first responds with physical symptoms, looking as if "he might have been having a heart attack" (173). Finally, away from the guests, Billy "remembered it shimmeringly" (177), but does not travel back in time to this particular event. The Dresden bombings and their effect are too painful to relive, and at first even too frightening to remember. The strong physical and psychological reaction to the barbershop quartet, which even disturbs Billy's usually normal outward appearance, thus shows how deeply Billy has buried his Dresden memories.

This suppression of memories from parts of the trauma is typical of PTSD sufferers. It goes hand-in-hand with other techniques of evasion. As has been shown, individuals try to protect themselves from the painful experience by avoiding any feelings, thoughts or conversations, and activities, places or people that could cause recollections (DSM-IV-TR 468). Billy demonstrates all of these symptoms. He hardly ever talks about his experiences in the war, even eluding the topic when his wife questions him about it (121-123). This behavior is in accordance with studies of prisoners of war which "report with astonishment that the men never discussed their experiences with anyone. Often those who married after liberation never told even their wives or children that they had been prisoners" (Herman 89).

Connected with the avoidance, and also a symptom of PTSD, is another striking feature of Billy's behavior, namely his diminished general responsiveness to the world around him. His range of emotions is severely restricted throughout the novel. He is described as one who "never got mad at anything" (30) and bears everything without reaction, since "[e]verything was pretty much all right with Billy" (157). This restricted range of affect shows itself most prominently in the much repeated phrase "so it goes" with which Billy reacts passively and without emotion to tragedy and death. Billy's behavior can easily be described by the terms "psychic numbing" (115) or "psychic closing-off" (126), which Robert J. Lifton used for labeling the reactions towards death in survivors of the Hiroshima bombing.[6] For Billy, avoidance and "psychic numbing" function as a protective shield against the horror of memory and offer him the possibility of living an "outwardly normal" (175) life by suppressing his trauma. However, it is impossible for Billy to prevent completely the intrusion of his memories because the events have destroyed him on the inside which now mirrors the ruins he saw in Dresden. At first, he follows the conventional way of seeking help by committing himself to a mental hospital since he felt "that he was going crazy" (100). Yet, just as mainstream American society does not provide an atmosphere conducive to recovery from the horrors of war, Billy is also failed by the psychiatric establishment of the time.[7] Neither providing an accurate diagnosis nor offering any coping mechanisms, it proves itself to be completely separated from true world experience. When Billy checks himself in, "the doctors agreed: He *was* going crazy" (100), but "[t]hey didn't think it had anything to do with the war. They were sure Billy was going to pieces because his father had thrown him into the deep end of the Y.M.C.A. swimming pool when he was a little boy, and had then taken him to the rim of the Grand Canyon" (100). Billy thus falls

---

[6] Donald Greiner was first to note the applicability of Lifton's ideas to Vonnegut's text. For further details see Donald Greiner's essay "Vonnegut's *Slaughterhouse-Five* and the Fiction of Atrocity" from 1973.

[7] At the time that Vonnegut wrote *Slaughterhouse-Five*, ostensibly about his own World War II experiences, PTSD was not an established diagnosis. One is left to wonder whether Billy (and/or Vonnegut?) would receive better psychiatric care today.

victim to the previous tendency in psychiatry to underestimate the role of "an external factor, something outside the person" (Kleber, Figley, and Gersons 11) in causing trauma and instead to focus only on one's "individual vulnerability as the reason for people's suffering" (Kleber, Figley, and Gersons 13).

Billy and his roommate and fellow war veteran Rosewater thus embark on their own path of "trying to re-invent themselves and their universe" (101) in order to cope with the war events. Specifically, in what has been referred to as "a desperate attempt to rationalize chaos" (Merrill and Scholl 69), they resort to science fiction. Billy thus claims that he was kidnapped by aliens from the planet Tralfamadore, where he was then displayed in a zoo. Tralfamadorian philosophy helps Billy deal with the horrible events and their consequences by reinterpreting their meaning, since the philosophy opposes the quest for making sense out of the occurrences. When he asks the Tralfamadorians why they picked him to be abducted, they tell him: " 'Why you? Why us for that matter? Why anything? Because this moment simply is. [...] There is no why' " (76-77). These beliefs also enable Billy to avoid some of the distress he feels when facing death:

> "When a Tralfamadorian sees a corpse, all he thinks is that the dead person is in bad condition in that particular moment, but that the same person is just fine in plenty of other moments. Now, when I myself hear that somebody is dead, I simply shrug and say what the Tralfamadorians say about dead people, which is 'So it goes.' " (27)

While the idea of Tralfamadore as a coping mechanism at first strikes one as bizarre, it nevertheless seems to be Billy's only option in a world clearly failing to provide him with a different path. As Leonard Mustazza points out, by indirectly identifying Kilgore Trout's science fiction novels as the source of Billy's ideas, "Vonnegut takes pains to show whence Billy's fantasy derives, and, in this regard, the novel proves to be quite realistic, a portrait of one of life's (especially war's) victims" (302). With the help of his Tralfamadorian fantasy and his idea of time travel, Billy conquers the effects of his trauma in a way that enables him to function. He controls his anxiety, so that nothing can surprise or scare him, and his symptoms of arousal are confined to his trouble in sleeping and his occasional bouts of weeping (61). However, as Herman points out, "the appearance of normal functioning [...] should not be mistaken for full recovery, for the integration of the trauma has not been accomplished" (165). The price Billy pays for appearing normal is high. Not only is he bound to a life of indifference, passivity, and a science fiction fantasy, but he can also never fully escape from his trauma which continues to intrude into his life.

Billy's trauma story is not the only one in the novel, but it is framed by that of the narrator, who is a fictionalized version of Vonnegut himself. While separated from Billy's story, the first chapter provides some of the "linking devices" (Klinkowitz 78); the Tralfamadorian "so it goes," the smell of "mustard gas and roses" (4, 7), and even a "Three Musketeers Candy Bar" (9), all of which appear again later in the text.[8] At the same time, the narrator interrupts Billy's story at several occasions to authenticate the events. The text implies that, because the horrible consequences of the bombing of Dresden are too far removed from normal experience to be easily reported, yet nevertheless truly happened, they can neither be completely fictionalized nor simply repeated through an eyewitness account. The novel thus becomes a mixture of autobiography and fiction, that simultaneously binds Vonnegut to, and distances him from, the text and its implications.

This need to develop new techniques to describe war experiences and particularly the bombing of Dresden, lies at the core of the trauma. As described previously, traumatic memories are usually not verbal, but surface as visual images (de Silva and Marks 166). Before they can be shared with others, they first have to be translated into language, a task that, difficult in itself, is complicated by processes of avoidance and denial. PTSD sufferers are often unable to recall important aspects of the trauma (DSM-IV-TR 468). This is a problem that the narrator faces when he simply cannot remember much about the war (14). Thus, even though he continuously tries to write the novel, he nevertheless feels unable to do so. Even after finally finishing the book after nearly a quarter of a century, he considers it "a failure" (22). In fact, as Peter Freese points out, "the thematic center of his novel [Dresden] is endlessly circumnavigated but never fully encountered" (221). This aspect of the novel is thus exactly what Herman understands as "the central dialectic of psychological trauma": the conflict between wanting to deny horrible events and at the same time wishing to share them (1).

This difficulty in expressing the events is enhanced by the political and societal denial surrounding them. The narrator shares Billy's experience that America does not offer an atmosphere that easily allows recovery, since there is no forum for a discussion of the events:

> I wrote the Air Force back then, asking for details about the raid on Dresden, who ordered it, how many planes did it, why they did it, what desirable results there had been and so on. I was answered by a man who, like myself, was in public relations. He said that he was sorry, but that the information was top secret still. (11)

Just as there is no public discussion of the events, there is also no discussion of them in private conversation. Since most of the victims of the air raids were Germans, the aggressors and major perpetrators of the war, the question of whether

---

[8] The "Three Musketeers Candy Bar" is directly related to a scene in which Billy's wife Valencia visits Billy in the mental hospital a few years after the war and eats a "Three Musketeer Candy Bar" (107). The significance of the image, however, lies in the time of the war. After the Battle of the Bulge, Billy is part of a group of soldiers called by one of them, Weary, "the Three Musketeers" (48). Weary later blames Billy for breaking up the (completely imagined) great union of the Three Musketeers and becomes obsessed with wanting Billy dead.

it is even legitimate to talk about the horrible and traumatizing aspects of the bombings is part of every discussion of them:

> I happened to tell a University of Chicago professor at a cocktail party about the raid as I had seen it, about the book I would write. He was a member of a thing called The Committee on Social Thought. And he told me about the concentration camps, and about how the Germans had made soap and candles out of the fat of dead Jews and so on.
> All I could say was, "I know, I know. I *know*." (10)

The desperate "'I know, I know. I *know*'" seems by no means Vonnegut's "expression of his exasperation at having to hear, once again, about the horror of the death camps" (275), as Philip Watts contends. Rather it is an acknowledgment of the difficulty and inability to talk or write about a topic which deeply affected one's psychology, but which at the same time cannot be separated from questions of guilt, since it necessarily includes portraying the perpetrators of the war, the Germans, as suffering. Consequently one needs to design one's own coping strategies and path of healing in order to deal with the horror of the Dresden air raids.

As has been shown earlier, writing can be an integral part of the treatment of posttraumatic stress. For Vonnegut, the recovery process is bound to literary production, and he himself views his work as "therapy" (Allen 109). His war, and particularly his Dresden, experience has not left him scarless. What we learn in the novel is corroborated by comments that the author has made in interviews, and together these point to an underlying trauma. Vonnegut especially emphasizes his amnesia with regards to Dresden:

> [T]he book was largely a found object. It was what was in my head, and I was able to get it out, but one of the characteristics about this object was that there was a complete blank where the bombing of Dresden took place, because I don't remember. And I looked up several of my war buddies and they didn't remember, either. They didn't want to talk about it. There was a complete forgetting of what it was like. There was all kinds of information surrounding the event, but as far as my memory bank was concerned, the center had been pulled right out of the story. (Allen 94)

Writing *Slaughterhouse-Five* thus meant the long and painful process of uncovering what Vonnegut had pushed out of his consciousness. Even though it is painful "to come face-to-face with the horrors on the other side of the amnesiac barrier" (Herman 184), it is a necessary step in recovery. However, the subject has to be approached with care, since successful recovery requires a balancing act: "[a]voiding the traumatic memories leads to stagnation in the recovery process, while approaching them too precipitately leads to a fruitless and damaging reliving of the trauma" (Herman 176). Vonnegut also does not face his suppressed memories directly, but slowly uncovers layer after layer to get to their core. The novel reflects this process of narrowing in on himself through the two trauma stories. Billy's story allows an indirect and detached exploration of the effects of the Dresden bombing, since the character is mostly fictional. The narrator's story, while on one level parallel to Vonnegut's, is on another level an integral part of a work of fiction. Moving himself from the factual to the fictional plane by creating the narrator thus still allows Vonnegut a degree of distance from himself and his experiences, a similar technique that Pennebaker and Greenberg, Wortman, and Stone found to be successful in their experiments on writing and healing (see Chapter 2). Consequently, the final point of recovery in this process of self-therapy is not achieved in the novel but rather comes with its completion:

> I felt after I finished *Slaughterhouse-Five* that I didn't have to write at all anymore if I didn't want to. It was the end of some sort of career. I don't know why, exactly. I suppose that flowers, when they're through blooming, have some sort of awareness of some purpose having been served. Flowers didn't ask to be flowers and I didn't ask to be me. At the end of *Slaughterhouse-Five*, [...] I had a shutting-off feeling, [...] that I had done what I was supposed to do and everything was OK. (Allen 107)

However, while *Slaughterhouse-Five* is the result of a successful self-treatment, telling the story does not mean that the trauma can then be forgotten. As in psychotherapy, which aims at "integration, not exorcism" (Herman 181) of the trauma, the Dresden experience does not lose its important position in Vonnegut's life after he completes the novel, but it can now be adequately integrated into the author's past. While the events no longer paralyze the writer, they are still available for further creative exploration, thus continuing as "the informing structure of all his novels" (Leeds 92). Yet Vonnegut has done more than heal himself. By publishing *Slaughterhouse-Five* and drawing the reader into his path of recovery, the stories of Billy, the narrator, and consequently Vonnegut take on a public dimension. Creating a story that mixes autobiography with fiction helps to turn the overwhelming and hard-to-grasp experience into a structured and controllable one, without concurrently sacrificing detail and complexity. While the story is different from the one experienced, it is not simplified, as these narratives of personal trauma usually become when translated into language, because the fictional layer returns the complexity into the text. In particular, the use of modern structural techniques, such as the following of Billy's wandering mind, gives the readers more immediate access to what it is like to live through such a traumatic experience as the Dresden bombings. The impact on the reader of a text such as *Slaughterhouse-Five* can thus be potent and surpass the limits of the concern for only an individual destiny. It draws attention to what we often need to suppress or deny when it is most important to remember; namely, the crippling nature of war and the terrible toll that modern warfare exacts on those forced to live through it.

6.2   Harry Mulisch

Not as well-known internationally as Vonnegut's *Slaughterhouse-Five*, but a bestseller in the Netherlands, and recently reissued in a new German translation, Harry Mulisch's *Het stenen bruidsbed* (*The Stone Bridal Bed*) offers another impressive attempt to deal through literature with the inner and outer destruction caused by the large area bombings in World War II. Mulisch's *Het stenen bruidsbed* was published in 1959, the key year in German postwar literature in which Böll, Grass, and Johnson shattered the silence surrounding the German past in their respective important novels, by establishing the Nazi years and German guilt as dominant topics of German literary production. Yet they did not much discuss the bombings and their psychological consequences in their works even though, as the previous chapters have shown, the bombings had deeply scarred German society. So, while German literature, caught up in guilt, trauma, and fear, remained largely silent about this part of World War II, Mulisch was able to fill this gap with his novel because of his position as a Dutch-language author. He could thus add yet another view to the multiple perspectives in dealing with the war offered by the three German authors in 1959. Not surprisingly though, the novel, which after its success in the Netherlands was translated into German for the first time in 1960, did not receive any attention in the country of its setting. In an interview, Mulisch recently uttered the suspicion that the lack of success was due to the fact that Germans in the Adenauer era did not care to have a Dutchman tell them about Dresden (*NZZ* 41). However, the lack of interest in Gert Ledig's *Vergeltung* a few years before the publication of *Das steinerne Brautbett*, as well as the previously described societal and cultural situation in Germany in the 1950s and early 1960s, suggest rather that the German public at this point was not yet ready to face the complex issue of the bombings regardless of who was writing about them.

Unlike Vonnegut, Mulisch was not a witness to the Dresden raids in 1945. His novel is thus not in part the working through of a personal bombing trauma as *Slaughterhouse-Five*. Mulisch did observe Dresden in its destruction eleven years after the war when he was attending a Heine conference in the German Democratic Republic. He later described his experience in an interview:

> Eigentlich hatte ich vor, ein Buch über einen hohen Naziverbrecher zu schreiben. Aber dann sah ich die öden Ruinenhaufen, wo tatsächlich Menschen lebten und immer noch Steine klopften wie die Nibelungen bei Wagner. Da wusste ich, dass ich dieser totalen Gestaltlosigkeit etwas Geformtes entgegenzusetzen hatte. [...] Eines Nachts stieg ich aus einem Jazzclub, der in irgendeinem Ruinenkeller eingerichtet war, und ich fand mich völlig verlassen in der Luft. Es gab hier keine Häuser, keine Straßen, keine Topographie mehr. Ich musste mich buchstäblich am Sternenhimmel orientieren, um wieder in meine Unterkunft zu finden. (dsch 29)[9]

---

[9] "Originally I was planning to write a book about a Nazi high criminal. But then I saw the bleak piles of ruins where people were actually living and still hammered stones just like the Nibelun-

However, Mulisch's perception of the destruction of Dresden does not seem to be the only reason why he felt the Dresden bombings and their effects to be a fitting subject matter for his novel. Indeed, Mulisch over and over again returns to different aspects of the Second World War in his texts, suggesting that he is trying to understand and work through his experiences of the war with his writing. The author's obsession with World War II is not surprising. His biography reveals that the war has left him scarred similarly to his key character of *Het stenen bruidsbed*, the American bomber pilot Corinth, whose face after a war injury resembles the ruins of Dresden, the city he had bombed just before his accident. The son of an Austrian father who collaborated with the Nazis and a Jewish mother, most of whose relatives were killed in concentration camps, Mulisch spent his childhood torn between victim and perpetrator. While hating his father for his involvement with the Nazis, he was also aware that it was his collaboration that saved his mother's life. Mulisch once fittingly summarized his paradoxical background as "more than having 'lived through' the war, I *am* the Second World War" (van der Paardt 204). It is thus not surprising that Mulisch chose a setting such as Dresden to explore further questions of guilt and responsibility and outer and inner destruction as a consequence of conflict and war. In Mulisch's words:

> Alles ist so ironisch [...]. Wenn mein Vater nicht bei den Deutschen mitgemacht hätte, hätte meine Mutter nicht überlebt. Denn als die mal verhaftet wurde, hat mein Vater seine hohen Freunde eingeschaltet, und sie wurde freigelassen. Was soll man darüber denken? Als Schriftsteller schreibt man dann eben über Schuld und Verantwortung. (Lebert and Weber)[10]

Het stenen bruidsbed is set in Dresden in 1958, where the protagonist of the novel, American dentist and former bomber pilot Norman Corinth takes part in a dental conference. However, his true motives for the trip to Dresden in the middle of the Cold War can be found in his war experiences which are interjected into the text as three flashbacks. Here it is revealed that Corinth is actually returning to Dresden because he was involved in the bombing of the city in February of 1945 and personally committed a particularly cruel act when shooting at civilians who were trying to protect themselves from the raging fires in the Elbe river. Shortly afterwards, he was seriously wounded when his plane went down. Corinth is presented as deeply injured by his experiences, both internally

---

gen in Wagner. Then I knew that I had to counter this complete shapelessness with something formed and ordered. [...] One night I climbed up out of a jazz club, which had been set up somewhere in one of the cellars under the ruins and I found myself completely alone in the air. There were no houses, no streets, no topography. I literally had to use the stars in the sky for orientation in order to find my accommodations again."

[10] "Everything is so ironic [...]. If my father hadn't collaborated with the Germans, my mother wouldn't have survived. Once, when she was arrested, my father informed his friends in high places and she was let go. What should one think about that? As a writer the consequence is that one writes about guilt and responsibility."

and externally. The novel's point of view is limited mainly to Corinth's own perspective and his confrontation with the past is mediated through his interaction with several characters. He starts an affair with the attractive organizer of the conference, Hella Viebahn, who had been imprisoned in a concentration camp during the Nazi years. He also spends much time with his West German colleague Schneiderhahn whose puzzling background and intentions Corinth tries to decipher throughout most of the novel. In addition, the plot is interspersed with short conversations with his chauffeur Günther and the hotel manager Ludwig. The book ends with another act of (self-)destruction by Corinth who crashes a car into the ruins and then, seriously injured, sets it on fire.

Vonnegut's passive protagonist Billy Pilgrim is a strikingly different personality than the older, harsh, and somewhat rough Norman Corinth (who, incidentally, is hardly ever mentioned by his first name). While Billy is somewhat naive and a completely innocent victim of the bombings and war in general, Corinth is a man of action, but also ripped apart by guilt. He was an active participant in the destruction of Dresden and went beyond any call of duty as a soldier, purposefully shooting at and murdering the women, children, and old people who had found protection in the river. Still, the two men are in many ways similarly affected by their respective war experiences. Billy is completely emotionally detached from his surroundings, his life, and his past; Corinth blocks out all emotional reactions. Corinth's detachment clearly reveals itself in the first section of the novel, which introduces and describes the protagonist. It is fittingly entitled: "(But Without Feeling)" and portrays a man marked by internal and external destruction.[11] Corinth's face is so severely scarred that it is similar to the broken landscape surrounding him in Dresden and for which he was partially responsible as a bomber pilot. He looks almost animal-like, his face is a patchwork of pieces of dead blue and white skin (10) without hair or eyelashes (11). The scars prevent him from forming most natural facial expressions that would normally accompany any emotional state. Like many who suffer from the effects of trauma, while able to build an outwardly normal life with a dental practice, marriage, and friends, he is unable to form any close and meaningful bonds with other people. The relationship to his wife is cold and distant, and harmony is maintained mainly through her consumption of a large number of medications (12). Similarly, when he starts an affair with Hella in Dresden, it is based solely on his near-animalistic sexual desires, but not on any emotional involvement: "[…] he felt his body. Saliva shot into his mouth, and he had to swallow. His horniness barked dutifully: a cold animal, and he thought: Of course, of course, I want her" (18-19).[12]

---

[11] Harry Mulisch, *Het stenen bruidsbed* (Amsterdam: de bezige bij, 1959) 9. Translation by the author based on the German translation by Gregor Seferens: Harry Mulisch, *Das steinerne Brautbett* (Frankfurt a. M.: Suhrkamp 1995). Subsequent references appear parenthetically in the text and refer to the Dutch edition of the work. The original text is provided in footnotes.
"(Maar zonder emotie)"

Corinth's feelings of detachment and alienation do not only play out with regards to others, but also to himself. Several times, Corinth perceives his body and mind/soul as being two separate entities. The schisms between body and mind are immediate reactions to situations that remind him of the past. For example, after he arrives in Dresden and is led into his room, he finds that his window overlooks the destroyed city. He also becomes a witness to a large number of dead, and nearly dead, flies struggling at this very window. As the hotel manager Ludwig explains: "Every year the same. They escape from the wind into the houses. What can you do? It is a tradition in Dresden to die on a large scale" (27-28).[13] Corinth's reaction indicates that the statement reminds him of his past involvement in the mass killing, specifically his horrific deed of shooting innocent civilians who were trying to escape from the deadly fire by resting in the river – a memory he clearly tries to suppress. Corinth's mind cannot handle the return to the place of his terrible actions and the schism occurs:

> He saw himself, lying there on the bed, in a tower, in Dresden . . . smoking and constantly drinking and looking at the ceiling. [. . .] He thought, if I am not conscious of being in Dresden where am I then? [. . .] He remembered something he had read somewhere (or had he made it up himself?): *The soul travels by horse*. [. . .] At this point it was sailing a few hundred kilometers off the coast of Long Island [. . .]. It would only arrive when he would be long since back in Baltimore – months later, when he, with bare underarms sticking out of his white coat and a piece of plastic in front of his mouth, would be bending over a woman whose open mouth full of gold was facing the sky, filled with gray mountains of lead - *Dresden*. Only then would his soul go up the stairs with Ludwig and watch the dying flies (30-31).[14]

This dissociation between body and mind is typical of Corinth's pychological adaptation. The reader is told that "after the war he made do without himself for years" (31).[15] Like so many others who experienced the war and the bombings, Corinth is lost, his experiences have fragmented him and shaken the constants that usually give orientation to life. What are left are individual pieces that cannot form a whole any longer, a condition shared by the fields of ruins of the

---

[12] "[. . .] hij voelde zijn lichaam. Water liep in zijn keel. Zijn geilheid blafte, een koud dier van plicht, en hij dacht, natuurlijk, natuurlijk, ik wil haar hebben."

[13] "Ieder jaar hetzelfde. Ze vluchten voor de wind de huizen in. Wat wilt u? Het is traditie in Dresden, op grote schaal te sterven."

[14] Hij zag zichzelf liggen, op een bed in een torentje, in Dresden . . . rokend en onafgebroken drinkend keek hij naar het plafond. [. . .] Hij dacht, als ik niet het besef heb dat ik in Dresden ben, waar ben ik dan? [. . .] Hij herinnerde zich iets, dat hij ergens gelezen had (of had hij het zelf bedacht?): *De ziel gaat te paard*. [. . .] Op het ogenblik voer zij een paar hondred kilometer uit de kust van Long Island [. . .]. Zij zou pas aankomen, wanneer hij allang terug was in Baltimore, – maanden later, als hij met blote onderarmen uit zijn witte kiel en een stukje plastic voor zijn mond over een vrouw gebogen stond, die haar mond vol goud opensperde naar de hemel buiten, waarin grauwe bergen lood stonden: – *Dresden*. Dan pas zou zijn ziel met Ludwig de trap opkomen en naar de stervende vliegen kijken."

[15] "hij het na de oorlog jarenlang zonder zichzelf had gedaan."

destroyed cities.[16] Not surprisingly, Corinth directly identifies with them when trying to reflect on his state: "[...] he had the feeling of being broken down. His kidneys were two collapsed villas in ravaged gardens, his back was the burnt-out church from the street corner" (56).[17]

The split between body and soul also indicates the changed view of two other points of orientation, time and space. Like Billy, Corinth can think of himself as being in two different places in time at the same time, so that temporality loses its linear function in his perception. Sometimes the war appears to him so unreal that he thinks it had never happened, or occurred three thousand years ago (105). Then when he successfully blocks out his memories, he finds himself immediately back in the war through flashbacks and reliving the events in his thoughts as soon as he is reminded of them. The Dresden experience was thus so extreme that he perceives it as having been "outside of history," which at the same time makes it always present for him (82).[18] The constant struggle between suppression and intrusion causes him not only to feel lost in time, but also in space. It is as if he has ceased to exist: "Already while I experience something, I have never experienced it. Never have I been anywhere. [...] I am nowhere. When I die, they will bury an empty coffin" (74-75).[19]

While Billy's response to the events is one of passivity, similar to the role he was forced to take during the bombings as a victim on the ground, Corinth finally continues his role as the man of action and returns to Dresden in an attempt to face himself and his guilt. His state of confusion is symbolized by the structure of the hotel he stays in, which is a labyrinth of strange rooms and towers that are accessible only through odd paths. The house seems almost organically grown and is mysteriously organized around a "mother cell," a room with glass walls in which an old woman lies in a bed, and which is located within another room. Access to Corinth's room is difficult not only because he has to climb through many others in order to get to it, but also because the key to it is in a locked box whose key is inside of the box itself:

> "Where is the key to this closet, Eugène?"
> "I don't know," Eugène laughed, looking at Corinth.
> "Huh, always this nonsense," Ludwig said. "Of course, it is *in* the closet again."
> "Yes! Eugène laughed. (25)[20]

---

[16] The way his driver Günther reacts when they are lost in Dresden can be used to describe Corinth's own confused state: "Everywhere I recognize individual things, and then something else again, but I don't know how everything fits together" (41) ("Overal herken ik iets, en dan weer iets anders, maar hoe het in elkaar past, weet ik niet.")

[17] "[...] het was een gevoel van afbraak. Zijn nieren waren twee ingestorte villa's in woeste tuinen, zijn rug was de verkoolde kerk op het kruispunt."

[18] "het was buiten de geschiedenis"

[19] "Terwijl ik iets meemaak, heb ik het nooit meegemaakt. Nooit ben ik ergens geweest. [...] Ik ben nergens. Als ik sterf, is mijn kist leeg."

This scene is symbolic of Corinth's psychological condition. He returned to Dresden, to the center of his trauma and his guilt in order to confront his inner turmoil and destruction. He tries to find access to himself and hopes to overcome his guilt and to become whole again and reestablish his place in the world. He is thus striving for humanity and life (46), more instinctively than consciously, hoping that the resolution for his despair would be located at the source. This is symbolized by the "green whispering" (16) he starts to hear immediately after he arrives in Dresden, and which seems to come from the city, but which he cannot decipher.[21] Just as the key to the closet, being inside the closet itself, is hard to obtain, resolution is similarly difficult to achieve. While Dresden could be a place to make peace with the past, it also worsens his condition because it is full of reminders of this past.

Unfortunately, Corinth's hope for a return to wholeness is only an illusion. To Philippe Noble, Corinth "is a criminal of a 'modern' anonymous war, hidden in a big crowd of many. But he is also a criminal in the 'ancient' sense" (350), because he perpetrates senseless murder of innocents. After the bomb is dropped by his battle friend, the "eraser of cities" (111),[22] Corinth also wants to have a direct part in the battle:

> "Look! Look!" In the black water in the flickering shine of the flames the blue-eyed Corinth sees them: heads, skulls, melons, motionless. And then he laughs in the laugh of the victor and yells: "Shall I serenade them?" And everyone laughs, all the pilots [...], and then he ejects the bullets into the water in front of him, where skulls crack, sway, burst, come apart, jump around, sink, and everyone laughs, all the pilots, everyone laughs into the night and sings:
> "Adieu, mein kleiner Gardeoffizier, Adieu. Adieu, und vergiss mich nicht, und vergiss mich nicht." (112)[23]

Corinth's later feelings of profound guilt about these brutal murders lie at the center of his traumatized state. These feelings of responsibility and shame start to arise when he sees the burning city again from the plane shortly before going down, and suddenly gains some understanding that this was not a game, but that his acts had real consequences: "Slowly the bowl of fire disappeared beneath him, and he felt that there was something changing in him, not much, but deep inside of him. [...] with a feeling of being drained, he turned his gaze away and stared into the night. It had really happened" (194-195).[24] By having Corinth's

---

[20] " 'Waar is de sleutel van het kastje, Eugène?' 'Weet ik niet,' lachte Eugène naar Corinth. 'O, het is zo'n grappemaker,' zei Ludwig. '*In* het kastje natuurlijk weer.' 'Ja!' lachte Eugène."

[21] "groene gefluister"

[22] "de stedenverdelger"

[23] " '*Kÿk! Kÿk!*' In het zwarte water ziet hen onder het bevend schÿnsel van de overwinnaar en schreeuwt: 'Zal ik ze eens serenade geven?' En allen lachen, alle vliegers [...], en dan jaagt hÿ de kogels voor zich uit het water in, waar de hoofden spatten, tuimelen, botsen, springen, keilen, verzinken, en lacht, alle vliegers, allen lachen in de nacht, en zingen: 'Adieu, mein kleiner Gardeoffizier, Adieu, Adieu, und vergiss mich nicht, und vergiss mich nicht.' "

plane crash right after this incident, an accident in which he is badly injured by fire, Mulisch also etches this knowledge, like a mark of Cain, permanently on Corinth's face.

Back in Dresden over a decade after the incident, Corinth, when trying to deal with his guilt, continuously emphasizes to himself and others that the war against Germany and his role in it as a bomber pilot was justified, particularly also because he is Jewish. After seeing the depressing sight of the destroyed city of Berlin, but also the Hitler bunker when he arrives in Germany, he reminds himself of the cruelty of the Nazi regime:

> Here they had hurried around with their files [...] to a spider who was dragging a leg and lay in bed with a film star, sent by a pig full of medals in front of a mirror, in the name of a cockroach; here they had celebrated their blood wedding while their country was engulfed in the smoke coming from burning human flesh, killing others, they had rampaged over the planet. He thought, *shouldn't* we have come here, to bomb this nest into dust and ashes? (33)[25]

While one can hardly disagree with Corinth's standpoint in this matter, the situation becomes more complex for him in Dresden. Here, he is not only confronted with the ruins, but with the victims of his own depravity. In a bar he meets a couple who tell their story of escape from the fires. The woman turns out to have been a possible victim of Corinth's shooting since she lost her leg as well as her baby in such an incident. Throughout the novel, Corinth hopes to come to an understanding of himself and his situation by evaluating these different facets of guilt. As no other author who wrote about the bombings, Mulisch thus explores through his main character the issue of guilt involved in destruction and the large area bombings. Corinth, as a fighter for the victors, the liberators, and as a Jew is looking for justification of his past acts by exploring the cruelty of the German past. In the secret service man Schneiderhahn, whom Corinth watches intently throughout his stay, he finally (erroneously) thinks that he has found the personification of this evil since, because of some remarks by Schneiderhahn, Corinth believes that he had been an SS-dentist in a concentration camp. When he confronts him about it, Corinth tries to justify his involvement in the bombings by Schneiderhahn's guilt, portraying the pilots of the air raids as bringing deserved punishments for the committed crimes:

> "In Auschwitz," Corinth said quietly, "dentists are waiting at the exits of the gas chambers. When the doors open, dead naked bodies stand closely pressed together

---

[24] "*Langzaam gleed de schotel vuur voorbÿ en hÿ voelde, dat er iets in hem veranderde: haast niets, maar precies in het midden. [...] met een gevoel of hÿ hol werd, wendde hÿ zÿn ogen af en keek voor zich in de nacht. Het was waar gebeurd.*"

[25] "Hier hadden ze haastig rondgelopen met hun papieren [...] naar een manke spin die met een filmster in bed lag, van een dekoreerd zwijn voor een spiegel, namens een kakkerlak; hier hadden zij hun bloedbruiloft gevierd, hun land walmend van brandend mensenvlees, moordend over de planeet tuimelend. Hij dacht, hadden wij soms *niet* aan moeten komen vliegen om het nest in puin te gooien?"

in the chamber, because there is no room for them to fall down. [...] While workers search for gold and diamonds in the anus and the genitalia, SS-dentists use hooks and tongs to break gold teeth and crowns out of gums. [...] Wasn't it just like that? Correct me if I am wrong, *Herr Doktor*"

[...] As a participant of ten to twelve bombing attacks on Berlin, four on Hamburg, and, let's say, thirty on Mannheim, Cologne, Essen, Hannover and more, I could make accusations against you. I hope I was at least lucky enough to kill your father, your wife, and your child."(155-157)[26]

After this episode, Corinth feels "triumphant," as if he has got closer to what he was searching for in Dresden (160-161). However, his feelings of success are an illusion. Not only because Schneiderhahn was anything but an SS-dentist, on the contrary he worked for a foreign secret service throughout the Nazi period, but also because his idea that one's own past behavior and personal guilt can be erased by that of others simply cannot hold up. Both Dresden and Auschwitz are part of what the novel describes as an anti-history of deeds without reason or purpose:

Between the mass murders of the Huns and Hitler's concentration camps no time has passed. They lie next to each other at the bottom of eternity. *And Dresden lies there as well*, he thought. [...] We destroyed Dresden because it was Dresden, just like the Jews were butchered because they were Jews, there is nothing more to it. [...] The bombing of Dresden is part of Hitler, of Attila, of Timur-Leng. (130)[27]

However, these comments should not be misunderstood as an equating of the victimhood of the Jews who died in Auschwitz and of the Germans who lost their lives in the bombings of German cities, at least this is what Mulisch claims later in an interview. According to Mulisch, what he looks at is the comparability of the "Techniken des Tötens, die eine Kultur anwendet" (dsch 29):

Und ich habe mich schon gefragt, welcher Mord unmenschlicher ist: die Selektion an der Rampe, bei der die Täter – wenn man so will auf altmodische Weise den Opfern direkt ins Gesicht sehen, oder der Mord aus einer fliegenden Maschine, bei der die Täter, junge Menschen auch sie, gar nicht mitbekommen, was sie anrichten. Ich habe dann geschrieben, dass jeder unmenschlicher ist als der jeweils andere. (dsch 29)[28]

---

[26] " 'Tandartsen in Auschwitz,' zei Corinth zacht, 'wachten bij de uitgangen van de gaskamers. Als de deuren opengaan, staan de naakte doden stijf op elkaar geperst, want er is geen plaats om te vallen. [...] Terweijl arbeiders goud en briljanten uit de aarzen en geslachtsdelen halen, breken SS-tandartsen met haken en tangen en hamers de gouden kiezen en kronen uit de kaken.' [...] 'Was het zo niet? korrigeert u mij eens. Korrigeert u mij eens, *Herr Doktor*.' [...] 'Ik zou het u kunnen verwijten als deelnemer aan tien of twaalf bombardementen op Berlijn, vier op Hamburg en een stuk of dertig op Mannheim, Keulen, Essen, Hannover en weet ik veel. Hopelijk heb ik het geluk gehad, daarbij uw vader, vrouw en kind te raken.' "

[27] "Tussen de massacres van de Hunnen en de koncentratiekampen van Hitler is geen tijd verstreken. Zij liggen naast elkaar op de bodem van de eeuwigheid. Hij dacht,*en daar ligt Dresden*. [...] Wij gooiden Dresden kapot omdat het Dresden was, zoals de joden geslacht werden omdat het joden waren. Verder geen boodschap. [...] Het bombardement van Dresden is van Hitler, en van Attila, en van Timoer Lenk."

Corinth feels personal guilt because he did kill and he did so with pleasure. When drunk with the feeling of victory, he shoots the civilians in the river, committing a direct and individually terrible crime. The novel shows that the consequences of his actions and subsequent personal guilt cannot be erased by the knowledge that overall he was fighting for the right side.

The more Corinth wants to believe that his guilt can be, or has been, erased and that he is whole again, suppressing the knowledge that it will never leave him, the stronger his physical reactions become to stimuli in the environment. Not only is it common in people suffering from trauma experiences to have physical reactions to stressors connected with the events, but the connection of psychological condition and physical reaction is used effectively throughout the work to describe Corinth's inner state. Just as with Corinth's face, Mulisch again employs the physical to mirror the true psychological condition, showing that Corinth is increasingly losing control. When talking to Hella about his role in the bombings, he denies that he ever thinks about the events, but his body's reaction reveals his true inner state:

> "Hella, something is happening to me ..." Frightened she was looking at the pearls of sweat on his forehead and around his nose that became larger and larger. His eyes attached themselves to the room. Still, it became worse and worse, invisible: a vibration in the night in the deathlike objects, as they were not themselves any longer, an opening-up that in horrible ways was threatening him. Light, light, he thought, but he was unable to speak; he felt that he had to use all his strength. But what strength? How? Against what? Then he felt that it became weaker, as if a storm had suddenly died down, and it disappeared. (106)[29]

These attacks become worse throughout his stay in Dresden and the more he tries to suppress his guilty conscience.

In order not to lose control completely Corinth, instead of slowly leaving his artificial coping constructs behind and facing reality, gets more deeply involved in them. While Billy Pilgrim flees into the realm of fantasy and science

---

[28] "[...] the comparability of the techniques of killing which a culture employs: And I did ask myself, which type of murder was more inhuman: selection at the ramp, where the murderers – in traditional style, if you want, look directly into the faces of their victims, or murder from a flying aircraft, in which the killers, also young people, don't even realize what they are causing. I then wrote that each acts more inhuman than the other."
While it is true that Mulisch does not seem to equate the victims of the bombings and of the Holocaust in the novel or in his comments, but is more interested in the killers, it is questionable whether such a comparison between the pilots and German Nazi criminals is really necessary. Since Mulisch also emphasizes the importance of dealing with one's personal guilt, it seems counterproductive to explore such "rankings" in brutality as for each person the personal guilt weighs heaviest.

[29] " 'Hella, er is iets met me ...' Angstig keek zij naar de groeiende zweetdroppels op sijn voorhoofd, naast zijn neus. Zijn ogen vraten zich vast in de kamer. Nog steeds werd het erger, onzichtbaar: een nachtelijk sidderen in de doodstille dingen, alsof zij zichzelf niet meer waren, een opengaan, dat hem walglijk bedgreigde. Hijt dacht, licht, licht, maar kon niet spreken; hij voelde dat hij zijn krachten onmenselijk inspande maar welke? hoe? waartegen? Toen merkte hij dat het afnam, alsof een storm plotseling ging liggen, en het verdween."

fiction in order to deal with the effects of the war, Corinth looks for support in the distant past of ancient mythology. By limiting himself to the stereotypical characteristics of a Homeric hero, bound to the fate determined for him, he tries to explain his own actions within the framework of myth. The bombings and his killing of the people in the Elbe are thus translated into Homeric terms. The airplane was the warship on the way to Dresden or Troy, and the "blue-eyed Corinth" (35) was on a mission to conquer it. The shooting of the people in the river, in particular, shows Corinth fully embracing the role of the victor and thus of the destroyer. In Dresden he increasingly interprets the world and himself through myth. He reenacts his character, the destroyer, over and over again. In his essay "Erinnern, Wiederholen und Durcharbeiten" ("Remembering, Repeating, and Working-Through"), Freud had already pointed out the connection between repetition, or acting out, and the suppression of certain childhood events. Freud contends that "je größer der Widerstand ist, desto ausgiebiger wird das Erinnern durch das Agieren (Wiederholen) ersetzt sein" (*Gesammelte Werke* V. 10 130).[30] In this case this idea can be applied to the traumatic event as well. Freud views acting out as a way to remember the suppressed event from the past. Mulisch himself goes even farther and sees this repeated reenactment of the past as a typically human characteristic: "Es scheint so, als ob sich die Vergangenheit immer wiederhole. [...] Ich glaube der Mensch wiederholt immer. So sind die Menschen einfach. Man hat oft gedacht, dass man sie ändern kann. Das scheint nicht der Fall zu sein" (Kleinschmidt 17).[31] This path of reenacting the past is, as is typical for people suffering from trauma, a vicious circle. The more Corinth tries to rid his deeds from consciousness, the more violently he acts out his past role of the destroyer, which leads over and over again to new reminders of his actions and his personal guilt.

The reenactment of the role of the destroyer manifests itself in several ways. One is through the association of destruction with sex, that leads like a thread through the novel. The reference to a bridal bed in the title already points to this connection between the sexual and destruction. Right from the beginning, the destroyed Dresden looks to Corinth like "a bride, who, when she sees the groom, has ripped her veil in pieces" (16).[32] In the first flashback about the bombing of Dresden, Corinth connects the destruction of the city more directly with male sexual arousal: *The bombing had already started, up above the first machines were returning: Lancasters, those were the British. He felt the begin-*

---

[30] "the greater the resistance, the more extensively will acting out (repetition) replace remembering" (trans. 151).

[31] "It seems as if the past will always repeat itself. [...] I believe that humans always repeat themselves. That's how humans are. Often one has hoped that one can change them. This does not seem to be possible."

[32] By applying the symbol of the wedding to Dresden and the Nazis and their crimes, the "blood wedding" (33), Mulisch also establishes a connection between them and shows that the destruction of Dresden ultimately was a consequence of these devious acts.

ning of an erection and put himself, sweating, in position behind his canon" (37-38).[33] The "ejaculation" finally occurs when Corinth shoots his bullets at the people standing in the river in the second flashback, feeling victorious and in complete control. Incidentally, this second flashback occurs at the same moment that Corinth has intercourse with Hella, whom he had been obsessed about "conquering" sexually from the first moment he saw her. Just as his killing in the past is perceived to be a sexual encounter, by having sex with Hella he kills again in the present. Hella, already a victim of the Nazis, now also becomes one of Corinth's since she is emotionally destroyed by his lack of interest in her after she sleeps with him. Sexuality for Corinth is thus inherently linked to causing destruction, the actual opposite of its biological purpose of procreation. He embraces the archetype of the destroyer vigorously, as if it were his biological function.

Also significant and connected with the issue of power, sex, and destruction is the symbol of fire that is associated with Corinth and Dresden. It is through fire that Corinth is eternally bound to Dresden and fire has made him the broken person he is when he returns. As a bomber pilot, Corinth is one of the people who unleashed the firestorm and the devastation that followed it. He then is injured and marked for life by fire immediately after the attacks. After he returns to Dresden, different kinds of "fire" are continuously mentioned around him, and each time, Corinth is immediately reminded of his past.[34] At the same time, he is continuously directly involved with fire as well. He again is in the position of the fire-starter. At first, this role is involuntary. Early on, he nearly burns his room down with his cigarette: "He burnt his fingers and immediately stood next to his bed while beating on his clothes, the cigarette butt was smoldering on the bedside rug. Fire, he thought, treading out the butt; swaying he walked to the window" (33).[35] Similarly, at the first reception of the conference, Corinth, deep in thought, nearly burns his fingers with his cigarette before someone extinguishes it. In the final scene of the novel, however, Corinth again consciously acts out the role of the destroyer and fire-starter. He repeats his destructive act and the consequences of the past by crashing a car like a bomb into the ruins and then setting it on fire. The reader is left with the final image of a badly hurt, broken man, bleeding from his old injuries, caught up in a war that never ends and who continues to perpetuate destruction.

---

[33] "*De bombardementen moesten al begonnen zÿn, hoger keerden de eerste machines terug: Lancasters; dat waren de engelsen. Hÿ kreeg een begin van een erektie en ging zwetend in positie liggen achter zÿn kanon.*"

[34] Apart from the Dresden firestorm in 1945, the most extensive description of which is centrally located in the third chapter of the drama-like structure of the novel, Ludwig talks about the recent fire in a neighboring hotel. In addition, the text also frequently refers to lighting cigarettes, lighted cigarettes, cigarette smoke, and damage caused by cigarette burns.

[35] "Hij brande zijn vingers en stond meteen op zijn kleren slaand naast het bed, het peukje smeulde in de mat. Brand, dacht hij, trapte het uit, wankelde en ging voor het raam staan."

The last chapter of the novel thus skillfully brings together all the earlier motives and symbols and ultimately confirms Hella's assessment that " '[t]he war is only over, when the last, who has lived through it, has died' " (95).[36] It starts out with Hella, Corinth's victim through sexual destruction, who now finds herself also caught in a repetitive cycle but, contrary to Corinth, as the ultimate victim. Schneiderhahn, the other important character in the novel, also becomes a victim of Corinth's destructive force. Enraged, Corinth tracks him down to his hotel and beats him up. While Schneiderhahn thinks this happens because Corinth still believes that he was a Nazi criminal and wants to punish him for it, he is actually beaten up because Corinth has learned that he lied about his past. While it seems strange at first that this would be the reason for Corinth to attack Schneiderhahn, the act becomes more understandable when one considers the role Schneiderhahn played in the eyes of the former bomber pilot. As has been pointed out Corinth, by projecting all his guilt onto Schneiderhahn, tries to relieve himself of his own personal guilt. While his physical reactions from the start reveal this strategy to be nothing but an illusion, Corinth has to face the truth when he finds out that Schneiderhahn had indeed lied, and had instead been working against the Nazis. Corinth's destructive rage is caused by his knowledge that the personal guilt he has brought onto himself cannot be redeemed and will never disappear; his self-destructive act and nearly complete repetition of the past events in the final pages of the novel confirm this acknowledgement.

With *Het stenen bruidsbed* Mulisch offers an impressive description of the psychological consequences of the bombings, not only for the people on the ground, but also for the pilots above. It is not a work of therapy in the sense that *Slaughterhouse-Five* was ten years later for Vonnegut, who had actually experienced the air raids. The fact that Mulisch was not directly involved in the bombings might also explain why he had little trouble writing about Dresden so soon after the war and immediately after he observed the destruction in the city in the 1950s. Still, while not therapeutic in the direct sense, the topic enabled Mulisch, whom critics have described as a moralist (Pelt 168), to explore better his difficult relationship to the past caused by his unique background and the questions of responsibility and guilt he has been struggling with ever since the war. By restricting the perspective predominantly to that of an American pilot, he offers a unique angle by which to analyze the various guilt issues involved in the Dresden bombing as well as in the Second World War in general. Mulisch's deep insight into the two poles of the war conflict, the victim and the perpetrator and the complexities that can complicate this relationship, as well as his perspective from the outside as a Dutch writer, seemed to have allowed him to explore these issues of guilt surrounding the bombings in more depth than any other author. His approach is similar to the understanding of guilt that Jaspers developed in his lectures on *Die Schuldfrage*. Mulisch, like Jaspers, shows that

---

[36] " 'De oorlog is pas afgelopen, wanneer de laatste die hem mee heeft gemaakt, is gestorven.' "

guilt can arise in many different ways, but never can one kind of guilt be erased by another. In addition, Mulisch warns against the idea of collective guilt as absolving personal guilt, just as Jaspers disqualifies it in his text. When Corinth tries to see Schneiderhahn as the representative of all of German guilt, actually projecting all war guilt, no matter by whom it was committed, onto him he effectively negates all individual guilt. It helps him to try to diffuse his personal act of horror in an unspecific collective. Schneiderhahn for him is not a person, but simply a figure representing an unspecified whole. Yet Mulisch makes clear that this is, at least for the individual, the wrong strategy. Schneiderhahn indeed is an individual with his own personal characteristics and an individual past. Mulisch stresses that both trying to minimize one's own guilt by seeing it erased by acts committed by others as well as hoping to hide one's own acts of horror behind the idea of collective guilt are not acceptable ways of dealing with one's past deeds.

Choosing an American pilot as his protagonist, Mulisch does not minimize German guilt and does not compare Dresden bombing victims to the victims of the Holocaust. The novel leaves plenty of room to explore German atrocities and makes clear that the horror created by Germans to which Corinth refers is completely real. Mulisch sends a message that Germans should not think that their own guilt is atoned for because they suffered from the bombings and horrors committed by others. They should not hide behind a collective guilt that would effectively take away responsibility from each individual. Yet by making Corinth, an American, a protagonist who has committed a cruel act, albeit against Germans, and who now breaks apart because of its consequences, Mulisch widens the perspective to be truly an international one. Modern war situations, he points out, even if mainly characterized by their anonymity and lack of emphasis on the individual fighter, still lead to acts that cause personal guilt. In the example of World War II, Mulisch shows that while many of these acts are committed by the original culprits, the Germans, they are not necessarily restricted to them. Personal guilt can arise in many situations and due to many different people – be it, as in Corinth's case, the needless killing of civilians on his bomber missions or, as in Mulisch's father's case, collaboration with the Nazis. War leaves behind many victims, perpetrators and some who fall somewhere between these two extreme poles. According to Mulisch, one way or another all of them have to carry the burden of an endless presence of their past experiences and deeds. By writing this novel, Mulisch also indicates that this state is not only limited to the people concerned directly, but can affect future generations who have to live with the deeds and destinies of their fathers and mothers and somehow have to try to make sense of them.

6.3   Henri Coulonges

The French novel *L'Adieu à la femme sauvage* (*Farewell, Dresden*) by Henri Coulonges was published in 1979 and is the story of Johanna, a twelve year old girl from Dresden, who barely survives the 1945 firestorm, and her later wanderings in search of a place of safety. In the bombings, she loses her friend Hella, her sister Grete, and effectively her mother Leni who is left almost speechless and passive after suffering a mental breakdown in response to the attacks and her other daughter's death. Narrated mostly through Johanna's eyes the author, using the innocence of the child's perspective, tries to convey a picture of the collapse of world order at the end of the war, characterized by destruction, the breakdown of bonds and family structures, displacement, and uncertainty.

When the bombing of Dresden starts, Johanna and her friend Hella are enjoying themselves at the circus across the river from the Old City. Instead of staying there until the alarm is over, Johanna and Hella try to make it home to the other side of the Elbe, thus entering directly into the chaos of flames and death that is raging through the town. Here, houses explode around them and whole streets are engulfed in flames, so they need to move constantly to escape the all-consuming fires. Their wanderings in the chaos leave them completely disoriented, both in space and time. Since most streets are blocked off by fires and smoke, they cannot follow any known path that would lead to their homes. Instead, they move about in circles, in need of finding shelter. Just as their knowledge of the city streets cannot help them to find the right way, time has lost its organizing function and becomes meaningless in the horror of the bombings:

> "There's no use running, Hella," she said matter-of-factly. "We won't have time to get home."
> [...] "Why are you sitting there," [said Hella.] "We have to find shelter! Hurry!"
> Johanna shook off her torpor, stood up and looked at her watch. It was ten past one. When had it begun? Three hours ago? Four?[37]

When the two girls get separated in the chaos, Johanna is ready to give up, not caring any longer what will happen to her without the support of her companion: "Before she had time to wonder what was happening, the blast knocked her down. [...] She had no pain anywhere, not even where she had been burned on her forehead. At last she felt good again. *I'll just go on lying here*, she thought. *It*

---

[37] Henri Coulonges, *Farewell, Dresden* (New York: Summit, 1989) 25. Subsequent references appear parenthetically in the text. The original French passages and page numbers are provided in the footnotes.

" 'Hella, dit-elle d'un ton détaché. Ce n'est pas la peine. On n'aura pas le temps de rentrer de toute façon.' [...] 'Pourquoi tu ne bouche pas? Il faut trouver un abri tout de suite ...' Son ton patétique eut pour mérite de sortir Johanna de sa torpeur. Elle se leva et regarda l'heure à sa montre. Il était une heure dix. Cela faisait trois heures, ou quatre heures, que tout avait commencé?" (37)

would have been senseless to run like that all night" (35).[38] However, the horror of wild screams by burned victims around her drive her away, and immediately start haunting her: "The scream she had heard resounded again in her" (36).[39]

Miraculously, she finds her friend again, which gives Johanna new strength, but Hella herself has been severely affected by the events around her. After seeing people flattened into the pavement, as she tells Johanna, she is wrapped in "bewilderment" and "indifference," a state that finally leads to her death in the firestorm by a collapsing glass roof, in front of Johanna's eyes.

When Johanna makes it home the next morning, she hopes for comfort and guidance from her mother. Instead, her family structure is completely destroyed because of the bombings. Her sister is dead, their house a ruin and her mother is left almost infant-like from the shock:

> Johanna looked at her, overwhelmed. Her mother's expressive face, once full of dimples, smiles and mischievous winks, [...] was now ashen and lifeless. Johanna sat down beside her and pressed her cheek against hers.
> "I'm here, Mutti," she said softly. "I'm with you."
> Leni didn't answer. [...] Not knowing what to do, Johanna scrutinized her face, watching for a quiver of her lips or a flicker of her eyes. But she saw nothing. It was as if she found a landscape she had known and loved darkened by fog, unrecognizable. (54)[40]

It is now up to Johanna to take over the adult role of the guide, setting the two off on wanderings in a world that has completely lost any order. The search for safety and comfort that had started with the bombings thus continues throughout the whole novel. They first end up in the house of the leader of the Dresden children's choir outside the city, who Johanna had met after she had found her way out from the firestorm and who coincidentally knows her mother and is in love with her. Since this state of affairs creates conflicts between the child and the choir master, and Johanna's mother needs psychological treatment, Johanna and Leni move on to Prague to stay with an old friend of the family. Here, Johanna

---

[38] "Avant qu'elle ait eu le temps de se demander ce qui se passait, le souffle d'une détonation violente l'avait précipitée à terre. [...] Elle n'avait mal nulle part, même plus à son front. Enfin elle se sentait bien. 'Je vais rester là tranquille, se dit-elle. J'allais quand même pas courir comme ça toute la nuit' " (55-56).

[39] "il y eut un cri [...] qui se propagea soudain dans son crâne comme dans une chambre d'écho" (56).

[40] "Johanna la regarda, anéantie. Cette oasis de fossettes, de sourires furtifs et de clins d'oeil malicieux qu'était le visage mobile et pétillant de sa mère [...], ce visage béni était devenu d'une fixité livide et tragique. Johanna s'accroupit à coté d'elle et posa sa joue contre la sienne. 'Je suis là, Mutti, lui murmura-t-elle tendrement à l'oreille. Je suis là avec toi ...' Léni ne répondit pas [...]. Indécise sur ce qu'il convenait de faire, Johanna scruta le visage de sa mère avec anxiété, à l'affût d'une lueur passagère dans ses yeux ou d'une crispation fugitive de ses lèvres. Mais rien, rien. C'était comme si, revenant après un cataclysme dans un paysage qu'elle avait jadis aimé [...], elle le retrouvait, assombri par le brouillard, impracticable, méconnaissable" (91).

experiences the collapse of Hitler-Germany, the passing of their family friend and her mother's violent death.

At the same time, Prague citizens are starting to take revenge on the Germans and collaborators on the streets. There is no place for Johanna any longer in this world. After everything around her has collapsed, Johanna finally becomes completely indifferent to her destiny. She can only identify with others who have now lost their place in society and joins a group of women who had worked for the Germans and were now being punished by the crowds. Yet this is not a political statement for Germany on Johanna's part. She remains the innocent victim, but now embraces this role instead of fighting it:

> Something strange was happening: she felt lighter with every step she took. [...] Johanna saw a group of terrified women huddled beside an overturned truck. All their hair had been cut off and they had been beaten. Two men took one of them by the arms and dragged her through the frenzied crowd. [...] Johanna darted through the crowd. Before the men could stop her, she reached the woman and said in German, "Give me your hand."
>
> [...] It seemed to Johanna that the onlookers had all fallen silent, because their shouts didn't concern her anymore. She squeezed the woman's hand harder and raised it, with their fingers intertwined, toward the sun. It was as if she had been reunited with Leni and, hand in hand, they were entering eternity together. (284-285)[41]

The novel contains strong scenes about the horror of the bombing war and manages to evoke touching and graphic descriptions of the Dresden air raids. It convincingly depicts the breakdown of order which came both with the destruction of the city and the end of the Third Reich, affecting all areas of one's own life and of society in general. Yet overall the novel is not as convincing as it could be in its approach to the bombing experience and its consequences. Apart from some rather far-fetched coincidences in plot (for example the relationship between Leni and the choir leader), there are two issues which weaken the novel. One is the neglect of a more complex discussion of (German) guilt, the other a lack of psychological depth in the characters.

"There are no gratuitous descriptions of carnage and violence, no talk about politics and Nazis, and most of all, no judgment. Johanna could be any girl in any country" (Reichel 13). With these words a reviewer in the Los Angeles Times praised Coulonges' book when it appeared in English translation (*Farewell,*

---

[41] "elle se sentait à chaque pas plus légère. [...] Elle vit un groupe de femmes terrifiées qui se trouvaient là, serrées les unes contre les autres, à côté d'une camionnette renversée. [...] Deux hommes la [une femme] prirent chacun par le bras et elle se débattit. Ils l'entraînèrent. [...] Johanna subitement se mit à courir, traversa la foule d'un seul élan et, avant que les hommes en brassard aient pu intervenir, s'approcha de la femme. 'Ta main', lui demande-t-elle. [...] Johanna eut l'impression que la foule s'était tue, ou que leurs cris s'étaient perdus dans des contrées inconnues qui ne la concernaient plus. Elle serra plus fort la main de la femme et la leva bien haut, enlacée dans la sienne, vers le soleil. C'était comme si elle entrait lentement, au bras de Léni retrouvée, dans l'éternité" (567-569).

Dresden) in 1989. However, does this really strengthen the novel as the reviewer implies? Choosing Johanna's naive child perspective, Coulonges indeed seems to try to minimize the need to address the political background of the events. Many times, he emphasizes the innocence of the child. As Annette, one of Johanna's friends puts it: "We're paying for something we didn't do. By 'we' I mean people our age, and even little children. You, your poor friend, Franz, me – look at what's happened to us. We didn't deserve this" (113).[42] While it is of course valid that the children were innocent, one of the problems of Coulonges' text is that this state has been expanded to almost every character in the novel. No one seems to carry any responsibility, everyone is good and decent. There is some evil lurking in the background, concentration camps are mentioned once or twice and one of the children thinks "we all had it coming" (113),[43] but the only time this evil really breaks out is when a group of deserters from Vlasov's army hit and rape Johanna's mother Leni. Yet is it an accident that they are, while fighting for Germany, actually Russian soldiers? Otherwise, one is almost always only confronted with the evil of others, the bombings and later the revenge killings in Prague. By almost completely denying the political background of the story he tells, Coulonges oversimplifies his plot. It would have been wise to consider and present the fact that politics and guilt are part of any war. When writing about World War II in Germany, one necessarily also writes about the Nazi past - particularly if one leaves it out of the text. The complexity of the issue of the bombings cannot be completely understood if questions of guilt and responsibility are ignored since these feelings influence strongly the reaction to the air raids.

Andrea Barnet in her review of the novel pinpoints another problem in the work when she talks about the lack of psychological depth of the text in which Coulonges "too often [...] remains outside his characters, instead of illuminating their inner lives or giving us more insight into the psychic dislocations they suffer as all order around them crumbles" (Barnet 19). Indeed, Coulonges often seems to be unclear about how to represent his characters' reactions to the experience of trauma. Just like the invented trauma stories produced during the experiments about trauma, writing, and healing that were discussed previously (see Chapter 2), his novel appears too contrived and regularly slips into the melodramatic. Part of the problem is a discrepancy between the content of the work and its form. The novel deals with chaos and disorder, the breaking down of structures and constants in Johanna's life such as place, status, and time. She loses her house and becomes a wanderer. In addition, the family dynamics are broken apart because she suddenly finds herself in the role of the caregiver and provider. This causes the biggest change in her life since, while still a child, she

---

[42] "On a payé alors qu'on n'avait rien fait. Nous, les enfants. Toi, ta copine, Franz, moi, tous on a payé plus ou moins cher alors qu'on ne le méritait pas" (199).

[43] "Que ça devait arriver. Qu'on l'a bien mérité" (199).

also has to be an adult, which throws her out of the linear natural development of growing up. However, the form does not reflect these changes in Johanna's life, as the book follows a strictly chronological order of events and uses a completely traditional style of narration. The discrepancy between a content completely out of the ordinary and a form following traditional story-telling patterns is one reason why Coulonges' work is much less impressive and convincing for the reader than the other two Dresden novels by Mulisch and Vonnegut. In contrast to Coulonges, both these authors try to implement postmodern techniques in their novels in order to recreate the destruction, fragmentation, and chaos they are depicting in their contents.

Mulisch, for example, replicates the fragmented inner state of his protagonist and that of his environment by creating a montage of "regular text" dealing with the stay in Dresden in the 1950s, and which itself is a mixture of interior monologues (both in third and first person), stream of consciousness, conversations, and authorial descriptions, with quotations and flashback episodes from the past. Since Corinth embraces antiquity in order to deal with his situation and also to express his relationship to the past, Mulisch uses a Homeric style in the flashback episodes. He also sets off the different parts visually, through regular and cursive type, so that *Het stenen bruidsbed* achieves an image of fragmentation on all levels of the text. At the same time, the recurrence of certain symbols, such as fire and sex, make clear that the present state is a consequence of past events and this gives the novel a sense of unity.

Vonnegut, like Mulisch, uses the same combination of coherence, achieved with his "linking devices," and fragmentation, caused by breaking up any chronology by simply following Billy's "time travel." Furthermore, he interrupts the illusion by adding self-reflections and narrative comments and by blurring the distinction between fact and fiction. He also mixes different genres. As ancient Greek literature enters Mulisch's novel, so does science fiction become part of Vonnegut's. In the spirit of this genre, Vonnegut uses comedy, irony, and fantasy to try to approach the outrageous events. Employing these new techniques and devices, both works create a form that complements the experiences they describe, giving the readers real insight into the inner and outer consequences of otherwise incomprehensible traumatic events – a quality Coulonges' *L'Adieu à la femme sauvage* never fully achieves.

The shortcomings in Coulonges' approach illustrate how difficult it is to depict traumatic events successfully through literature. In the case of the air raids against Germany during World War II, it is particularly challenging since there are complex relationships to politics and guilt to consider. The international treatment of the bombings as exemplified in these three novels about Dresden shows that the air raids are not only a specifically German topic, but can hold powerful messages about the realities and effects of war for an international audience. Their successes and failures also make clear that it is and will always be difficult to create convincing and appropriate literary narratives about the air war in Germany. Making the bombings a topic of literature opens up the opportunity to explore history from a different angle and points to many difficult issues involved in the war, yet it also combines two challenging tasks. The first is that one needs to describe events that are located far outside normal human experience and that can have incomprehensible shattering consequences both internally and externally. The second is that it is impossible to talk about the air raids without also exploring issues of guilt and responsibility.

The three novels on Dresden discussed here reveal that, while authors need to address similar issues to produce a successful text, writers from outside Germany can confront the bombing experience more directly than their German counterparts. Obviously the fact that a novel like *L'Adieu à la femme sauvage* which hardly deals with the guilt issues involved, can appear and not cause a scandal, would not have been possible if the author had been German. While Coulonges' failure to include the complex guilt issues in his text can simply be understood as resulting in a weaker novel or a failed attempt to try something new, for a German writer the book would be seen as a political statement and could mark him forever as an author with revisionist tendencies. The novels described here and the experiments their writers are willing to undertake in their books, as compared to the uneasy treatment the bombings receive in most German literature, illuminate once more the problematic relationship of German literature to this part of the German past. The difficult psychological situation in response to the air raids that German authors faced when trying to write about them was accompanied by enormous political pressures, much stronger than those that non-German authors experienced. Even though these forces have been weakening over time, they still seem largely responsible for the fact that up to this date some of the most gripping and artistically boldest literary writing on the air war and its consequences has been provided by a Dutch and an American author.

Chapter 7
Conclusion

While the bombings during World War II are often assumed to have been traumatic for the population, their psychological consequences have not been sufficiently explored in Germany. This lack of attention to the topic, which at first seems puzzling when one reflects on the air raids' far-reaching effects, can be explained both by coping mechanisms involving denial and suppression and the complicated issues of German guilt, shame, and responsibility deeply linked to such a study. Yet when striving at a complete picture of World War II and Germany's 20th century past, it is necessary to look at this aspect of the German war experience and its consequences despite the sensitivity of the issue. The literary works about the bombings reveal themselves to be excellent sources by which to gain a better understanding of the events and their impact. While they bear witness to the difficulty of Germans in dealing with all aspects of their past, they still manage to offer powerful descriptions of the air raids and their specific psychological consequences.

As has been shown, the direction of trauma studies currently propagated in the humanities is only partially fit to grasp the psychological damage the bombings have caused in a large number of individuals who experienced them. Based on the assumption that our life in the postmodern world is entirely based on trauma, even if many have never lived through a traumatic event, the current theoretical approach makes it difficult to address and characterize actual individual trauma experiences. Furthermore, it gives little consideration to trauma survivors whose roles are not clearly defined as innocent victims. The criteria established in psychiatry for acute and posttraumatic stress disorder to look at the available literary accounts help gain a deeper, and – what is particularly important in this complex case – a more objective understanding of what it meant to have experienced the bombings. In response to the trauma, all works display a variety of dissociate symptoms of ASD, often coupled with those of avoidance, intrusion, and arousal as described for PTSD. The people are portrayed as emotionally numb, often feeling as if they are in a daze, and as if the events around them were not really happening. They are reduced to their instincts, simply reacting to what is happening without being able to pause for reflection. Particularly striking is the feeling of having fallen out of time that characterizes all the works. During an attack, time as measured by clocks becomes unimportant as it does not provide any ordering function in the chaos of an event beyond ordinary human experience. Even when the bombardment is over, this feeling continues. After living through the experience, many perceive themselves as if they have fallen out of history and were "suspended" in time. They are captured in the trauma that repeatedly intrudes into their lives through flashbacks, dreams, and thoughts, which makes it increasingly difficult to carry on with life as before. Survivors of the bombings thus perceive themselves as separate and outside of the normal parameters of everyday life, more or less pretending to be normal. This inner destruction is a mirror of the external devastation the bombings caused, often entailing a literal loss of one's space and place in society. It is thus not surprising that in nearly all accounts, inhabitants are constantly and often aimlessly on the move.

In a second step, the psychiatric approach helps explain not only the behavior of the literary characters encountered in the works, but also sheds light on the situation of the authors themselves, who were often deeply affected by the trauma as well. In addition to literary production, the texts can be read as self-therapeutic endeavors, giving the author the possibility of overcoming the trauma experience by communicating it through language. Yet as the works reveal and trauma research confirms, this step involves a painful and complicated process due to the discrepancy of existing language and literary patterns with the magnitude of the events.

Interwoven with the authors' explorations of the psychological effects of the trauma are politico-cultural issues. Engrained in the texts, particularly in stylistic decisions, are also coping mechanisms concerning German guilt. Early narratives avoid connecting the bombing experience to questions of German responsibility by interpreting them as events that can have a positive effect on individual, artistic development as in Hans Erich Nossack or on societal improvement, as in Wolfgang Borchert. The only way these immediate reactions to the bombings can deal with the German role in the events is by excluding this issue from their texts. The cool audience response to Gert Ledig's *Vergeltung*, in which he portrays the horror of the bombings more realistically and also touches on questions of German responsibility, exemplifies how deeply engrained these coping mechanisms were in German society as a whole.

Alexander Kluge and Walter Kempowski also aim at giving a true account of the horror of the bombings and the collective aspect of the experience by creating a realm of objectivity. To avoid getting emotionally involved and to achieve authenticity, they stay in the genre of documentary literature and employ the technique of the montage. Located on the fringes of fiction writing, the two authors' approaches have a number of similarities. However, the differences between them actually highlight the important role fiction can play in successfully representing trauma, an assessment also supported by recent trauma studies. Even though Kempowski arranges only authentic materials, such as diaries and letters, Kluge, who invents many of his sources and characters, offers the reader the more impressive and capturing report about the bombings. In comparison, Kempowski's voices are often handicapped by their inability to express convincingly an event so beyond all normal experience.

Dieter Forte does not exclude emotional involvement in his mixture of autobiographical and fictional elements. This style provides most access among the German literary depictions to both the horror and the short and long term psychological effects of the bombings. Fiction is here revealed as a possible path to overcoming difficulty with the representation of personal experiences as, by allowing distance between the writer and his text, it acts as a shield against the destructive forces of the author's vivid memories. Still, in no other German text does the author's trauma lurk as closely under the surface as in these novels and the story is at times driven to a point where fiction breaks down under the pressure of the urge to unburden oneself. The combination of this style with the carefully constructed side stories that provide the historical context, create a powerful and chilling portrait of the bombings and their effect both on individuals and on German society as a whole.

Yet it is essential to contrast these portrayals of the bombings with those that offer a different perspective in order to grasp the full complexity of the issues involved. The Jewish-German accounts by Werner Schmidt, Victor Klemperer, Wolf Biermann, and Günter Kunert make particularly clear how the bombings themselves, the experience of them, and their depiction is linked to issues of German guilt and responsibility. Even though the bombings were deeply troubling and traumatizing for these authors as well, they marked the arrival of freedom from persecution and were thus also positive and welcome events. It is important to keep this double meaning of the air raids in mind, no matter whose account one reads, as it can help not to lose perspective of the political realities of the time.

A topic so deeply concerned with the destruction of Germany and so undeniably linked to questions of German guilt and responsibility at first seems as if it should almost exclusively be a theme of German literature. However, as this study has shown, some of the most powerful literary works about the bombings stem from non-German authors. Particularly Kurt Vonnegut and Harry Mulisch, and to a lesser extent also Henri Coulonges illustrate that the bombings can provide the material for large literary works and are of international concern. Vonnegut and Mulisch's novels convince both through their innovative form and their depth of content. While both writers also work through their own conflicts and traumas in their texts, they still have more distance to the events than their German counterparts and seem thus freer and less tortured in their attitude towards them. By filling this gap between author and event with fiction, they create moving and stylistically convincing works which explore both the long-lasting psychological effects and the questions surrounding guilt and shame.

The wide variety of literary accounts that depict the bombings with vastly different approaches and styles, gives an indication of the complexities of such an experience both in its physical and psychological consequences and in its historical implications, as well as in its containability in language. Even though for many writing about the air raids meant attempting to overcome one's own tendencies to suppress the events, a good number of authors rose to the challenge and managed to offer insight into the horror of such traumatic experiences. W. G. Sebald's thesis about a general taboo in German literature about the topic thus cannot hold. Yet when considering the attitudes of the general public and literary critics, who indeed rarely discussed the air raids or the literature about them, Sebald's assessment seems more accurate. However, even here, the question of how much of this ambivalence was collective and how much was rather founded on individual choices, needs to be examined more closely.

While Sebald's assertions and explanations do not necessarily withstand scrutiny, the attention he received for his claims points to an interesting new development in Germany. Suddenly, a topic that had hardly ever risen to the surface of German consciousness, receives wide attention by writers, critics, and the general population alike. More writers now (re)visit the theme of the bombings, as exemplified in Forte's recent novels and Kempowski's *Echolot* project, as well as Biermann's recent reflections about his bombing experiences. Kluge also decided to include the Halberstadt text in his new collection of stories, *Chronik der Gefühle*. Particularly significant, however, is the fact that now both readers and critics pay attention to these works and show great interest in this part of German history. Sebald's Zurich lectures caused such a stir among critics that they were published in book form soon afterwards. It was also due to the discussion of the literature of the bombings that Gert Ledig's forgotten novels were reissued with large success. Jörg Friedrich's *Der Brand* was also an immediate bestseller.

Why are Germans suddenly eager to address this difficult issue almost 60 years after the war? In the case of the writers, the narratives are marked by the awareness that it is important to write and speak about the bombings before even the last living witnesses, those who experienced the air raids as children, are gone. This motif of sharing one's memories with the world is coupled with a wish to unburden some of the horror one contained inside since the bombings took place. For some, it just takes these many years to overcome the muting psychological impact of the events as well as to design strategies which help avoid being misread as supporting the zero-sum games so popular in regard to the bombings.

For the general population, the belated concern for the experience of the air raids seems part of a larger trend to try to redefine German identity after reunification. With one of the most obvious reminders of the consequences of National Socialism and the war reversed, established identity patterns in both states are reconsidered in order to come up with a self-definition which would reflect the new Germany that emerged after 1989/90. As has been seen at other important turning points after 1945, one's relationship to history, particularly that to the Nazi era, often plays an integral part in identity formation. However, it is an illusion to think that the topic is now, several decades after the bombings, less complex or controversial than it was in the years before, as the newly gained public interest and its relationship to identity formation can have largely different motives. Many of the generations who did not experience the war or the immediate postwar era now wish to develop a more complex understanding of their past and their heritage when entering a new era. Even though rarely discussed, the experience of the bombings and the accompanying vast destruction became an integral and formative part of the identity of those who lived through them. It colored their behavior and views and thus also the development of Germany after 1945 and the life of the generations after them who lived with the constant shadow of events they could not comprehend. In order to understand both the war generation and the history of Germany in its entirety, as well as their own position in this world, many now find it essential to learn about all parts of Germany's past and gain a complete picture of the Nazi period and its consequences. Others, however, try to achieve what they call a "normalization" of German identity by bringing the air raids into public discussion. While acting under the pretext of trying to urge for peace in remembering the cruelty of war through the bombings, their interest is often not a more complete understanding of history, but its relativization, an attempt to achieve a shift of emphasis away from Germans as perpetrators.

Yet shrouding the bombings and their impact on the population in silence because of this problematic situation only empowers the very people who are proponents of these misleading ideas. By discussing the topic and by analyzing the bombings' effects objectively and in the proper historical context, one not only gains a more complete understanding of German history, history in general, and the devastating effects of war on civilians, but can actually help end revisionist arguments that attempt to misuse the topic to justify the wish to forget German guilt and responsibility. This work is an attempt to understand better an important period in German history and literature, as well as German attitudes towards it today. At the same time it aims at offering new ways of exploring the general effects of war on civilians and the trauma it often entails. It is hoped that this study can be a step in the path towards a more in-depth understanding of the complex relationship between war, trauma, historical guilt, and the production of literature.

Works Cited

Aberbach, David. *Surviving Trauma: Loss, Literature and Psychoanalysis.* New Haven: Yale UP, 1989.

Allen, William Rodney, editor. *Conversations with Kurt Vonnegut.* Literary Conversation Series. Jackson: UP of Mississippi, 1988.

American Psychiatric Association. *Diagnostic and Statistical Manual of Mental Disorders III.* Washington, 1980.

American Psychiatric Association. *Diagnostic and Statistical Manual of Mental Disorders IV-TR.* Washington, 2000.

Anonymous. "Dichter, dichte . . .; Wolf Biermann legt *Alle Gedichte* vor." *Neue Zuercher Zeitung* 29 Jan. 1996: 18.

Anonymous. "Die Frau, die Stadt und der Krieg; Harry Mulischs *Steinernes Brautbett.*" *Neue Zuercher Zeitung* 6 Jan. 1996: 41.

Asch, Kenneth. "Rebuilding Dresden." *History Today* 49 (1999): 3–4.

Babinski, J. and J. Froment. *Hystérie-pithiatisme et troubles nerveux d'ordre réflexe en neurologie de guerre.* Paris: Masson, 1918.

Bal, Mieke, Jonathan Crewe, and Leo Spitzer, editors. *Acts of Memory: Cultural Recall in the Present.* Hanover: UP of New England, 1999.

Barnet, Andrea. "War's Booted Night." *The New York Times* 12 Mar. 1989: 19.

Barnouw, Dagmar. "Opening and Closing the Past in Postward German Literature: Time, Guilt, Memory, and the Critics." *Legacies and Ambiguities: Postwar Fiction and Culture in West Germany and Japan.* Ed. Ernestine Schlant and J. Thomas Rimer. Baltimore: Johns Hopkins UP, 1991. 227–248.

Bender, L. and A. Blau. "The Reaction of Children to Sexual Relations with Adults." *American Journal of Orthopsychiatry* 7 (1937): 500–518.

Beseler, Hartwig and Niels Gutschow. *Kriegsschicksale Deutscher Architektur.* Neumünster: Wachholtz, 1988.

Biermann, Wolf. *Alle Lieder.* Köln: Kiepenheuer und Witsch, 1991.

Biermann, Wolf. *Alle Gedichte.* Köln: Kiepenheuer und Witsch, 1996.

Biermann, Wolf. *Wie man Verse macht und Lieder.* Köln: Kiepenheuer und Witsch, 1997.

Biller, Maxim. "Unschuld mit Grünspan. Wie die Lüge in die deutsche Literatur kam." *Deutsche Literatur 1998.* Ed. Volker Hage. Stuttgart: Reclam, 1999. 278–283.

Bloom, Harold. Introduction. *Kurt Vonnegut.* Ed. Harold Bloom. Modern Critical Views. Broomall: Chelsea, 2000. 1–2.

Bodman, Frank. "War Conditions and the Mental Health of the Child." *British Medical Journal* 11 (1941): 486–488.

Boelich, Walter. "Wie die Deutschen mit ihrer Geschichte umgehen." *Gegen den Versuch, Vergangenheit zu verbiegen: Eine Diskussion um politsche Kultur in der Bundesrepublik aus Anlaß der Frankfurter Römerberggespräche 1986.* Ed. Hilmar Hoffmann. Frankfurt a. M.: Athenäum, 1987. 61–82.

Böll, Heinrich. "Die Stimme Wolfgang Borcherts: Nachwort zu Wolfgang Borchert *"Draußen vor der Tür"* und ausgewählte Erzählungen." *Wolfgang Borchert.* Ed. Gordon J. A. Burgess. Hamburger Bibliographien Band 24. Hamburg: Hans Christians, 1985. 15–20.

Böll, Heinrich. *Billiards at Half-Past Nine.* New York: Penguin, 1994.

Böll, Heinrich. *Billiard um halb zehn.* 1959. München: dtv, 1997.

Borchert, Wolfgang. "Billbrook." *Das Gesamtwerk.* Hamburg: Rowohlt, 1949. 75–93.

Borchert, Wolfgang. "Hamburg." *Das Gesamtwerk.* Hamburg: Rowohlt, 1949. 72–74.

Borchert, Wolfgang. "Dann gibt es nur eins!" *Draußen vor der Tür und ausgewählte Erzählungen.* Hamburg: Rowohlt, 1956. 110–112.

Borchert, Wolfgang. "Das ist unser Manifest." *Draußen vor der Tür und ausgewählte Erzählungen.* Hamburg: Rowohlt, 1956. 112–117.

Borchert, Wolfgang. "Die Küchenuhr." *Draußen vor der Tür und ausgewählte Erzählungen.* Hamburg: Rowohlt, 1956. 103–105.

Borchert, Wolfgang. "Generation ohne Abschied." *Draußen vor der Tür und ausgewählte Erzählungen.* Hamburg: Rowohlt, 1956. 108–110.

Borchert, Wolfgang. "Hamburg 1943." *Wolfgang Borchert: Allein mit meinem Schatten und dem Mond: Briefe, Gedichte und Dokumente.* Ed. Gordon J. A. Burgess and Michael Töteburg. Hamburg: Rowohlt, 1996. 252.

Bowie, Andrew. "New Histories: Aspects of the Prose of Alexander Kluge." *European Studies* 12 (1982): 180–208.

Bowlby, John. Foreword. *Surviving Trauma: Loss, Literature and Psycho-analysis.* Ed. David Aberbach. New Haven: Yale UP, 1989. vi–viii.

Brendler, Konrad. "Working Through the Holocaust: Still a Task for Germany's Youth." *Beyond Trauma: Cultural and Societal Dynamics.* Ed. Rolf J. Kleber, Charles A. Figley, and Berthold P. R. Gersons. The Plenum Series on Stress and Coping. New York: Plenum, 1995. 249–275.

Breuer, Joseph and Sigmund Freud. *Studien über Hysterie.* Wien: Deuticke, 1895.

Brison, Susan J. "Trauma Narratives and the Remaking of the Self." *Acts of Memory: Cultural Recall in the Present.* Ed. Milke Bal, Jonathan Crewe, and Leo Spitzer. Hanover: UP of New England, 1999. 39–54.

Brockmann, Stephen. "German Literature, Year Zero: Writers and Politics, 1945–1953." *Stunde Null: The End and the Beginning Fifty Years Ago.* Ed. Geoffrey J. Giles. Washington: German Historical Institute, 1997. 59–74.

Broer, Lawrence R. *Sanity Plea: Schizophrenia in the Novels of Kurt Vonnegut.* Revised edition. Tuscaloosa: U of Alabama P, 1994.

Buruma, Ian. *The Wages of Guilt: Memories of War in Germany and Japan.* New York: Penguin, 1994.

Cameron, Linda D. and Gregory Nicholls. "Expression of Stressful Experiences Through Writing: Effects of a Self-Regulation Manipulation for Pessimists and Optimists." *Health Psychology* 17 (1998): 84–92.

Carp, Stefanie. *Kriegsgeschichten: Zum Werk Alexander Kluges.* München: Fink, 1987.

Caruth, Cathy, editor. *Trauma: Explorations in Memory.* Baltimore: Johns Hopkins UP, 1995.

Caruth, Cathy. *Unclaimed Experience: Trauma, Narrative, and History.* Baltimore: Johns Hopkins UP, 1996.

Clausen, Bettina. "Rückläufige Jugend: Bemerkungen zu Borchert und zum frühen Borchert-Erfolg." *"Pack das Leben bei den Haaren": Wolfgang Borchert in neuer Sicht.* Ed. Gordon Burgess and Hans-Gerd Winter. Hamburg: Dölling und Galitz, 1996. 224–237.

c.m. "Der Wiederaufbau eines Mythos." *FAZ* 18 Apr. 2000: 4.

Connelly, Mark. *Reaching for the Stars. A New History of Bomber Command in World War II.* New York: Tauris, 2001.

Coulonges, Henri. *Farewell, Dresden.* New York: Summit, 1989.

Coulonges, Henri. *L'Adieu á la femme sauvage.* Paris: Stock, 1979.

Cowell, Alan. "Victor and Vanquished Mourn Dresden's War Dead." *The New York Times* 14 Feb. 1995: A6.

Creamer, Mark, Philip Burgess, and Phillipa Pattison. "Reaction to Trauma: A Cognitive Processing Model." *Journal of Abnormal Psychology* 101 (1992): 452–459.

Culbertson, Roberta. "Embodied Memory, Transcendence, and Telling: Recounting Trauma, Re-establishing the Self." *New Literary History* 26 (1995): 169–195.

Dagerman, Stig. *German Autumn.* 1947. London: Quartet Books, 1988.

Dalgleish, Tim. "Cognitive Theories of Post-traumatic Stress Disorder." *Post-Traumatic Stress Disorders: Concepts and Therapy.* Ed. William Yule. Wiley Series in Clinical Psychology. Chichester: Wiley, 1999. 193–220.

Daly, R. J. "Samuel Pepys and Post-Traumatic Stress Disorder." *Brit. J. Psychiat.* 143 (1983): 64–68.

de Silva, Padmal and Melanie Marks. "Intrusive Thinking in Post-Traumatic Stress Disorder." *Post-Traumatic Stress Disorders: Concepts and Theory.* Ed. William Yule. Chichester: Wiley, 1999. 161–175.

Delau, Reinhard. "Ein Stadtbild in der Diskussion: Erstarrt Dresden zur historischen Kulisse?" Online. Lexis-Nexis Academic Universe. 8 Aug. 2001. *Sueddt. Zeitung* 26 Apr. 1994.

Diefendorf, Jeffry M. "The New City: German Urban Planning and the Zero Hour." *Stunde Null: The End and the Beginning Fifty Years Ago.* Ed. Geoffrey J. Giles. Washington: German Historical Institute, 1997. 89–103.

Dirschauer, Johannes. *Tagebuch gegen den Untergang: Zur Faszination Victor Klemperers.* Gießen: Psychosozial-Verlag, 1997.

dsch. "Wir Bestraften, aufwachsend in zerstörten Städten – Vor fünfzig Jahren ging Dresden unter: Gespräch mit Harry Mulisch." *Frankfurter Allgemeine Zeitung* 13 Feb. 1995: 29.

Dürr, Volker. Introduction. *Coping with the Past: Germany and Austria After 1945.* Ed. Kathy Harms, Lutz R. Reuter, and Volker Dürr. Madison: U of Wisconsin P, 1990. 3–21.

Düwel, Jörn and Niels Gutschow. *Städtebau in Deutschland im 20. Jahrhundert: Ideen, Projekte, Akteure.* Stuttgart: Teubner, 2001.

Eitinger, Leo. "Pathology of the Concentration Camp Syndrome." *Archives of General Psychiatry* 5 (1961): 371–379.

Elm, Theo. "Draußen vor der Tür: Geschichtlichkeit und Aktualität Wolfgang Borcherts." *"Pack das Leben bei den Haaren": Wolfgang Borchert in neuer Sicht.* Ed. Gordon Burgess and Hans-Gerd Winter. Hamburg: Dölling und Galitz, 1996. 262–279.

Erichsen, John. *On Concussion of the Spine, Nervous Shock, and Other Obscure Injuries of the Nervous System.* London: Longmans, 1875.

Farrell, Kirby. *Post-Traumatic Culture: Injury and Interpretation in the Nineties*. Baltimore: Johns Hopkins UP, 1998.

Felman, Shoshana and Dori Laub. *Testimony: Crises of Witnessing in Literature, Psychoanalysis, and History*. New York: Routledge, 1992.

Fickert, Kurt. "The Reality-Truth Relationship in Wolgang Borchert's Work." *Germanic Notes* 22 (1991): 9–11.

Forte, Dieter. *Der Junge mit den blutigen Schuhen*. Frankfurt a. M.: Fischer, 1995.

Forte, Dieter. *In der Erinnerung*. Frankfurt a. M.: Fischer, 1998.

Forte, Dieter. *Schweigen oder sprechen*. Ed. Volker Hage. Frankfurt a. M.: Fischer, 2002.

Forte, Dieter. "Menschen werden zu Herdentieren: Dieter Forte über W. G. Sebalds Luftkrieg Thesen und eigene Erinnerungen an die Bomben." *Der Spiegel* 3 Apr. 1999: 220–223.

Freese, Peter. "Kurt Vonnegut's *Slaughterhouse-Five* and the Fiction of Atrocity." *Historiographic Metafiction in Modern American and Canadian Literature*. Ed. Bernd Engler and Kurt Müller. Beiträge zur englischen und amerikanischen Literatur. Paderborn: Schöningh, 1994. 209–222.

Freud, Sigmund. "Remembering, Repeating and Working-Through." *The Standard Edition of the Complete Psychological Works of Sigmund Freud*. Volume 17. London: Hogarth Press. 1919. 147–157.

Freud, Sigmund. *Gesammelte Werke*. London: Imago, 1947.

Freud, Sigmund. "The Aetiology of Hysteria." *Standard Edition*. Volume 3. London: Hogarth P. 1962.

Freud, Sigmund. *Freud Studienausgabe*. Ed. Alexander Mitscherlich, Angela Richards, and James Strachey. Frankfurt: Fischer, 1972.

Freud, Sigmund. "Introduction to Psycho-Analysis and the War Neurosis." *Essential Papers on Posttraumatic Stress Disorder*. Ed. Mardi J. Horowitz. New York: New York UP, 1999. 99–115.

Friedrich, Jürgen. *Der Brand: Deutschland im Bombenkrieg 1940-1945*. München: Propyläen, 2002.

Gerstenberger, Heide. "Meine Prinzipien über das Deutschtum und die verschiedenen Nationalitäten sind ins Wackeln gekommen wie die Zähne eines alten Mannes." *Im Herzen der Finsternis: Victor Klemperer als Chronist der NS-Zeit*. Ed. Hannes Heer. Berlin: Aufbau-Verlag, 1997. 10–20.

Gesellschaft zur Förderung des Wiederaufbaus der Frauenkirche Dresden e. V. "Die Frauenkirche zu Dresden". http://www.frauenkirche-dresden.org 20 July 2001.

Gesellschaft zur Förderung des Wiederaufbaus der Frauenkirche Dresden e. V. Dresden ruft. Dresden.

Gidron, Yori, Tuvia Peri, John F. Connolly, and Arieh Y. Shalev. "Written Disclosure in Posttraumatic Stress Disorder: Is it Beneficial for the Patient." *Journal of Nervous and Mental Disease* 184 (1996): 505–507.

Giordano, Ralph. "Dresden, Februar 1945 – Ein Brief an Roman Herzog." *taz* 2 Jan. 1995: 10.

Glaser, Hermann. *1945: Ein Lesebuch*. Frankfurt a. M.: Fischer, 1995.

Golier, Julia and Rachel Yehuda. "Neuropsychological processes in posttraumatic stress disorder." *Psychiatric Clinics of North America* 25 (2002): 317–340.

Grass, Günter. "'. . . dass ich ein Instrument bin'; Ein Gespräch mit dem Schriftsteller Günter Grass." *Neue Zuercher Zeitung* 16 May 1998: 65.

Grass, Günter. *Schreiben nach Auschwitz: Frankfurter Poetik-Vorlesung*. Frankfurt a. M.: Luchterhand, 1990.

Greenberg, Melanie A., Camille B. Wortman, and Arthur A. Stone. "Emotional Expression and Physical Health: Revising Traumatic Memories or Fostering Self-Regulation." *Journal of Personality and Social Psychology* 71 (1996): 588–602.

Greiner, Donald. "Vonnegut's *Slaughterhouse-Five* and the Fiction of Atrocity." *Critique* 14 (1973): 38–51.

Guetg, Marco. "Unermüdlicher Sammler von Alltäglichkeiten." *Sonntagszeitung* 5 Dec. 1999: 67.

Güntner, Joachim. "Der Luftkrieg fand im Osten statt." *Deutsche Literatur 1998*. Ed. Volker Hage. Stuttgart: Reclam, 1999. 271–275.

Hage, Volker. "Feuer vom Himmel." *Der Spiegel* 12 Jan. 1998: 138–141.

Hage, Volker. "Kälte und Hunger hören nie auf: Dieter Fortes Romantrilogie." *Deutsche Literatur 1998*. Ed. Volker Hage. Stuttgart: Reclam, 1999. 127–132.

Hage, Volker. "Die Angst muß im Genick sitzen." *Der Spiegel* 4 Jan. 1999: 160–164.

Hage, Volker and Walter Kempowski. "Das hatte biblische Ausmaße." *Der Spiegel* 27 Mar. 2000: 264–268.

Harpprecht, Klaus. "Stille, schicksallose." *Deutsche Literatur 1998*. Ed. Volker Hage. Stuttgart: Reclam, 1999. 267–269.

Heidelberger-Leonard, Irene. "'Auschwitz werden die Deutschen den Juden nie verzeihen.' Überlegungen zu Günter Kunerts Judesein." *Günter Kunert: Beiträge zu seinem Werk*. Ed. Manfred Durzak and Hartmut Steinecke. Hanser, 1992. 252–266.

Hell, Julia. "History as Trauma, or, Turning to the Past Once Again: Germany 1949/1989." *South Atlantic Quarterly* 96 (1997): 911–947.

Hennig, Falko. "Kaffee und Kuchen bei Kempowski." *taz* 1 Sept. 1999: 23.

Herbst, Jurgen. *Requiem for a German Past: A Boyhood Among the Nazis*. Madison: U of Wisconsin P, 1999.

Herf, Jeffrey. *Divided Memory: The Nazi Past in the Two Germanys*. Cambridge: Harvard UP, 1997.

Herman, Judith. *Trauma and Recovery*. New York: Plenum, 1997.

Hirsch, Marianne. *Family Frames: Photography, Narrative and Postmemory*. Cambridge: Harvard UP, 1997.

Hirsch, Marianne. "Projected Memory: Holocaust Photographs in Personal and Public Fantasy." *Acts of Memory: Cultural Recall in the Present*. Ed. Mieke Bal, Jonathan Crewe, and Leo Spitzer. Hanover: UP of New England, 1999. 2–23.

Hof, Holger and Dieter Forte. "Dem Zeitstrom entgegen: Gespräch mit Holger Hof." *Vom Verdichten der Welt: Zum Werk von Dieter Forte*. Ed. Holger Hof. Frankfurt a. M.: Fischer, 1998. 200–217.

Horowitz, Mardi J., editor. *Essential Papers on Posttraumatic Stress Disorder*. New York, NY: New York UP, 1999.

Horowitz, Mardi J. "A Model of Mourning: Change in Schemas of Self and Other." *Essential Papers on Posttraumatic Stress Disorder*. Ed. Mardi J. Horowitz. New York: New York UP, 1999. 253–273.

Huyssen, Andreas. *Twilight Memories: Marking Time in a Culture of Amnesia*. New York: Routledge, 1995.

Huyssen, Andreas. "On Rewritings and New Beginnings: W. G. Sebald and the Literature About the *Luftkrieg*." *Zeitschrift für Literaturwissenschaft und Linguistik* 124 (2001): 72–90.

Jacobs, Peter. *Im Kern ein deutsches Gewächs: Eine Biographie*. Berlin: Aufbau Taschenbuch Verlag, 2000.

Janet, Pierre. *The Major Symptoms of Hysteria: Fifteen Lectures Given in the Medical School of Harvard University*. New York: MacMillan, 1920.

Jarausch, Konrad H. "1945 and the Continuities of German History: Reflections on Memory, Historiography, and Politics." *Stunde Null: The End and the Beginning Fifty Years Ago*. Ed. Geoffrey J. Giles. Washington: German Historical Institute, 1997. 9–24.

Jaspers, Karl. *The Question of German Guilt*. Dial P, 1947.

Jaspers, Karl. *Die Schuldfrage*. 1946. München: Piper, 1965.

Kacandes, Irene. "Narrative Witnessing as Memory Work: Reading Gertrud Kolmar's *A Jewish Mother*." *Acts of Memory: Cultural Recall in the Present*. Ed. Milke Bal, Jonathan Crewe, and Leo Spitzer. Hanover: UP of New England, 1999. 55–71.

Kaplan, Harold and Benjamin J. Sadock, editors. *Comprehensive Textbook of Psychiatry/IV*. 6th edition. Baltimore: Williams and Wilkins, 1995.

Kempowski, Walter. *Das Echolot: Ein kollektives Tagebuch*. Volume 1. München: Knaus, 1993.

Kempowski, Walter. *Das Echolot: Fuga furiosa*. Volume 4. München: Knaus, 1999.

Kilb, Andreas. "Es bellen die Mörser, es rasseln die Ketten." *FAZ* 17 Oct. 2000: 21.

Kleber, Rolf J., Charles A. Figley, and Berthold P. R. Gersons, editors. *Beyond Trauma: Cultural and Societal Dynamics*. The Plenum Series on Stress and Coping. New York: Plenum, 1995.

Kleinschmidt, Klaus. "Das Buch benutzt mich, wie ich das Buch benutze: Harry Mulisch im Gespräch." *Neue Zuercher Zeitung* 4 Oct. 1993: 17.

Klemperer, Victor. *Und so ist alles schwankend: Tagebücher Juni bis Dezember 1945*. Berlin: Aufbau Verlag, 1996.

Klemperer, Victor. *LTI*. 1947. Leipzig: Reclam, 1998.

Klemperer, Victor. *Ich will Zeugnis ablegen bis zum letzten: Tagebücher 1933-1945*. Ed. Walter Nowojoski. 1995. Berlin: Aufbau Taschenbuch Verlag, 1999.

Klinkowitz, Jerome. *Slaughterhouse-Five: Reinventing the Novel and the World*. Twayne's Masterworks Studies. Boston: Twayne, 1990.

Kluge, Alexander. "Eröffnungsbilanz des 21. Jahrhunderts: ein Gespräch mit Alexander Kluge über seine *Chronik der Gefühle*." *Neue Zuercher Zeitung* 16 Dec. 2000: 82.

Kluge, Alexander. *Neue Geschichten. Hefte 1-18:'Unheimlichkeit der Zeit'*. Frankfurt a. M.: Suhrkamp, 1977.

Kohlhaas, Ellen. "Ein Mahnmal für den Frieden." *FAZ* 9 June 1996: 26.

Kraske, Bernd M. "Briefe Wolfgang Borcherts an Karl Ludwig Schneider." *Wolfgang Borchert*. Ed. Gordon J. A. Burgess. Hamburger Bibliographien Band 24. Hamburg: Hans Christians, 1985. 38–56.

Krell, Detlef. "Offene Wunden." *taz* 14 Feb. 1995: 5.

Kulick, Holger. "Die Narbe wächst." Online. 20 Aug. 2001. *Spiegel Online* 19 May 2001.

Kunert, Günter. *Unter diesem Himmel. Gedichte.* Berlin/DDR: Neues Leben, 1955.

Kunert, Günter. *Vor der Sintflut. Das Gedicht der Arche Noah.* München: Hanser, 1985.

Kunert, Günter. *Erwachsenenspiele: Erinnerungen.* 1997. München: dtv, 1999.

Kunert, Günter. *Gedichte.* Stuttgart: Reclam, 1999.

Kurowski, Franz. *Der Luftkrieg über Deutschland.* Düsseldorf: Econ, 1977.

LaCapra, Dominick. "Trauma, Absence, Loss." *Critical Inquiry* 25 (1999): 696–727.

LaCapra, Dominick. *Writing History, Writing Trauma.* Baltimore: Johns Hopkins UP, 2001.

Lau, Jörg. "Heilige Krieger." *taz* 20 Apr. 1996: 15.

Lebert, Stephan and Antje Weber. "Tot sein kann ich immer noch. Schriftsteller Harry Mulisch über seinen Vater, die Kollegen und den Nobelpreis." *Sueddeutsche Zeitung* 4 June 1994.

Leeds, Marc. "Beyond the Slaughterhouse: Tralfamadorian Reading Theory in the Novels of Kurt Vonnegut." *The Vonnegut Chronicles: Interviews and Essays.* Ed. Peter J. Reed and Marc Leeds. Contributions to the Study of World Literature. Westport: Greenwood, 1996. 91–102.

Leicht, Robert. "Nur das Hinsehen macht uns frei: Wir und unsere Vergangenheit: Die deutsche Geschichte läßt sich nicht retuschieren." *Historikerstreit: Die Dokumentation der Kontroverse um die Einzigartigkeit der nationalsozialistischen Judenvernichtung.* München: Piper, 1987. 361–366.

Leys, Ruth. *Trauma: A Genealogy.* U of Chicago P, 2000.

Lifton, Robert J. *History and Human Survival.* New York: Vintage, 1971.

Lifton, Robert J. and Cathy Caruth. "An Interview with Robert J. Lifton." *Trauma: Explorations in Memory.* Ed. Cathy Caruth. Baltimore: Johns Hopkins UP, 1995. 128–147.

Lifton, Robert J. and Eric Olson. "The Human Meaning of Total Disaster: The Buffalo Creek Experience." *Essential Papers on Posttraumatic Stress Disorder.* Ed. Mardi J. Horowitz. New York: New York UP, 1999. 206–231.

Long, Jonathan. "History, Narrative, and Photography in W. G. Sebald's *Die Ausgewanderten.*" *Modern Language Review* 98 (2003): 117–137.

Macksoud, Mona S., Atle Dyregrov, and Magne Raundalen. "Traumatic War Experiences and Their Effects on Children." *International Handbook of Traumatic Stress Syndromes.* Ed. John P. Wilson and Beverly Raphael. New York: Plenum, 1993. 625–633.

Maier, Charles S. "Immoral Equivalence: Revising the Nazi Past for the Kohl Era." *Reworking the Past: Hitler, the Holocaust, and the Historians' Debate.* Ed. Peter Baldwin. Boston: Beacon P, 1990. 38–44.

Malt, Ulrik Fredrik. "Traumatic Effects of Accidents." *Individual and Community Responses to Trauma and Disaster.* Ed. Robert J. Ursano, Brian G. McCaughey, and Carol S. Fullerton. Cambridge: Cambridge UP, 1994. 103–135.

Markovits, Andrei S. "Coping with the Past: The West German Labor Movement and the Left." *Coping with the Past: Germany and Austria After 1945.* Ed. Kathy Harms, Lutz R. Reuter, and Volker Dürr. Madison: U of Wisconsin P, 1990. 219–232.

Martin, Russell. *Picasso's War.* New York: Dutton, 2002.

Maue, Karl-Otto. "Aufbruch-Skepsis-Rechtfertigung: Drei Strategien im literarischen Feld der Nachkriegszeit am Beispiel der Hamburger Autoren Axel Eggebrecht, Hans Erich Nossack und Hans Friedrich Blunck." *"Liebe, die im Abgrund Anker wirft": Autoren und literarisches Feld im Hamburg des 20. Jahrhunderts.* Ed. Inge Stephan and Hans-Gerd Winter. Hamburg: Argument, 1989. 175–196.

Mazzoleni, Donatella. "The City and the Imaginary." *Space and Place: Theories of Identity and Location.* Ed. Erica Carter, James Donald, and Judith Squires. London: Lawrence and Wishart, 1993. 285–301.

McCewan, Bruce S. "The Neurobiology and Neuroendocrinology of Stress. Implications for Post-traumatic Stress Disorder from a Basic Science Perspective." *Psychiatric Clinics of North America* 25 (2002): 469–494.

McFarlane, Alexander C. "The Severity of Trauma: Issues about its Role in Posttraumatic Stress Disorder." *Beyond Trauma: Cultural and Societal Dynamics.* Ed. Rolf J. Kleber, Charles R. Figley, and Berthold P. R. Gersons. New York: Plenum P, 1995. 31–54.

McFarlane, Alexander C. and Nicholas Potts. "Posttraumatic Stress Disorder: Prevalence and Risk Factors Relative to Disasters." *Posttraumatic Stress Disorder: A Comprehensive Text.* Ed. Philip A. Saigh and J. Douglas Bremner. Needham Heights: Allyn and Bacon, 1999. 92–102.

McFarlane, Alexander C., Rachel Yehuda, and C. Richard Clark. "Biologic Models of Traumatic Memories and Post-traumatic Stress Disorder. The Role of Neural Networks." *Psychiatric Clinics of North America* 25 (2002): 253–270.

Meadows, Elizabeth A. and Edna B. Foa. "Cognitive-Behavioral Treatment of Traumatized Adults." *Posttraumatic Stress Disorder: A Comprehensive Text*. Ed. Philip A. Saigh and J. Douglas Bremner. Needham Heights: Allyn and Bacon, 1999. 376–390.

Meier, Bettina. "Goethe in Trümmern: Vor vierzig Jahren: Der Streit um den Wiederaufbau des Goetheshauses in Frankfurt." *The Germanic Review* 43 (1988): 183–188.

Meinecke, Friedrich. *Die deutsche Katastrophe*. Wiesbaden: Brockhaus, 1946.

Meinecke, Friedrich. *The German Catastrophe*. Boston: Beacon, 1950.

Merrill, Robert and Peter A. Scholl. "Vonnegut's *Slaughterhouse-Five*: The Requirements of Chaos." *Studies in American Fiction* 6 (1978): 65–76.

Miller, Laurence. *Shocks to the System: Psychotherapy of Traumatic Disability Syndromes*. New York: Norton, 1998.

Mirtschev, Bogdan. "Ausgeliefert an das Unaussprechliche: Daseinskrise und innere Konflikte der Heimkehrerfigur im literarischen Werk von Wolfgang Borchert." *"Pack das Leben bei den Haaren": Wolfgang Borchert in neuer Sicht*. Ed. Gordon Burgess and Hans-Gerd Winter. Hamburg: Dölling und Galitz, 1996. 170–181.

Mitscherlich, Alexander and Margarete Mitscherlich. *The Unfähigkeit zu trauern: Grundlagen kollektiven Verhaltens*. München: Piper, 1967.

Mittig, Hans-Ernst. "Künstler in Schuldgefühlen: 'Denkmal für die ermordeten Juden Europas'." *Geschichtswissenschaft und Öffentlichkeit: Der Streit um Daniel J. Goldhagen*. Ed. Johannes Heil and Rainer Erb. Die Zeit des Nationalsozialismus. Frankfurt a. M.: Fischer, 1998. 279–294.

Mommsen, Wolfgang J. "The Germans and Their Past: History in Political Consciousness in the Federal Republic of Germany." *Coping with the Past: Germany and Austria After 1945*. Ed. Kathy Harms, Lutz R. Reuter, and Volker Dürr. Madison: U of Wisconsin P, 1990. 252–269.

Mulisch, Harry. *Het stenen bruidsbed*. Amsterdam: De bezige bij, 1959.

Mulisch, Harry. *Das steinerne Brautbett*. Frankfurt a. M.: Suhrkamp, 1994.

Müller, Lothar. "Späte Vergeltung." *FAZ* 28 Oct. 1999: 57.

Mustazza, Leonard. "Vonnegut's Tralfamadore and Milton's Eden." *Essays in Literature* 13 (1986): 299–312.

Neffe, Jürgen. "Geliebte Dickmadame." *Der Spiegel* 2 Oct. 2000: 292–301.

Niven, Bill. *Facing the Nazi Past: United Germany and the Legacy of the Third Reich.* New York: Routledge, 2002.

Noble, Philippe. "La Guerre de Troie a Toujours Lieu." *Etudes Germaniques* 39 (1984): 347–361.

Nolte, Ernst. "Zwischen Geschichtslegende und Revisionismus." *Historikerstreit: Die Dokumentation der Kontroverse um die Einzigartigkeit der nationalsozialistischen Judenvernichtung.* München: Piper, 1987. 13–35.

Nossack, Hans Erich. "Brief an Hermann Kasack." *Dieser Andere.* Ed. Christof Schmid. Frankfurt a. M.: Suhrkamp, 1976. 13–31.

Nossack, Hans Erich. *Der Untergang.* 1948. Frankfurt a. M.: Suhrkamp, 1996.

Orr, Scott P., Linda J. Metzger, and Roger K. Pitman. "Psychophysiology of Post-traumatic Stress Disorder." *Psychiatric Clinics of North America* 25 (2002): 271–293.

Paul, Jürgen. "Dresden: Suche nach der verlorenen Mitte." *Neue Städte aus Ruinen: Deutscher Städtebau der Nachkriegszeit.* Ed. Klaus von Beyme et al. München: Prestel, 1992. 313–333.

Paul, Jürgen, Thomas Kantschew, and Uwe Kröger. *Der Wiederaufbau der Frauenkirche zu Dresden: Eine Aufgabe von nationaler und internationaler Bedeutung.* 3rd edition. Dresden: Gesellschaft zur Förderung des Wiederaufbaus der Frauenkirche Dresden e. V., 1998.

Pelt, Will F. "Strömungen in der modernen niederländischen Literatur." *Kwartalnik Neofilologiczny* 2 (1975): 161–171.

Pennebaker, James W. "Putting Stress into Words: Health, Linguistic, and Therapeutic Implications." *Behaviour Research and Therapy* 31 (1993): 539–548.

Pennebaker, James W. "Telling Stories: The Health Benefits of Narrative." *Literature and Medicine* 19 (2000): 3–18.

Pennebaker, James W., Michelle Colder, and Lisa K. Sharp. "Accelerating the Coping Process." *Journal of Personality and Social Psychology* 58 (1990): 528–537.

Pennebaker, James W. and Martha E. Francis. "Cognitive, Emotional, and Language Processes in Disclosure." *Cognition and Emotion* 10 (1996): 601–626.

Pepys, Samuel. *The Shorter Pepys.* Ed. Robert Latham. London: Bell and Hyman, 1985.

Piers, Craig C. "Remembering Trauma: A Characterological Perspective." *Trauma and Memory*. Ed. Linda M. Williams and Victoria L. Barnyard. Thousand Oaks: Sage, 1999. 57–65.

Prasad, J. "Psychology of Rumors: A Study of the Great Indian Earthquake of 1934." *British Journal of Psychology* 26 (1934): 1–15.

Preisendoerfer, Bruno. "30 Tage Weltkrieg." *Die Woche* 26 Nov. 1999: 8.

Rabinbach, Anson. "Beyond Bitburg: The Place of the 'Jewish Question' in German History after 1945." *Coping with the Past: Germany and Austria After 1945*. Ed. Kathy Harms, Lutz R. Reuter, and Volker Dürr. Madison: U of Wisconsin P, 1990. 187–218.

Rabois, Dana, Sonja V. Batten, and Terence M. Keane. "Implications of Biological Findings for Psychological Treatments of Post-traumatic Stress Disorder." *Psychiatric Clinics of North America* 25 (2002): 443–462.

Raddatz, Fritz J. "'I'd Rather Be Dead than Think the Way Kunert Does': Interview with Wolf Biermann and Günter Kunert." *New German Critique* (1981): 45–55.

Reemtsma, Jan Philipp. "Und auch Opas M.G.: Wolfgang Borchert als Veteran." *"Pack das Leben bei den Haaren": Wolfgang Borchert in neuer Sicht*. Ed. Gordon Burgess and Hans-Gerd Winter. Hamburg: Dölling und Galitz, 1996. 238–249.

Reents, Edo. "Geschichte zum Verschlucken: Zum Erscheinen von *Echolot*, Teil II: über den Archivar Walter Kempowski." *Sueddt. Zeitung* 11 Oct. 1999: 17.

Reichel, Sabine. "A Child at the Bombing of Dresden: Farewell Dresden by Henri Coulonges." *Los Angeles Times* 26 Feb. 1989: 13.

Reiss, Hans. "Victor Klemperer (1881-1960): Reflections on his 'Third Reich' Diaries." *German Life and Letters* 51 (1998): 65–92.

Richards, David and Karina Lovell. "Behavioural and Cognitive Behavioural Interventions in the Treatment of PTSD." *Post-Traumatic Stress Disorders: Concepts and Therapy*. Ed. William Yule. Wiley Series in Clinical Psychology. Chichester: Wiley, 1999. 239–266.

Roberts, David. "Die Formenwelt des Zusammenhangs: Zur Theorie und Funktion der Montage by Alexander Kluge." *Zeitschrift für Literatur und Linguistik* 46 (1982): 104–119.

Rode, Ulrike. "Ledig entläßt niemanden aus dem Inferno." *Tages-Anzeiger* 18 Nov. 1999: 66.

Roos, Peter. "Den Toten schlägt keine Zeit." *FAZ* 19 Jan. 2000: 44.

Rosellini, Jay. "Kunerts langer Abschied von Brecht – Biermanns Annäherung an Kunert." *Günter Kunert: Beiträge zu seinem Werk.* Ed. Manfred Durzak and Hartmut Steinecke. Hanser, 1992. 267–294.

Rosellini, Jay. *Wolf Biermann.* Beck'sche Reihe Autorenbücher. München: Beck, 1992.

Rossi, Aldo. *The Architecture of the City.* Cambridge: MIT P, 1982.

Ruby, Andreas. "Las Vegas an der Elbe." Online. 8 Aug. 2001. *Zeit.de* 46 (2000).

Rudolph, Ekkehart and Hans Erich Nossack. "Hans Erich Nossack." *Aussage zur Person: Zwölf deutsche Schriftsteller im Gespräch mit Ekkehart Rudolph.* Tübingen: Erdmann, 1977. 178–191.

Ryan, Judith. *The Uncomplicated Past: Postwar German Novels and the Third Reich.* Detroit: Wayne State UP, 1983.

Saigh, Philip A. and J. Douglas Bremner. "The History of Posttraumatic Stress." *Posttraumatic Stress Disorder: A Comprehensive Text.* Ed. Philip A. Saigh and J. Douglas Bremner. Needham Heights: Allyn Bacon, 1999. 1–17.

Scheer, Maximilian. "An Rhein und Ruhr." *In Deutschland unterwegs: Reportagen, Skizzen, Berichte 1945-1948.* Ed. Klaus R. Scherpe. Stuttgart: Reclam, 1982. 201–221.

Schirrmacher, Frank. "Luftkrieg. Beginnt morgen die deutsche Nachkriegsliteratur." *Deutsche Literatur 1998.* Ed. Volker Hage. Stuttgart: Reclam, 1999. 262–267.

Schmidt, Werner. *Leben an Grenzen.* Frankfurt: Suhrkamp, 1993.

Schneider, Peter. "German Postwar Strategies of Coming to Terms with the Past." *Legacies and Ambiguities: Postwar Fiction and Culture in West Germany and Japan.* Ed. Ernestine Schlant and J. Thomas Rimer. Baltimore: Johns Hopkins UP, 1991. 279–288.

Schoeller, Wilfried F. "Gert Ledigs lange verschollen gewesener Roman *Vergeltung.*" *Sueddt. Zeitung* 11 Dec. 1999: 4.

Schröder, Claus B. *Draußen vor der Tür: Eine Wolfgang-Borchert-Biographie.* Berlin: Henschel, 1988.

Sebald, W. G. *Schwindel. Gefühle.* 1990. Frankfurt a. M.: Fischer, 1994.

Sebald, W. G. *Nach der Natur.* Frankfurt a. M.: Fischer, 1995.

Sebald, W. G. *Die Ringe des Saturn.* 1992. Frankfurt a. M.: Fischer, 1997.

Sebald, W. G. *Luftkrieg und Literatur.* München: Hanser, 1999.

Sebald, W. G. *On the Natural History of Destruction.* New York: Random House, 2003.

Shakespeare, William. *King Henry IV. The Riverside Shakespeare.* Boston: Houghton Mifflin, 1974. 847–929.

Smyth, Joshua M., Arthur A. Stone, Adam Hurewitz, and Alan Kaell. "Effects of Writing About Stressful Experiences on Symptom Reduction in Patients with Asthma or Rheumatoid Arthritis." *Journal of the American Medical Association* 281 (1999): 1304–1309.

Stark, James L. *Wolfgang Borchert's Germany: Reflections of the Third Reich.* Lanham: UP of America, 1997.

Steele, Jonathan. "The Night it Rained Fire." *The Guardian (London)* 9 Feb. 1995: T2.

Stephan, Inge. "'Hamburg ist für alles Künstlerische immer lähmend gewesen': Formen der Mythologisierung Hamburgs bei Hans Erich Nossack." *"Liebe, die im Abgrund Anker wirft": Autoren und literarisches Feld im Hamburg des 20. Jahrhunderts.* Ed. Inge Stephan and Hans-Gerd Müller. Hamburg: Argument, 1989. 294–316.

Sturken, Marita. "Narratives of Recovery: Repressed Memory as Cultural Memory." *Acts of Memory: Cultural Recall in the Present.* Ed. Milke Bal, Jonathan Crewe, and Leo Spitzer. Hanover: UP of New England, 1999. 231–248.

Sullivan, Gregory M. and Jack M. Gorman. "Finding a Home for Post-Traumatic Stress Disorder in Biological Psychiatry: Is it a Disorder of Anxiety, Mood, Stress, or Memory?" *Psychiatric Clinics of North America* 25 (2002): 463–468.

Süskind, W. E. "Der geschichtliche Augenblick." *In Deutschland unterwegs: Reportagen, Skizzen, Berichte 1945-1948.* Ed. Klaus R. Scherpe. Stuttgart: Reclam, 1982. 307–312.

Tal, Kali. *Worlds of Hurt: Reading the Literatures of Trauma.* Cambridge: Cambridge UP, 1996.

Terr, Lenore C. "Childhood Trauma and the Creative Product: A Look at the Early Lives and Later Works of Poe, Wharton, Margritte, Hitchcock, and Bergman." *Psychoanalytic Study of the Child* 42 (1987): 545–572.

Terr, Lenore C. "Terror Writing by the Formerly Terrified: A Look at Stephen King." *Psychoanalytic Study of the Child* 44 (1989): 369–390.

Trende, Klaus and Wolf Biermann. *Schmerz der Freiheit: Ein Gespräch.* Cottbus: Fabrik Verlag, 1997.

Trimble, Michael R. "Post-Traumatic Stress Disorder: History of a Concept." *Trauma and Its Wake: The Study and Treatment of Post-Traumatic Stress Disorder.* Ed. Charles R. Figley. Brunner/Mazel Psychosocial Stress Series 4. New York: Brunner/Mazel, 1985. 5–14.

Trimborn, Jürgen. "Das 'Wunder von Dresden': der Wiederaufbau der Frauenkirche. Ein kritischer Blick auf das 'größte Rekonstruktionsprojekt des Jahrhunderts'." *Die Alte Stadt: Vierteljahreszeitschrift für Stadtgeschichte, Stadtsoziologie und Denkmalpflege* 97 (1997): 127–150.

Trindler, Helen and Paul M. Salkovskis. "Personally Relevant Intrusions Outside of the Laboratory: Long-term Suppression Increases Intrusion." *Behaviour Research and Therapy* 32 (1994): 833–842.

Ullrich, Volker. "Ach, wie wir gelitten haben." *Die Zeit* 18. Dec. 2002: 45.

van der Kolk, Bessel A. and Onno van der Hart. "The Intrusive Past: The Flexibility of Memory and the Engraving of Trauma." *Trauma: Explorations in Memory.* Ed. Cathy Caruth. Baltimore: Johns Hopkins UP, 1995. 158–182.

van der Paardt, Rudi. "A Unity of Opposites: The Paradoxical Oeuvre of Harry Mulisch." *The Low Countries: Arts and Society in Flanders and the Netherlands. A Yearbook.* Ed. Jozef Deleu. Flemish-Netherlands Foundation Stichting Ons Erfdeel, 1994-1995. 204–207.

Vogt, Jochen. "Der ratlos-rastlose Erzähler Alexander Kluge: Eine romantheoretische Annäherung." *Alexander Kluge.* Ed. Heinz Ludwig Arnold. Text und Kritik. München: edition text+kritik, 1985. 9–21.

Watts, Philip. "Rewriting History: Celine and Kurt Vonnegut." *The South Atlantic Quarterly* 93 (1994): 265–278.

Weathers, Frank W., Brett T. Litz, and Terence M. Keane. "Military Trauma." *Traumatic Stress: From Therapy to Practice.* Ed. John R. Freedy and Stevan E. Hobfoll. The Plenum Series on Stress and Coping. New York: Plenum, 1995. 103–128.

Weisaeth, Lars. "Psychological and Psychiatric Aspects of Technological Disasters." *Individual and Community Responses to Trauma and Disaster.* Ed. Robert J. Ursano, Brian G. McCaughey, and Carol S. Fullerton. Cambridge: Cambridge UP, 1994. 72–102.

Weizsäcker, Richard von. *Von Deutschland aus.* München: dtv, 1987.

Wong, Cheryl M. "Post-traumatic Stress Disorder: Advances in Psychoneuroimmunology." *Psychiatric Clinics of North America* 25 (2002): 369–383.

Young, Allen. *Harmony of Illusions: Post-Traumatic Stress Disorder.* Princeton, NJ: Princeton UP, 1995.

Yule, William, Ruth Williams, and Stephen Joseph. "Post-Traumatic Stress Disorder in Adults." *Post-Traumatic Stress Disorders: Concepts and Therapy.* Ed. William Yule. New York: John Wiley and Sons, 1999. 1–24.

Index